SOURCES OF WEAPON
SYSTEMS INNOVATION IN THE
DEPARTMENT OF DEFENSE

THE ROLE OF IN-HOUSE RESEARCH AND DEVELOPMENT, 1945–2000

By Thomas C. Lassman

Center of Military History
United States Army
Washington, D.C., 2008

CONTENTS

Since the end of World War II, civilian and military policymakers have sought to understand and improve the institutional processes involved in the development of modern weapons systems. The persistent calls for institutional, managerial, and organizational reform suggest that such tasks have not always been easy nor clearly defined. This study is intended to bring some historical clarity to that problem by identifying and examining the patterns of organizational and institutional change that guided in-house weapons research and development (R&D) over the course of the past six decades. Specifically, it details the history of weapons R&D in the major laboratories owned and operated by the Army, the Navy, and the Air Force between 1945 and 2000. At the same time, the monograph complements a larger multivolume historical effort that is currently analyzing the policies, procedures, and institutions that guided the development, production, and procurement of major weapon systems during the same period. Together they constitute the on-going Defense Acquisition History Project.

The Department of Defense spends hundreds of billions of dollars every year to keep U.S. forces equipped with state-of-the-art weapon systems. Research and development is an essential component of this process. It is the foundation upon which all weapon systems are built once requirements have been set. Although they outsourced a significant share of their research requirements during the Cold War, the Army, the Navy, and the Air Force also maintained extensive in-house R&D establishments whose laboratories turned out many products, ranging from fundamental knowledge in physics, chemistry, and other scientific disciplines to complete prototype weapon systems. What set the services apart from one another, however, was the extent to which they managed and organized their respective R&D programs.

In the Army, research, development, and production proceeded alongside one another in the manufacturing arsenals that had been in continuous operation since the beginning of the nineteenth century, despite actions taken by some Army leaders to separate these functions organizationally as a necessary prerequisite to the development of technologically advanced weapon systems. The Navy, by contrast, maintained a sharper organizational division of labor between R&D and production. Established in 1923, the Naval Research Laboratory operated independently of the Navy's material bureaus, where, like the Army's arsenals, technological innovation had historically depended on the close coordination of research, development, and production. Created in 1947, the Air Force relied more heavily than the Army and the Navy on the private sector for new knowledge and skills. But it also operated an extensive network of in-house laboratories, the management and organization of which periodically shifted between the extremes of independence from and subordination to the Air Force's production and procurement functions. Throughout all three services, a disjunction sometimes existed between the formulation of R&D policies at the management level and the implementation of those policies in the laboratory. These relationships and other patterns of organizational change are highlighted in the study and should help DoD acquisition managers to understand the current acquisition environment and successfully navigate their way through it as they seek to make informed decisions about future weapons development across an increasingly broad spectrum of activities.

Washington, D.C.   Jeffrey J. Clarke
August 15, 2008   Chief of Military History

THE AUTHOR

Thomas C. Lassman was born and raised in Pittsburgh, Pennsylvania. He received a B.A. degree in history from Washington University in 1991 and M.A. and Ph.D. degrees in the history of science from Johns Hopkins University in 1996 and 2000, respectively. Before joining the U.S. Army Center of Military History as a contract historian in 2005, he worked at the Chemical Heritage Foundation in Philadelphia and the Center for History of Physics at the American Institute of Physics in College Park, Maryland.

PREFACE

When I began working on this monograph as a contract historian for the Defense Acquisition History Project at the U.S. Army Center of Military History (CMH) in June 2005, I knew very little about American military history. My knowledge of the field was limited to a few periods and events directly relevant to the subject of my doctoral dissertation. That gap has since narrowed significantly, thanks in no small part to the input and expertise provided by my colleagues on the project. Glen Asner, Nancy Berlage, and Chris Dachi first introduced me to the Defense Acquisition History Project, and Jeffrey Clarke, then Chief Historian (now Chief of Military History), hired me to write this monograph. I am especially grateful to them and to Alfred Goldberg, Stuart Rochester, Richard Stewart, and Louis Galambos for their encouragement and guidance.

Dr. Clarke and Dr. Stewart, currently Chief Historian, carefully read and critiqued the entire manuscript. Elliott Converse, whose research and writing on the history of weapon systems acquisition in the Department of Defense during the early years of the Cold War has served as a model for my own work, also provided invaluable comments and support. He has been an outstanding colleague, friend, and mentor. I am equally indebted to J. Ronald Fox, whose encyclopedic knowledge of the weapons acquisition process and detailed critiques of my chapters improved the manuscript immeasurably. Alisa Robinson, Chief of CMH's Editorial Branch, guided the final version through the editing and publication process. James McDonald, of the Office of the Deputy Undersecretary of Defense (Science and Technology), reviewed the manuscript for public release.

I must extend a very special thanks to my daily lunchtime companions at CMH—Walter Poole, Edgar Raines, Walton Moody, and Philip Shiman. Their friendship sustained me throughout the research and writing process, and I am also grateful to them for helping me learn the ins and outs of American military history. I also thank David Allen, Carolyn Halladay, and Shannon Brown for their assistance on the project.

I am grateful to the librarians and archivists in the Library and Archives Branch at CMH who helped me identify and locate source materials. I am especially indebted to Patricia Ames and Lenore Gardner, both of whom patiently tracked down many journal articles, books, and unpublished documents. Without their help, conducting the research for this study would have been a far more arduous process than it turned out to be. I rarely experienced problems with my office computer equipment, thanks to the technical support provided by Jeffrey Noone. Cheryl Eddens, CMH's security manager, helped me obtain a security clearance and the required identification badges and building passes to work at CMH and other Defense Department installations in the Washington D.C. area.

Several outside reviewers generously gave their time to read and comment on the manuscript. Professor David Hounshell at Carnegie Mellon University, whose own work on the history of American industrial research frames much of the analysis in the pages that follow, provided an outstanding critique that encouraged me to rethink some of the major themes and arguments. So did Glen

Asner, whose recent Ph.D. dissertation on the impact of military contracting on industrial R&D during the Cold War will likely set the standard for future scholarship in the field. Professor Robert Kargon, my graduate advisor at Johns Hopkins University, also read and critiqued the manuscript. Herbert Fusfeld joined the research staff of the Frankford Arsenal as a physicist in 1941. In April 2005, just before I joined the acquisition history project, Dr. Fusfeld discussed with me his research at the arsenal during World War II, and he also reviewed an early draft of chapter 2. Jeffrey Barlow at the Naval Historical Center kindly reviewed chapter 3. Michael Neufeld at the Smithsonian Institution's National Air and Space Museum recommended several important sources on the history of the Army's rocket and missile programs.

Finally, I am very grateful to my family and friends who have always supported me and my love of history. Research and writing can be a lonely experience. It was for me until the fall of 2005, when I met Rebecca Osthus. Her presence in my life has been nothing less than joyous.

Although this study is the result of a collective effort, I alone am fully responsible for any errors of fact and interpretation.

Washington, D.C.   Thomas C. Lassman
August 24, 2008

SOURCES OF WEAPON SYSTEMS INNOVATION IN THE DEPARTMENT OF DEFENSE

THE ROLE OF IN-HOUSE RESEARCH AND DEVELOPMENT, 1945–2000

CHAPTER ONE

Introduction: The Sources of Weapon Systems Innovation

This study of weapons research and development (R&D) in the Army, the Navy, and the Air Force complements a larger, multivolume history of weapons acquisition in the Department of Defense, covering the period 1945 to 2001. The series examines the policies, procedures, and institutional environment that guided the development and procurement of major weapon systems, such as tanks, artillery, strategic and tactical aircraft, ballistic missiles, surface ships, and nuclear submarines.[1] Because of its brevity, imposed by a one-year contract with the U.S. Army Center of Military History, this monograph does not examine all of the in-house laboratories owned and operated by the military services. It concentrates instead on major facilities and programs that illustrate the scope and content of weapons R&D at specific points in time throughout the postwar period. The goal is not to be comprehensive but rather to provide a broad historical overview of the Defense Department's internal R&D operations and highlight the patterns of organizational change that guided the development of major weapon systems.

Toward that goal, this study focuses on laboratory research in the physical sciences. It omits federally funded research and development centers, many of which did not support bench science in the laboratory. The Rand Corporation, the Mitre Corporation, and the Institute for Defense Analysis, for example, fit into this latter category. Also omitted are civilian government laboratories, even though they routinely provided technical services, and in some cases complete weapon systems, to the military departments. Representative examples of institutions in this category include the National Advisory Committee for Aeronautics, the National Bureau of Standards, and the nuclear weapons laboratories and production facilities owned by the Department of Energy and its predecessor, the Atomic Energy Commission.[2]

---

[1] The series, which was still in progress at the U.S. Army Center of Military History at the time this study was completed (fall 2006), comprises five narrative volumes and one documentary volume.

[2] On the National Bureau of Standards, see Rexmond C. Cochrane, *Measures for Progress: A History of the National Bureau of Standards* (Washington, D.C.: U.S. Department of Commerce, 1966); Elio Passaglia with Karma A. Beal, *A Unique Institution: The National Bureau of Standards, 1950–1969* (Washington, D.C.: U.S. Department of Commerce, 1999); and James F. Schooley, *Responding to National Needs: The National Bureau of Standards Becomes the National Institute of Standards and Technology, 1969–1993* (Washington, D.C.: U.S. Department of Commerce, 2000). The history of the National Advisory Committee for Aeronautics is examined in Alex Roland, *Model Research: The National Advisory Committee for Aeronautics, 1915–1958*, 2 vols. (Washington, D.C.: National Aeronautics and Space Administration, 1985). On the Atomic Energy Commission, see the official three-volume history: Richard G. Hewlett and Oscar E. Anderson, *The New World, 1939–1946*, vol. 1 of *A History of the United States Atomic Energy Commission* (University Park: Pennsylvania State University Press, 1962); Richard G. Hewlett and Francis Duncan, *Atomic Shield, 1947–1952*, vol. 2 of *A History of the United States Atomic Energy Commission* (University Park: Pennsylvania State University Press, 1969); and Richard G. Hewlett and Jack M. Holl, *Atoms for Peace and War, 1953–1961: Eisenhower and the Atomic Energy Commission*, vol. 3 of *A History of the United*

Admittedly, these omissions are to some extent arbitrary, determined more by space and time constraints than by any comprehensive, theoretically informed argument that would necessitate the elimination of one type of research and development organization in favor of another. But the larger goal of understanding the historical evolution of the weapons acquisition process *within* the Department of Defense after World War II precludes coverage of the entire federal R&D establishment.

World War II marked the beginning of a massive and permanent restructuring of the institutional relationship between the civilian scientific establishment and the military services in the United States. Prior to 1940, with few exceptions, weapons research and development was concentrated in production facilities owned and operated by the Army and the Navy. The Army's primary source of technological innovation and weapons acquisition had been, for more than a century, the system of manufacturing arsenals that developed and produced everything from rifles and small-arms ammunition to field guns and tanks. Similarly, the latest advances in shipbuilding technology originated in the Navy's technical bureaus and an interconnected network of shipyards and docks. The Air Force, which did not achieve independent status from the Army until 1947, followed a somewhat different strategy, relying much more heavily than the Army and the Navy on private industry for new technical knowledge. In all cases, however, the end of World War II signaled the beginning of a protracted decline of the R&D laboratories attached to the manufacturing facilities owned and operated by the military services as the government began shifting more of its resources for the development and production of new weapons technologies to private-sector institutions.

To be sure, some service facilities, such as the Naval Research Laboratory, continued to thrive after the war, but the outsourcing of R&D continued unabated. Although technologically sophisticated in their own right, the in-house laboratories managed by the Army, the Navy, and the Air Force were not equipped to handle the anticipated R&D requirements of new high-speed aircraft, nuclear submarines, and other weapon systems employing the latest advances in solid-state electronics, jet propulsion, and atomic energy. Industry and academia provided much of the requisite expertise to develop and manufacture these technologies for an expanding military establishment. This trend persisted throughout the Cold War.[3]

During World War II, the federal government relied on the private sector to develop and produce the massive quantities of weapons needed by the military services. The absence of a large peacetime military establishment, compounded by the debilitating effects of the Great Depression and policies favoring

---

States Atomic Energy Commission (Berkeley: University of California Press, 1989). Also useful are Peter J. Westwick, *The National Labs: Science in an American System, 1947–1974* (Cambridge, Mass.: Harvard University Press, 2003); and Robert W. Seidel, "A Home for Big Science: The Atomic Energy Commission's Laboratory System," *Historical Studies in the Physical and Biological Sciences* 16 (1986): 135–75.

[3] For a concise overview of the weapons production facilities operated by the Army, the Navy, and the Air Force during the Cold War, see Philip Shiman, *Forging the Sword: Defense Production During the Cold War* (Champaign, Ill.: Construction Engineering Research Laboratoriesa, U.S. Army Corps of Engineers, July 1997).

isolationism in international affairs during the interwar period, had left the system of arsenals, shipyards, and in-house laboratories without sufficient resources to support the wartime mobilization. This gap was filled by new emergency agencies that coordinated the operational requirements of the military services and the research, development, and manufacturing capabilities of business and industry. The Office of Scientific Research and Development (OSRD), for example, distributed most of the federal funds allocated for R&D to industrial and university laboratories, where scientists and engineers collaborated with their government counterparts to produce the atomic bomb, microwave radar, the radio proximity fuse, and a host of other state-of-the-art weapons vital to the war effort. The Defense Plant Corporation and the War Production Board carried out similar functions, coordinating industrial R&D and allocating public funds to expand the production of steel, synthetic rubber, pharmaceuticals, aviation fuel, and other critical wartime materials.[4] Although these and other emergency agencies were quickly dismantled after the war, their institutional legacies became permanent fixtures in a newly reconstituted, postwar scientific establishment in which the government had become the largest single source of funding for academic research in the physical sciences. Moreover, the end of World War II did not result in the complete demobilization of the armed forces and the scientific and industrial infrastructure that had been built by the government to develop and produce new weapons. Deteriorating relations with the Soviet Union and the subsequent onset of the Cold War after 1945 set the United States on a course toward permanent military preparedness that would last for nearly fifty years.[5]

The extent to which the government was expected to maintain its new function as a source of scientific progress, economic prosperity, and military security in peacetime became the centerpiece of a fierce political struggle between civilian and government science policymakers during the last days of World War II. A leading spokesman in this debate was Vannevar Bush, wartime director of the Office of Scientific Research and Development and one of the major architects of America's postwar science policy. In his landmark report, *Science—The Endless Frontier*, Bush argued that scientific research of the type normally conducted in universities rather than government laboratories would be the principal source of industrial innovation, military security, and economic growth. In Bush's mind, the government would simply make funds available for scientific study, and the recipient private-sector institutions would determine for themselves how those resources should be allocated. Bush and his allies in Congress favored

---

[4] See David M. Hart, *Forged Consensus: Science, Technology, and Economic Policy in the United States, 1921–1953* (Princeton: Princeton University Press, 1998), chap. 5; and Peter Neushul, "Science, Technology, and the Arsenal of Democracy: Production Research and Development during World War II" (Ph.D. diss., University of California, Santa Barbara, 1993).

[5] On American-Soviet relations and the changing geopolitical environment during the Cold War, see Melvyn P. Leffler, *A Preponderance of Power: National Security, the Truman Administration, and the Cold War* (Stanford: Stanford University Press, 1992); John Lewis Gaddis, *The United States and the Origins of the Cold War, 1941–1947* (New York: Columbia University Press, 1972); and Gaddis, *Strategies of Containment: A Critical Appraisal of American National Security Policy during the Cold War* (New York: Oxford University Press, 2005).

the establishment of a new civilian agency—the National Research Foundation (later the National Science Foundation)—to distribute public funds for basic research to colleges and universities. Bitter debates in Congress, however, prevented passage of the foundation's enabling legislation until 1950, thereby allowing the military services to fill the void left after OSRD had closed five years earlier.[6] In 1946, for example, the Navy established the Office of Naval Research (ONR) as an independent organization separate from the technical bureaus to fund academic and industrial research in the physical sciences. By the end of the decade, ONR was a major source of government funding for basic research in the United States. The other services followed ONR's lead, organizing their own contracting offices to support research in new fields of science and engineering recently opened up during the war.[7]

The impetus toward greater reliance on contracting rather than in-house government research and development after World War II was also driven by the tremendous growth and diversification of the scientific disciplines during the previous half century. Throughout most of the nineteenth century, the United States had been an intellectual backwater in such fields as theoretical physics and organic and physical chemistry; the major developments in these fields originated in Europe. By 1900, however, the United States boasted a

---

[6] On Bush, OSRD, and postwar research policy, see G. Pascal Zachary, *Endless Frontier: Vannevar Bush, Engineer of the American Century* (New York: Free Press, 1997); Nathan Reingold, "Vannevar Bush's New Deal for Research: Or the Triumph of the Old Order," *Historical Studies in the Physical and Biological Sciences* 17 (1987): 299–344; Reingold, "Choosing the Future: The U.S. Research Community, 1944–46," *Historical Studies in the Physical and Biological Sciences* 25 (1995): 301–28; Larry Owens, "The Counterproductive Management of Science in the Second World War: Vannevar Bush and the Office of Scientific Research and Development," *Business History Review* 68 (Winter 1994): 515–76; Daniel J. Kevles, "The National Science Foundation and the Debate over Postwar Research Policy, 1942–1945: A Political Interpretation of *Science—The Endless Frontier*," *Isis* 68 (March 1977): 5–26; Jessica Wang, "Liberals, the Progressive Left, and the Political Economy of Postwar American Science: The National Science Foundation Debate Revisited," *Historical Studies in the Physical and Biological Sciences* 26 (1995): 139–66; and J. Merton England, *A Patron for Pure Science: The National Science Foundation's Formative Years, 1945–1957* (Washington, D.C.: National Science Foundation, 1982).

[7] On the expansion of military funding for R&D and its impact on private-sector institutions during the Cold War, see, for example, Harvey M. Sapolsky, *Science and the Navy: The History of the Office of Naval Research* (Princeton: Princeton University Press, 1990); Nick A. Komons, *Science and the Air Force: A History of the Air Force Office of Scientific Research* (Arlington, Va.: Historical Division, Office of Information, Office of Aerospace Research, 1966); Paul K. Hoch, "The Crystallization of a Strategic Alliance: The American Physics Elite and the Military in the 1940s," in vol. 1 of *Science, Technology, and the Military*, ed. Everett Mendelsohn, Merritt Roe Smith, and Peter Weingart (Dordrecht, The Netherlands: Kluwer Academic Publishers, 1988); Robert W. Seidel, "Accelerators and National Security: The Evolution of Science Policy for High-Energy Physics, 1947–1967," *History and Technology* 11 (1994): 361–91; Seidel, "Accelerating Science: The Postwar Transformation of the Lawrence Radiation Laboratory," *Historical Studies in the Physical Sciences* 13 (1983): 375–400; Thomas J. Misa, "Military Needs, Commercial Realities, and the Development of the Transistor, 1948–1958," in *Military Enterprise and Technological Change: Perspectives on the American Experience*, ed. Merritt Roe Smith (Cambridge, Mass.: MIT Press, 1985); Stuart W. Leslie, *The Cold War and American Science: The Military-Industrial-Academic Complex at MIT and Stanford* (New York: Columbia University Press, 1993); John W. Servos, "Changing Partners: The Mellon Institute, Private Industry, and the Federal Patron," *Technology and Culture* 35 (April 1994): 221–57; Paul Forman, "Behind Quantum Electronics: National Security as Basis for Physical Research in the United States, 1940–1960," *Historical Studies in the Physical and Biological Sciences* 18 (1987): 149–229; Daniel J. Kevles, "Cold War and Hot Physics: Science, Security, and the American State, 1945–56," *Historical Studies in the Physical and Biological Sciences* 20 (1990): 239–64; and Peter Galison and Bruce Hevly, eds., *Big Science: The Growth of Large-Scale Research* (Stanford: University Press, 1992).

small but steadily growing network of research universities supported by the personal fortunes of wealthy industrialists, such as Andrew Carnegie and John D. Rockefeller. From these humble beginnings emerged a domestic scientific community that, by 1940, had already assumed international standing in the physical sciences, especially in the new fields of atomic, nuclear, and solid-state physics. Similarly in the case of industry, many large manufacturing companies had established centralized research laboratories after 1900 to capitalize on the latest developments in these and other scientific and engineering disciplines.[8] The military services aggressively tapped this diversified academic and industrial knowledge base during World War II, and they would continue to do so after the war was over, to meet evolving weapons requirements.

The rapid postwar growth of the civilian research infrastructure matched the continued diversification of key sectors of the industrial economy into the defense business. The huge demand for war materials had prompted businesses across the country to add manufacturing capacity (at government expense) for everything from aircraft parts and optical equipment to torpedoes and artillery shells. Although many companies jettisoned or closed their military operations after 1945 and prepared to re-enter civilian markets, others chose to remain in the defense business by purchasing government-owned production facilities built during the war. The firms pursuing this latter strategy were as diverse as the defense markets they served. Some companies, such as the aircraft and electrical equipment manufacturers, had always provided hardware to the military services, even during peacetime, and they simply added more capabilities to these core businesses. In other cases, firms that had cut their teeth on military contracts during the war viewed the rapid growth potential in new defense markets as an effective means to offset cyclical behavior in existing civilian product lines. Typically, such firms diversified into defense-related fields through outside acquisitions or by expanding their internal R&D operations. The latter strategy was especially common in large, science-based corporations during the early years of the

---

[8] On the rise of research universities and the growth of the scientific and engineering communities in the United States, see, for example, Daniel J. Kevles, *The Physicists: The History of a Scientific Community in Modern America* (Cambridge, Mass.: Harvard University Press, 1987); Helge Kragh, *Quantum Generations: A History of Physics in the Twentieth Century* (Princeton: Princeton University Press, 1999); John W. Servos, *Physical Chemistry from Ostwald to Pauling: The Making of a Science in America* (Princeton: Princeton University Press, 1990); Laurence R. Veysey, *The Emergence of the American University* (Chicago: University of Chicago Press, 1965); Roger L. Geiger, *To Advance Knowledge: The Growth of American Research Universities, 1900–1940* (New York: Oxford University Press, 1986); Robert E. Kohler, *Partners in Science: Foundations and Natural Scientists, 1900–1945* (Chicago: University of Chicago Press, 1991); and Bruce Seely, "Research, Engineering, and Science in American Engineering Colleges, 1900–1960," *Technology and Culture* 34 (April 1993): 344–86. On the growth of science-based industries and the corresponding expansion of corporate research and development, see Alfred D. Chandler Jr., *Strategy and Structure: Chapters in the History of the American Industrial Enterprise* (Cambridge, Mass.: MIT Press, 1962); Chandler, *The Visible Hand: The Managerial Revolution in American Business* (Cambridge, Mass.: Belknap Press of Harvard University Press, 1977); David A. Hounshell, "The Evolution of Industrial Research in the United States," in *Engines of Innovation: U.S. Industrial Research at the End of an Era,* ed. Richard S. Rosenbloom and William J. Spencer (Boston: Harvard Business School Press, 1996); and John Kenly Smith Jr., "The Scientific Tradition in American Industrial Research," *Technology and Culture* 31 (January 1990): 121–31.

Cold War, when research in cutting-edge fields, such as solid-state physics and semiconductor electronics, was expected to be a major source of new technologies, both civilian and military.[9] Consequently, the growth of captured markets for military hardware in a broad range of manufacturing industries after World War II accelerated the shift in defense spending for R&D from the in-house laboratories operated by the military services to a wide variety of private-sector businesses that now had the technical capabilities to meet critical defense requirements.

At the end of World War II, it was by no means certain that the government arms industry would decline at the expense of the private sector, but there were clear signs that the business community was in a more favorable position to grow and expand than the old-line arsenals and shipyards operated by the Army and the Navy. During the depression years, the business community had been brought to its knees as the government struggled to revive an economy eviscerated by overproduction and anemic consumer demand.[10] The onset of war, however, reversed this trend and helped revive the economy. Driven by huge infusions of capital from the government for new manufacturing capacity, the industrial sector experienced a spectacular recovery that continued into the postwar period. Given these institutional circumstances and the fact that the government found it increasingly difficult to compete against industry and academia for the best scientific and engineering talent, it is perhaps not surprising that the outsourcing of R&D functions to the private sector by the military services became increasingly pervasive as the Cold War progressed.[11]

In a similar fashion, organizational and policy changes within the military services and the Office of the Secretary of Defense (OSD) favored, with varying degrees of success, the separation of R&D from the more common production functions handled by the arsenals and shipyards. This outcome reinforced the ongoing shift of in-house research and development functions from the services to industrial and academic contractors. In some cases, it spawned entirely new types of R&D organizations that provided technical expertise not otherwise available in the Department of Defense. Representative examples include the federally funded research and development centers, a new breed of private, not-for-profit institutions that performed operations research and systems analysis

---

[9] For a general historical overview of the growth and diversification of American manufacturing industries after World War II, see Alfred D. Chandler Jr., "The Competitive Performance of U.S. Industrial Enterprises since the Second World War," *Business History Review* 68 (Spring 1994): 1–72. One need only page through the issues of business and industry trade journals, such as *Aviation Week, Electronics, Fortune,* and *Business Week,* from the 1950s and 1960s to see how attractive the defense business had become to firms that manufactured commercial products for civilian markets.

[10] Although industrial production declined during the depression, corporate investment in research and development increased. See David C. Mowery and Nathan Rosenberg, *Technology and the Pursuit of Economic Growth* (Cambridge: Cambridge University Press, 1989), chap. 4.

[11] See Aaron L. Friedberg, *In the Shadow of the Garrison State: America's Anti-Statism and Its Cold War Grand Strategy* (Princeton: Princeton University Pres, 2000); Hart, *Forged Consensus,* chaps. 6–7. See also Alan Brinkley, *The End of Reform: New Deal Liberalism in Recession and War* (New York: Alfred A. Knopf, 1995); and Paul A. C. Koistinen, *Arsenal of World War II: The Political Economy of American Warfare, 1940–1945* (Lawrence: University of Kansas, 2004).

and engineering required for the integration of increasingly complex technologies employed in weapon systems.[12]

Meanwhile, a managerial revolution in the Department of Defense that began under the direction of defense secretary Robert McNamara in the early 1960s further eroded the independence of the military services. Throughout the decade, the services gradually lost their ability to set policy as McNamara concentrated decision-making authority concerning all facets of weapons acquisition, including R&D, under civilian control in the Office of the Secretary of Defense. Increased outsourcing of research, development, and production was one consequence of McNamara's specific brand of centralization. This trend was reversed somewhat in the 1970s as OSD delegated more responsibility back to the services, but the growth of R&D in the private sector continued, especially in the following decade as defense spending increased dramatically during the presidency of Ronald Reagan. A similar scenario played itself out in the 1990s. Although procurement levels declined to fit new policies that favored a smaller, more mobile force structure, federal investment in R&D remained steady to maintain the technological superiority of new weapon systems.[13]

R&D in the Army, the Navy, and the Air Force was conducted in a variety of institutional settings during the Cold War. Evaluation centers at several Air Force bases, for example, handled full-scale testing of airframes, jet engines, rocket motors, and aerial weapon systems, while the laboratories at the Army's principal manufacturing arsenals developed stronger and more reliable metal alloys used in the production of field guns, projectiles, and armor. Meanwhile, large, centralized laboratories, such as the Naval Research Laboratory and the Naval Ordnance Laboratory, supported a broad range of technical activities, from fundamental studies in nuclear and solid-state physics to the development of mines, torpedoes, and other ordnance materials. The Naval Research Laboratory had no institutional equivalent in the Army and the Air Force. Still, all of these types of R&D organizations— weapons testing facilities, factory laboratories, and centralized laboratories separate from production units—existed in each of the military services.

Chapter 2 of this study examines the content and scope of research and development in the United States Army after World War II. Because this study focuses on R&D programs that supported major weapon systems, however, emphasis is placed on the laboratories attached to the Army's six largest

---

[12] For a general historical survey of the federally funded research and development centers, see *A History of the Department of Defense Federally Funded Research and Development Centers* (Washington, D.C.: Office of Technology Assessment, June 1995).

[13] Roger R. Trask and Alfred Goldberg, *The Department of Defense, 1947–1997: Organization and Leaders* (Washington, D.C.: Historical Office, Office of the Secretary of Defense, 1997), 1–53. See also the essays by Elliott Converse, Walter Poole, Shannon Brown and Walton Moody, Andrew Butrica, and Philip Shiman in Shannon A. Brown, ed., *Providing the Means of War: Historical Perspectives on Defense Acquisition, 1945–2000* (Washington, D.C.: U.S. Army Center of Military History and Industrial College of the Armed Forces, 2005). On industrial research in the United States during the 1980s and 1990s, see Margaret B. W. Graham, "Corporate Research and Development: The Latest Transformation," *Technology and Society*, no. 2/3 (1985): 179–95; and Robert Buderi, *Engines of Tomorrow: How the World's Best Companies Are Using Their Research Labs to Win the Future* (New York: Simon and Schuster, 2001).

manufacturing arsenals: Picatinny (New Jersey), Frankford (Pennsylvania), Watertown (Massachusetts), Watervliet (New York), Rock Island (Illinois), and Springfield (Massachusetts). To be sure, this narrow selection of facilities omits other laboratories owned and operated by the Army. The Signal Corps, for example, operated a large and diversified electronics R&D program based at Fort Monmouth, New Jersey. Although significant in its own right, work in this field focused primarily on the development of communications equipment incorporated into weapon systems produced either in the arsenals or in industry. Unlike the Ordnance Department, which managed the arsenal system, the Signal Corps did not manufacture complete weapon systems of its own. The Chemical Warfare Service, by contrast, operated extensive R&D and weapons production facilities, but a discussion of chemical weapons technologies remains outside the scope of this study.[14]

Although research and development in the Army arsenals typically focused on the solution of immediate problems encountered in the production of field guns, howitzers, ammunition, and other weapons, it also included studies in more speculative fields of science—such as solid-state physics—that, in some cases, emulated research underway in academic and industrial institutions. Even in such instances, research of this type remained closely tied to development and production, a defining feature of technological innovation in the arsenals, which sometimes contradicted policies handed down by the Army Staff to maintain a clear organizational separation between each of these functions. Similar conflicts involving management policy, the execution of R&D in the laboratory, and weapons production on the factory floor existed in the Navy and the Air Force during the same period. Meanwhile, after 1945, the arsenal system entered a period of protracted decline as the Army shifted more of its resources for weapons research and development from in-house facilities to private-sector industrial and academic contractors. The Army began scaling back its arsenal operations in the 1960s. Ordnance production ceased at Watertown Arsenal and Springfield Armory before the decade was out. Manufacturing operations at Frankford Arsenal shut down in 1977.

Like the Army, the Navy originally depended on its own in-house facilities and those of industry for technical expertise. The earliest source of such knowledge existed in the system of shipyards and docks that the federal government established at the beginning of the nineteenth century. By the end of World War II, the Navy's technical capabilities had expanded significantly. In addition to the shipyards, it owned and operated a network of research and development laboratories, most of which were assigned to the Navy's three material bureaus: ordnance, aeronautics, and ships. Representative examples, discussed in Chapter 3, include the Naval Ordnance Laboratory (Maryland), Naval Proving Ground (Virginia), Naval Ordnance Test Station and Naval Electronics Laboratory (both in California), David Taylor Model Basin (Maryland), Naval Aircraft Factory (Pennsylvania), and the Crane Naval Ammunition Depot (Indiana). These

---

[14] The multivolume history of weapons acquisition, of which this monograph is a part, does not examine chemical and biological weapons, either.

facilities, working in collaboration with industrial contractors, played major roles in the development of nuclear-powered propulsion systems for submarines and surface ships, the Sidewinder air-to-air missile, and Polaris, the first submarine-launched nuclear missile.

In 1923, the Navy established the Naval Research Laboratory in Washington, D.C., to pursue a broader and more diversified R&D program independent of the immediate technical support functions handled by the bureaus. This type of institution was unique to the Navy; its equivalent did not exist in the Army and the Air Force. The Navy did, however, establish a contracting unit—the Office of Naval Research (ONR)—in 1946 to fund academic and industrial research unrelated to specific weapons requirements. Moreover, ONR served as the model for the Army and the Air Force, both of which set up similar contracting organizations—the Army Research Office and the Office of Air Research—to support long-term research in private-sector institutions. The founding of ONR (and its counterparts in the Army and the Air Force) also signaled the beginning of a larger shift of Defense Department resources for R&D from the in-house service laboratories to outside contractors.

Chapter 4 examines the growth and diversification of the Air Force's in-house R&D facilities after World War II. Because its primary technology of choice—the airplane—is a more recent innovation, the Air Force has a history of research and development that lacks the long, deep institutional legacies found in the Army and the Navy. Originally an organizational element of the Army, the Air Force did not achieve status as an independent service until 1947. Prior to separation, research and development had been dispersed among a diverse group of public and private-sector institutions: the domestic aircraft manufacturers, the National Advisory Committee for Aeronautics, the National Bureau of Standards, and the air arm's own in-house R&D facilities. Major internal R&D operations were located at Wright Field in Ohio. After the war, however, the scale of Air Force R&D grew rapidly to include new electronics and communications programs at Rome Air Development Center near Syracuse, New York, and the Cambridge Research Laboratories outside Boston. The Arnold Engineering Development Center in Tennessee handled testing and development of all types of aircraft engines and rocket motors, while the evaluation centers at Edwards (California), Kirtland (New Mexico), Holloman (New Mexico), and Patrick (Florida) Air Force bases supported similar functions on complete aircraft and ballistic missile delivery systems. In addition to supporting these ongoing technical activities, the Air Force laboratories also diversified—both internally and through external contracts—into more speculative fields of science and technology, such as artificial intelligence and laser and particle-beam weapons.

Finally, it is necessary to include a brief note on the source materials and the research methodology used to produce this monograph. There is no synthetic history of research and development in the Department of Defense or in the individual military services during the Cold War. The published secondary literature, most of which is cited in the chapters that follow, focuses on specific laboratories and contracting offices, R&D programs, or high-level management policies. This study has also drawn heavily on a wide variety of articles and reports published in weekly news magazines and military and industry trade journals. Time and space limitations precluded further historical research in relevant manuscript collections maintained by the armed services and public and private repositories. Only through rigorous analysis of pertinent archival materials—a time-consuming and costly process—would it have been possible to contextualize this study further and add historical depth to the information gleaned from published sources. Consequently, the arguments and conclusions presented in the pages that follow, while supported by the evidence cited in the footnotes, are more suggestive than definitive. This outcome should not discourage the reader but rather serve as a guide for additional historical research on an otherwise neglected, important topic in the history of science, technology, and the military in modern America. This study has only begun to explore the content, scope, organization, and management of the Army's arsenal system and the sprawling network of laboratories and testing facilities operated by the Navy and the Air Force, which, taken together, constituted a substantial segment of the federal R&D establishment after 1945. Filling the gaps in the general framework presented here is a task left to other historians and future projects.

Research and Development in the Army

During World War II, the United States turned out unprecedented quantities of guns, ordnance, aircraft, and ships to equip American and allied combat forces fighting in Europe and Asia. Firms in the steel, automobile, aircraft, electrical, and other critical manufacturing industries suspended commercial operations to help the War Department meet the rapidly growing demand for all types of military hardware. Perhaps nowhere was the demand more acute and the transition from civilian to military production more difficult than in the Army. Like the other military services, the Army was responsible for the design, fabrication, and procurement of ordnance materials. The centerpiece of this effort was the Army's arsenal system, which provided much of the technical knowledge and manufacturing expertise used by corporate America to mass-produce everything from small-arms ammunition and artillery shells to field guns and tanks. During the postwar period, however, the arsenal system played an important but steadily diminishing role as the Army and the other military services turned to academia and industry for the latest advances in science and technology to support ongoing production programs.[1]

The origins of the arsenal system in the United States can be traced back to the earliest days of the Republic, when the federal government established in-house production facilities to meet the expanding weapons requirements of the regular army and the state militias. The Springfield (Massachusetts) Armory was established in 1794.[2] Watervliet Arsenal (New York) was founded in 1813, and Watertown (Massachusetts) and Frankford (Pennsylvania) arsenals followed three years later. The two remaining arsenals, Rock Island (Illinois) and Picatinny (New Jersey), were established in 1862 and 1880, respectively. Springfield produced rifles and other small arms, whereas Watervliet pioneered the development and manufacture of large-caliber guns and artillery. Watertown produced howitzers and seacoast and antiaircraft guns. Frankford manufactured

---

[1] On the arsenal system during World War II, see Constance McLaughlin Green, Harry C. Thomson, and Peter C. Roots, *The Ordnance Department: Planning Munitions for War*, in *United States Army in World War II, The Technical Services* (Washington, D.C.: Office of the Chief of Military History, 1955); and Harry C. Thomson and Lida Mayo, *The Ordnance Department: Procurement and Supply*, in *United States Army in World War II, The Technical Services* (Washington, D.C.: Office of the Chief of Military History, 1960). Also on wartime weapons production, see R. Elberton Smith, *The Army and Economic Mobilization*, in *United States Army in World War II, The War Department* (Washington, D.C.: Office of the Chief of Military History, 1959). For a general overview of weapons production facilities owned and operated by the Army, the Navy, and the Air Force during the Cold War, see Philip Shiman, *Forging the Sword: Defense Production during the Cold War* (Champaign, Ill.: Construction Engineering Research Laboratoriesa, U.S. Army Corps of Engineers, July 1997).

[2] Also founded in 1794, the Harpers Ferry Armory was destroyed during the Civil War. On the history of this armory, see Merritt Roe Smith, *Harpers Ferry Armory and the New Technology: The Challenge of Change* (Ithaca, N.Y.: Cornell University Press, 1977).

small-arms ammunition, artillery projectiles, fuzes, gun cartridges, and optical and fire control instruments. Rock Island manufactured artillery recoil mechanisms, gun carriages, and combat vehicles. Picatinny Arsenal was the Army's primary source of explosives, propellants, bombs, and other munitions. All six arsenals were assigned to the Ordnance Department, which had played a seminal role in the mechanization of arms production in the United States during the nineteenth century.[3] Established by an act of Congress in 1812, the Ordnance Department was one of the seven independent technical services operated by the Army at the end of World War II.[4]

That the government routinely favored a policy of rapid postwar demobilization often left the arsenal system without the requisite institutional resources to maintain an extensive manufacturing capability on standby status. Taking its place was a more diversified in-house research and development function to help the industrial sector meet ordnance production requirements in time of war. The extent of this transformation was especially evident during World War I, when industrial firms converted their manufacturing operations to focus on the mass production of weapons developed in the arsenals.[5] Even during World War II, following another significant expansion in manufacturing capacity, the arsenal system produced less than 10 percent of the Army's total ordnance require-

---

[3] In addition to the six principal manufacturing arsenals, the Ordnance Department also owned and operated repair and storage facilities, typically referred to as arsenals or depots. Prior to 1940, major operations were located at Augusta Arsenal (Georgia), Benecia Arsenal (California), Ogden Arsenal (Utah), Raritan Arsenal (New Jersey), and San Antonio Arsenal (Texas). The Army also operated a network of proving grounds responsible for weapons testing and evaluation. See, for example, F. B. Pletcher, "Aberdeen Proving Ground," *Iron Trade Review* 73 (18 October 1923): 1091–96; "Some Recent Advances in Ballistics," *Journal of Applied Physics* 16 (December 1945): 773–80; "Metallurgical Activities at Aberdeen Proving Ground," *Metal Progress* 59 (April 1951): 499–502; J. P. Hammill, "Research in Ballistics," *Ordnance* 44 (September-October 1959): 235–38; W. D. Hodges, "New Role for Aberdeen," *Ordnance* 56 (September-October 1971): 132–35; Levin H. Campbell Jr., *The Industry-Ordnance Team* (New York: McGraw-Hill, 1946), 46–53; Herman H. Goldstine, *The Computer from Pascal to von Neumann* (Princeton: Princeton University Press, 1993), part 2; and David H. Devorkin, *Science with a Vengeance: How the Military Created the Space Sciences after World War II* (New York: Springer-Verlag, 1992), chap 7.

[4] Like the Ordnance Department, the Quartermaster Corps, Corps of Engineers, Signal Corps, Transportation Corps, Medical Department, and the Chemical Warfare Service operated their own research laboratories or maintained institutional connections to outside R&D organizations. For a discussion of the scope and content of these functions at the end of World War II, see the articles under the general title, "Mobilization of Scientific Resources—V: The U.S. Army," in the April 1945 issue of the *Journal of Applied Physics*. See also the review articles and reports of research findings published in *Army Research and Development News Magazine*, a monthly periodical introduced by the Office of the Chief of Research and Development in December 1960. On the Ordnance Department and its contributions to the development of American manufacturing technology, see David A. Hounshell, *From the American System to Mass Production, 1800–1932: The Development of Manufacturing Technology in the United States* (Baltimore: Johns Hopkins University Press, 1984); Merritt Roe Smith, "Army Ordnance and the 'American System' of Manufacturing, 1815–1861," in *Military Enterprise and Technological Change: Perspectives on the American Experience*, ed.. Merritt Roe Smith (Cambridge, Mass.: MIT Press, 1985); and Smith, "Military Arsenals and Industry before World War I," in *War, Business, and American Society: Historical Perspectives on the Military Industrial Complex*, ed. Benjamin Cooling (Port Washington, N.Y.: Kennikat Press, 1977).

[5] Smith, "Military Arsenals and Industry before World War I," esp. 35–41. The sharp rise in the outsourcing of weapons production to industry during the war was matched, albeit on a much smaller scale, by a major expansion of manufacturing capacity in the arsenals. See W. H. Tschappat, "The Manufacturing Arsenals and Their Equipment," *American Machinist* 78 (14 February 1934): 141–44.

ments.[6] After 1945, the six old-line arsenals, while still maintaining extensive production capabilities, were essentially repositories of an accumulated knowledge base that supported, on behalf of industry, the design and development of ordnance and associated weapons delivery systems.[7] Of the $2 billion set aside for weapons production by the Ordnance Department in 1958, for example, 90 percent of that amount was earmarked for distribution to industrial contractors through the arsenal system.[8]

Consequently, the manufacturing firms that had relied on the arsenals and other service laboratories to jump-start arms production during World War II rapidly built up their own in-house technical capabilities afterward to meet the anticipated demand for increasingly sophisticated military hardware. Expanding internal R&D functions also mitigated the likelihood of technological obsolescence inherent in arms production. This transformation was especially evident among those companies that moved aggressively into the electronics and guided missile fields. These state-of-the-art technologies, not the conventional weapons traditionally developed in the arsenals, were expected to play a leading role in a future war.[9]

---

[6] Wartime expenditures for the construction of additional production capacity in the old-line arsenals exceeded $300 million. The Ordnance Department and the other technical services also built new manufacturing facilities from scratch. The Detroit Arsenal, for example, was established by the Ordnance Department to manufacture tanks (a function previously assigned to the Rock Island Arsenal), and the Chemical Warfare Service built the Pine Bluff (Arkansas), Rocky Mountain (Colorado), and Huntsville and Redstone (Alabama) arsenals to produce chemical agents and explosives for artillery shells, bombs, and other types of ammunition. The government, largely through the Defense Plant Corporation, also financed the construction of weapons production facilities operated by industrial contractors. After the war, these government-owned, contractor-operated (GOCO) plants were either placed on standby status or continued operating at reduced production levels. In some cases, manufacturing facilities were purchased outright by the contractors. Throughout the postwar period, the military services gradually disposed of their GOCO plants and other in-house operations. Smith, *The Army and Economic Mobilization*, 497–98, 501.

[7] Post–World War II production levels at the arsenals varied according to the supply needs of the military services. The arsenals generally operated on standby status during peacetime, scaling back manufacturing functions and focusing instead on research and development. During wartime (Korea, Vietnam), however, production of conventional weapons in the arsenals rose sharply to match a much larger expansion of output by private industry. The manufacture of more specialized equipment in the arsenals, such as guided missile launchers, typically did not exceed the pilot production state. Shiman, *Forging the Sword*, 24, 39–43; C. M. Wesson, "Adequate National Defense Requires Modernized Army Arsenals," *Machinery* 45 (July 1939): 737; Thomson and Mayo, *The Ordnance Department: Procurement and Supply*, 12.

[8] J. H. Hinrichs, "Army Ordnance Arsenals," *Ordnance* 43 (September-October 1958): 211.

[9] Shiman, *Forging the Sword*, 53–54, 64–66. In a deliberate move to diversify its defense business in the 1950s, General Motors scaled back tank and gun production in favor of establishing new markets in military electronics. The large airframe manufacturers, such as North American Aviation, Chance Vought, Lockheed, Martin, Northrop, and Douglas Aircraft, adopted a similar strategy. These and other firms diversified into the electronics and missile fields. "[T]he best way to win a foothold among the top 100 [defense contractors] is via the missile and electronics business: the big future contracts will be for rockets, electronic equipment, and other hardware of the nuclear-space age," *Business Week* reported in 1958. "The Pentagon's Top Hands," *Business Week* (20 September 1958): 39; H. W. Barclay, "General Motors Defense Research Laboratories," *Automotive Industries* 127 (1 December, 1962): 44. Many firms entered military markets for missiles and electronics through a combination of outside acquisitions and internal expansion of corporate R&D functions. See, for example, J. S. Butz, "United Has Proved Value of Research," *Aviation Week* 66 (3 June 1957): 200–13; R. Hawkes, "Convair Seeks Lead Through Research," *Aviation Week* 66 (3 June 1957): 215–30; P. J. Klass, "Bell Advances Avionics on Wide Front," *Aviation Week* 66 (3 June 1957): 235–51; E. Clark, "Martin's Research Is Broad, Varied," *Aviation Week* 66 (3 June 1957): 252–65; and "Chance Vought Stakes Its Future on Research Push," *Business Week* (23 July 1960): 104–08.

Research and development in the arsenals covered many fields within the scientific and engineering disciplines. This work included routine testing, analysis, and standardization of critical components for guns and ammunition and fundamental studies of the behavior and properties of constituent ordnance materials, especially metals and alloys. Laboratory investigations typically covered a broad range of activities, from exploratory research to pilot assembly work on the shop floor. This close working relationship among different types of research, development, and production had been a defining feature of technological innovation in the arsenal system for more than a century, and it remained largely intact throughout the postwar period. Such a symbiotic relationship was not, however, unique to the Army or to the other military services. It had also been one of the defining features of technological innovation in industry. Like their counterparts in the arsenals, researchers in industrial laboratories had been equally successful at extending the frontiers of science while at the same time using that knowledge to improve existing goods and services and introduce new commercial products.[10] Dividing research into distinct categories—for example, *basic, fundamental,* or *applied*—is exceedingly difficult in cases such as these where professional allegiances and disciplinary boundaries in science and engineering often overlapped. The fact that such definitional ambiguity imposes interpretive limits on the historian seeking to reconstruct the boundaries between different categories of knowledge within and across institutions further illustrates the extent to which research, development, and production were inextricably linked in the arsenal system.[11]

This chapter focuses on the multidirectional relationship among research , development, and production in the Army's six old-line manufacturing arsenals, and how it responded to broader changes in Defense Department policy and evolving patterns of institutional growth in the federal scientific research establishment after World War II. Major emphasis is placed on the content and scope of laboratory research in metallurgy, solid-state physics, and high-energy X-ray research. Research in these fields led to the development of improved metals and alloys, which enabled workers at Watertown and Frankford arsenals and the Springfield Armory—and their counterparts in industry—to manufacture more reliable artillery shells, gun tubes, recoil mechanisms, and other conventional ordnance materials. The same research also contributed to the ongoing development of more recent wartime weapons, such as missiles and rockets. Although it shared jurisdiction over these new technologies with the Navy and the Air Force, the Army nevertheless maintained a significant program

---

[10] For an introduction to the historical literature on American industrial research, see John Kenly Smith Jr., "The Scientific Tradition in American Industrial Research," *Technology and Culture* 31 (January 1990): 121–131; and David A. Hounshell, "The Evolution of Industrial Research in the United States," In *Engines of Innovation: U.S. Industrial Research at the End of an Era,* ed. Richard S. Rosenbloom and William J. Spencer (Boston: Harvard Business School Press, 1996).

[11] For an insightful discussion of this methodological problem and how historians have struggled with it in studies of R&D in academic, industrial, and government institutions, see Ronald R. Kline, "Construing 'Technology' as 'Applied Science': Public Rhetoric of Scientists and Engineers in the United States, 1880–1945," *Isis* 86 (June 1995): 194–221. For a broader analysis, see Donald E. Stokes, *Pasteur's Quadrant: Basic Science and Technological Innovation* (Washington, D.C.: Brookings Institution Press, 1997).

of rocket and missile development at Picatinny and Rock Island arsenals. In some cases, though rare, laboratory research in the arsenals extended the frontiers of knowledge in highly esoteric fields. In the early 1970s, for example, researchers at Watervliet Arsenal began studying superconductivity. Although it did not lead to any immediate practical results, this work produced new classes of stable superconducting materials that manifested superior electrical and magnetic properties.

Changing Institutional Patterns of Army Research and Development after World War II

That the arsenals maintained a close working relationship between R&D and production is understandable, given their mandate to provide the Army with the most technologically advanced ordnance and weapons delivery systems. What is perhaps more unusual, however, is the extent to which the arsenals maintained this culture of innovation during the postwar period, especially given the pressures exerted by the Army Staff and influential civilian scientists to separate research and development from production.[12] Emphasis on the rapid development and mass production of weapons during the war had forced the arsenals to relinquish most long-range, undirected research to the private sector. Established in 1941, the Office of Scientific Research and Development (OSRD) spearheaded this readjustment. It coordinated and distributed to universities and industrial firms federal funds for research in the physical sciences. "[M]uch of our basic research," wrote an Army officer stationed at Frankford Arsenal in 1943, "has been abandoned for the time being, in favor of applied research that might be termed more precisely, industrial engineering. The Army is therefore, more dependent upon universities and industrial laboratories for amplification of the research aspects of its many problems." OSRD managed more than two hundred research projects on behalf of the Ordnance Department during the war, including, among others, studies of the kinetics of nitration of chemicals

---

[12] The same trends also guided R&D policy in American industry after the war. Committed to the separation of research and development from production, corporate executives invested large sums of money in the construction and staffing of state-of-the-art laboratories located far away from manufacturing operations. Although such efforts typically produced a wealth of knowledge in diverse fields of science and technology, they contributed far less to the development of new products and commercial markets. In many cases, research in the engineering disciplines proved to be more valuable to the development of new products than even the most advanced basic research. See Hounshell, "The Evolution of Industrial Research in the United States," 45–51. Useful case studies include David A. Hounshell and John Kenly Smith Jr., *Science and Corporate Strategy: DuPont R&D, 1902–1980* (Cambridge: Cambridge University Press, 1988); John W. Servos, "Changing Partners: The Mellon Institute, Private Industry, and the Federal Patron," *Technology and Culture* 35 (April 1994): 221–57; Stuart W. Leslie, "Blue Collar Science: Bringing the Transistor to Life in the Lehigh Valley," *Historical Studies in the Physical and Biological Sciences* 32 (2001): 71–113; Scott G. Knowles and Stuart W. Leslie, "'Industrial Versailles': Eero Saarinen's Corporate Campuses for GM, IBM, and AT&T," *Isis* 92 (March 2001): 1–33; and Margaret B. W. Graham and Alec T. Shuldiner, *Corning and the Craft of Innovation* (New York: Oxford University Press, 2001). A similar strategy also guided R&D policy in science-based manufacturing firms that received weapons contracts from the Department of Defense. For an excellent analysis of the impact of military contracting on R&D in the defense industry after World War II, see Glen Ross Asner, "The Cold War and American Industrial Research" (Ph.D. diss., Carnegie Mellon University, 2006).

used in explosives, development of special fuels suitable for jet propulsion, and investigations of plastic deformation in metals.[13]

Although OSRD closed after the war, its institutional legacy continued to exert a profound influence on the institutions of science and technology in the military, including the Army arsenals. OSRD director Vannevar Bush, who had served as President Franklin Roosevelt's de facto science adviser during the war, favored the organizational separation of research and development from production. In his view, research of the type normally conducted in the leading universities ought to be the primary source of technological innovation, military security, and economic growth. Moreover, Bush believed that in-house government research was inferior to its academic equivalent. Relying on government laboratories for the advancement of science would only increase the likelihood of political and bureaucratic interference from the state.[14] Bush also served in several capacities as a civilian consultant to the military services after the war, and his views were shared by General Dwight Eisenhower and other senior Army officers familiar with the contributions that science had made to the allied victory.[15]

Senior officers in the Ordnance Department, however, believed that separating the management of research and development from production would only lead to greater inefficiencies and waste in the weapons procurement process. While proclaiming that the "freedom [of R&D] from control of those responsible for mass production is a great spur to development," one officer assigned to the Ordnance Department's Research and Development Service also acknowledged that "new weapons must be designed with ultimate mass manufacture in mind."[16] The Davies Committee, appointed by the Secretary of the Army in September 1953 to evaluate the organizational relationship between R&D and production, rendered a similar opinion. Composed primarily of former and current Ordnance Department personnel, the committee concluded that the separation of development from production and procurement would slow the pace of weapons innovation and also inhibit the necessary exchange of information between researchers working in the laboratory and weapons users operating in the field. In cases where specialized knowledge and expertise were needed, however, the committee recommended that the Ordnance Department contract

---

[13] L. S. Fletcher, "Research at a Government Arsenal in Cooperation with Universities," *Journal of Engineering Education* 33 (June 1943): 783; Green, Thomson, and Roots, *The Ordnance Department: Planning Munitions for War,* 217–19, 227; Campbell, *The Industry-Ordnance Team,* 154–55.

[14] On Bush's views, see his landmark report, *Science—The Endless Frontier: A Report to the President on a Program for Postwar Scientific Research* (Washington, D.C.: U.S. Government Printing Office, 1945). See also Nathan Reingold, "Vannevar Bush's New Deal for Research: Or the Triumph of the Old Order," *Historical Studies in the Physical and Biological Sciences* 17 (1987): 299–344.

[15] H. S. Aurand, "The Army's Research Program," *Mechanical Engineering* 68 (September 1946): 785–86. Bush served as chairman of the Research and Development Board, which had been established in 1947 to coordinate the research functions of the military services and advise the Secretary of Defense on scientific and technical matters.

[16] D. W. Hoppock, "How Army Ordnance Develops Weapons for Its 'Customers,'" *Product Engineering* 16 (June 1945): 361–62.

directly with scientists working in civilian research institutions. Predictably, the Ordnance Department endorsed the committee's recommendations.[17]

The growth and diversification of the postwar federal research establishment intensified the debates among senior Army officials and civilian experts about the relationship between R&D and weapons production. When OSRD and other temporary wartime agencies closed after 1945, the military services quickly filled the void by establishing new organizations to fund scientific research in universities and other private-sector institutions. The wartime success of OSRD and the likelihood of a larger postwar military establishment made the outsourcing of R&D especially appealing to key leaders in the military services. To be sure, the military leadership had already witnessed firsthand how effectively civilian science had been mobilized to develop the atomic bomb, microwave radar, the proximity fuse, and other critical wartime weapons. The establishment of the Office of Naval Research (ONR) in 1946, and the founding of similar extramural funding organizations in the Army and the Air Force shortly thereafter, likely exerted greater influence on the long-term viability of R&D in the arsenal system than did the debates about its internal structure and organization immediately after the war.[18] In 1946, for example, the Ordnance Department expected to allocate only one-third of the funds for research and development requested annually from Congress to the Army's arsenals and proving grounds; the remaining two-thirds were to be used "in placing contracts with research institutions and with manufacturers having strong scientific and engineering research organizations and the facilities suitable for the development of new weapons." Commenting specifically on the significance of this institutional division of labor, the Ordnance Department's director of R&D, Maj. Gen. Gladeon Barnes wrote, "Our war experience has taught us that this is the best possible way in which to conduct research and development in ordnance for the War Department."[19]

Back in the spring of 1946, General Eisenhower, who then served as Army chief of staff, announced the establishment of a new Research and Development Division assigned to the War Department General Staff. The purpose of this high-level staff organization was to coordinate the R&D operations of the Army and the Navy (an independent Air Force would not be established until 1947) with those of the civilian scientific and engineering communities.[20] The Army alone maintained a research budget of $280 million that year, one quarter of which was earmarked for fundamental studies in colleges and universities.[21] The

---

[17] James E. Hewes, *From Root to McNamara: Army Organization and Administration, 1900–1963* (Washington, D.C.: U.S. Army Center of Military History, 1975), 227.

[18] See Daniel J. Kevles, *The Physicists: The History of a Scientific Community in Modern America* (Cambridge, Mass.: Harvard University Press, 1987), chap. 22; Harvey M. Sapolsky, *Science and the Navy: The History of the Office of Naval Research* (Princeton: Princeton University Press, 1990); and Nick A. Komons, *Science and the Air Force: A History of the Air Force Office of Scientific Research* (Arlington, Va.: Historical Division, Office of Information, Office of Aerospace Research, 1966).

[19] G. M. Barnes, "Research Needs for Weapons," *Mechanical Engineering* 68 (March 1946): 197.

[20] "War Department Research and Development Division," *Science* 104 (18 October 1946): 369; "Army Puts Research, Development on Top General Staff Level," *Iron Age* 158 (3 October 1946): 95.

[21] "Science Dons a Uniform," *Business Week* (14 September 1946): 22. In 1947, the Army distributed

Ordnance Department created a formal coordinating function to handle R&D contracting in 1951, when it established the Office of Ordnance Research (OOR) at Duke University. Staffed by civilian and military scientists, OOR supported academic research in the sciences that had no direct relation to specific ordnance problems, although OOR did on occasion fund some fundamental work in the arsenal laboratories. "[OOR] is interested in the sciences having ordnance relevancy," wrote the director of OOR's Metallurgical and Engineering Sciences Division, "but proposals pertaining to applied or technical research design and development are not within the mission of this office."[22]

Similar attempts to create an Army-wide R&D organization had proved more problematic, primarily because the technical services did not want to lose operational control of functions that they had always managed themselves. They also resisted initiatives that sought to separate the management of research and development from production and procurement. The extent to which these bureaucratic customs prevailed had been clearly revealed in 1947, when the General Staff abolished the Research and Development Division and merged its functions into the Service, Supply, and Procurement Division (later the Logistics Division) under the direction of the Deputy Chief of Staff for Logistics. Under mounting pressure from civilian scientists within and outside the Army, however, the Deputy Chief of Staff for Logistics relinquished control of R&D to the new Office of the Chief of Research and Development, established on the Army Staff by the Secretary of the Army, in 1955.[23] Organizationally equivalent to the position of deputy chief of staff, this new office expanded three years later when the Army Science Advisory Panel lobbied successfully for the establishment of the Army Research Office to plan and coordinate the research and development functions of the Ordnance Department and the other six technical services.[24]

Although the establishment of the Army Research Office and the Office of the Chief of Research and Development once again elevated the status of R&D and made centralized planning a key component of the Army's R&D program,

---

more than two-thirds of its funds for research and development to industrial firms, universities, and other private research organizations. In most cases, new contracts for basic research were awarded to institutions to continue work previously funded by OSRD. "Army Reveals Plans to Industry," *Chemical and Engineering News* 25 (3 February 1947): 306.

[22] P. R. Kosting, "Metallurgy Research Program of the U.S. Army Office of Ordnance Research," *Journal of Metals* 9 (May 1957): 664 (quote); "Ordnance Research Program," *Army, Navy, Air Force Journal* 88 (16 June 1951): 1165; P. N. Gillon, "Army Ordnance Research," *Army, Navy, Air Force Journal* 92 (20 November 1954): 337, 339.

[23] For a detailed discussion of these events, see Hewes, *From Root to McNamara*, 217–58; and Elliott V. Converse, "The Army and Acquisition, 1945–1953," March 2003 (unpublished manuscript), U.S. Army Center of Military History, Fort Lesley J. McNair, Washington, D.C. I am indebted to Dr. Converse for sharing an early version of this manuscript with me.

[24] "ARO Coaching Army Research," *Chemical and Engineering News* 36 (15 September 1958): 38–39. Within a decade, ARO's six technical divisions (physical and engineering sciences, environmental sciences, behavioral sciences, life sciences, studies and analysis, data management) coordinated and monitored R&D projects in 60 Army laboratories, 225 colleges and universities, 161 nonprofit research institutions, and more than 300 private firms. W. J. Lynch, "Combat Superiority Aim of Army Research Program," *Defense Industry Bulletin* 5 (July 1969): 14, 16. For a brief review of the Army Research Office's programs and functions in the early 1990s, see W. A. Flood, "The Army Research Office," *IEEE Antennas and Propagation Magazine* 33 (February 1991): 17.

the execution of that function was still decentralized and controlled by the individual technical services under the direction of the Deputy Chief of Staff for Logistics. The Ordnance Department retained control of its own laboratories and funds and determined how resources for R&D would be allocated to those in-house facilities and also to academic and industrial contractors through the Office of Ordnance Research.[25] Much of this institutional leverage was lost, however, in an Army-wide reorganization in the early 1960s, thereby weakening the ability of the arsenals to maintain a viable production base and a competitive scientific and technological infrastructure.

Although the Deputy Chief of Staff for Logistics was responsible for integrating their functions into a unified weapons procurement system, the seven technical services essentially operated as separate supply organizations, each one responsible for specific components—armament, communications equipment, and so on. Efforts to reform and streamline this organizational structure had been attempted before, but it was not until the early 1960s that the Office of the Secretary of Defense (OSD) acted decisively to implement permanent changes. Coordination and operational efficiency suffered, especially in cases where the development of new weapon systems, such as missiles and rockets, cut across the jurisdictional boundaries of two or more technical services. Prompted by these structural problems in the procurement process and Defense Secretary Robert McNamara's predilection for centralized administrative control of weapons acquisition, the Pentagon deactivated the offices occupied by the Army's technical service chiefs in 1962 and combined the functions under their control into a new organization—the Army Materiel Command (AMC). This massive restructuring eliminated the authority of the technical service chiefs and merged into a single unit all phases of the Army's weapons acquisition process: R&D, testing and evaluation, procurement and production, inventory management, storage and distribution, and maintenance. Most of the installations previously assigned to the technical services were realigned into five major commodity commands that focused on hardware development: Weapons, Munitions, Missiles, Electronics, and Mobility. A separate Test and Evaluation Command conducted studies to certify operational readiness of the equipment developed in the commodity commands, while the Supply and Maintenance Command supervised field repairs and equipment distribution to the Army's operating units.

The reorganization intensified debates between advocates of the new materiel command and opponents, who believed that the merger of R&D with production and procurement would impede the longer term research needed to develop the most technologically advanced weapon systems. Partly in response to this ongoing conflict, the Army Staff created a two-tiered R&D organization within AMC. The five commodity commands assumed management control of most of the laboratories previously attached to the technical services. These laboratories conducted R&D to support each command's assigned mission and

---

[25] "Army Research Office," *Science* 128 (19 September 1958): 645–46; "U.S. Army Research Office Schedules Move to New Location in June," *Army Research and Development News Magazine* 3 (May 1962): 18.

commodity category. The new Weapons Command, for example, managed the laboratories and production facilities at Rock Island and Watervliet arsenals and Springfield Armory, while the Electronics Command supervised the old Signal Corps laboratories (renamed the Electronic Research and Development Laboratories) located at Fort Monmouth, New Jersey. The remaining laboratories, which conducted Army-wide research and development separate from the R&D underway in the commodity commands, reported directly to the AMC headquarters staff.[26]

Space limitations and this chapter's primary emphasis on the arsenal system preclude a detailed analysis of all the Army's laboratories, as well as of the organizational permutations that recast their functions and missions in the decades following AMC's establishment.[27] Some general patterns are discernable, however, and they help frame the more detailed examination of R&D in the arsenal system that follows in the section below. Despite the controversy that permeated the debates among civilian scientists, the Army Staff, and the technical service chiefs about the extent to which R&D should be divorced from production and procurement, a robust relationship between these functions remained intact in the arsenal system throughout the postwar period. At the same time, it is also true that the fading influence of the technical services hastened the decline of the arsenal system. No longer protected by the once-powerful and independent Ordnance Department, the arsenals lost some of their institutional flexibility and, as a result, were more vulnerable to the persistent drive toward government contracting that came to dominate the weapons acquisition process during the Cold War. This reality left fewer alternatives available to those arsenals already weakened by an increasingly competitive labor market for technical expertise and declining budgets for research, development, and production.[28] By 1980, Springfield and Frankford

---

[26] *Arsenal for the Brave: A History of the United States Army Materiel Command, 1962–1968* (Washington, D.C.: U.S. Army Materiel Command, 30 September 1969), chaps. 1, 4. Also on the formation of AMC, see Hewes, *From Root to McNamara*, chaps. 8–10.

[27] The following historical materials may be consulted for additional information on the content, scope, and restructuring of Army research and development outside the arsenal system. Institutional changes are covered in detail in *Army Research and Development News Magazine* and in the annual histories produced by the Army Materiel Command. Copies of the AMC annual histories are preserved at the Army Materiel Command Historical Office at Fort Belvoir, Virginia. *Arsenal for the Brave* also provides broad coverage of the Army's laboratory system as it evolved during the 1960s. On the latest major transformation of Army R&D—events culminating in the formation of the Army Research Laboratory at Adelphi, Maryland, in 1992—see the AMC annual histories mentioned above and also *A History of the Army Research Laboratory* (Adelphi, Md.: Army Research Laboratory, August 2003). Additional studies of Army R&D in some of the major AMC subordinate commands during the Cold War may be identified in Edgar F. Raines Jr., "U.S. Army Historical Publications Related to the U.S. Army in the Cold War Era: A Preliminary Bibliography," 22 July 1994 (unpublished manuscript), Histories Division, U.S. Army Center of Military History, Fort Lesley McNair, Washington, D.C.

[28] Even before the establishment of the Army Materiel Command in 1962, the Army faced institutional competition for qualified scientists and engineers to staff the arsenal laboratories. Employment patterns varied by technical field, but industrial firms generally paid higher salaries than government laboratories for qualified scientists and engineers. Watervliet and Rock Island arsenals, for example, experienced staffing shortfalls through the post–World War II period. In some cases, shortages forced the arsenals to contract out work previously conducted internally. See "Industry-Military Link Forged," *Business Week* (16 November 1946): 20–26; "Keeping Federal Labs Staffed," *Chemical and Engineering News* 11

arsenals had been permanently shuttered, and a third—Watertown Arsenal—had closed its weapons manufacturing facilities.[29]

The Content of Research and Development in the Arsenal System

Rapid demobilization of the industrial economy at the end of World War II brought a sharp reduction in employment and a corresponding reorientation of technical activities in the arsenal system. As production levels dropped, The Army placed renewed emphasis on the expansion of research and development to maintain technological readiness in what was becoming an increasingly hostile geopolitical environment prompted by the onset of the Cold War. Much of this work continued to focus on short-term practical problems, such as the improvement of manufacturing methods and materials and the overhaul of precision machine tools. Arsenal administrators and their superiors on the Army Staff also strove to capture the latest developments in science and technology that had opened up during the war. Microwave radar, the atomic bomb, and the proximity fuse were among the most significant and decisive wartime weapons that the United States had developed. The Army leadership expected that the technologies on which they were based would achieve similar results in the event of another war.

To prepare for that possibility, American military leaders harnessed the scientific community's expertise in many technical fields, especially the new and expanding disciplines of nuclear and solid-state physics. Research in nuclear physics, which had first taken American physicists by storm in the 1930s, experienced rapid growth after the war.[30] The military's interest in nuclear research during the postwar period was largely, but not completely, restricted to the development of tactical and strategic nuclear weapons and atomic-powered propulsion systems for the Navy's submarine fleet.[31] Responsibility for R&D was split three ways—among the Atomic Energy Commission (AEC) in-house laboratories

(11 November 1957): 42–26; P. A. Chadwell, "DOD and Service R&D Programs," *National Defense* 66 (October 1981): 44–47; *A History of Watervliet Arsenal, 1813 to Modernization 1982,* (Watervliet, N.Y.: Watervliet Arsenal, 1982): 174, 184; and *A History of Rock Island and Rock Island Arsenal from Earliest Times to 1954,* vol. 3 (1940–1954), (Rock Island, Ill.: Rock Island Arsenal, 1965), 597.

[29]"Materiel Development and Readiness Command Replaces AMC," *Army Research and Development News Magazine* 17 (January-February 1976): 4–5; "Watertown Arsenal Slated for Elimination in DoD Move," *Army Research and Development News Magazine* 5 (June 1964): 20; "Springfield Museum, Institute Replace Armory after Phaseout," *Army Research and Development News Magazine* 9 (June 1968): 5; "DoD Announces Frankford Arsenal Closing, AMC Depot System Realignment," *Army Research and Development News Magazine* 16 (January-February 1975): 4.

[30] See Kevles, *The Physicists,* esp. chaps. 14–15, 21–23.

[31] One important exception was the academic research in nuclear physics sponsored by the Office of Naval Research. This work was, by and large, generally more fundamental in nature, unrelated to specific weapons requirements. See, for example, Sapolsky, *Science and the Navy;* and S. S. Schweber, "The Mutual Embrace of Science and the Military: ONR and the Growth of Physics in the United States after World War II", in vol. 1 of *Science, Technology, and the Military,* ed. Everett Mendelsohn, Merritt Roe Smith, and Peter Weingart (Dordrecht, The Netherlands: Kluwer Academic Publishers, 1988).

and production facilities; the universities and industrial firms operating under AEC contracts; and the laboratories assigned to each of the military services.[32] Nuclear research in the Army's arsenals focused primarily on the effects of radiation on materials. Some related studies also were conducted to ensure effective mating of nuclear weapons to advanced missile-delivery systems. High-energy X-ray analysis of metal components used in gun and artillery assemblies is representative of the research done on materials, whereas the latter studies focused on the development, testing, and pilot production of launch vehicles for missiles and rockets capable of carrying both conventional and nuclear warheads.[33]

Picatinny Arsenal, located in northern New Jersey, forty miles west of New York City, played an important role in the Army's nuclear weapons program. Long known for the production of explosives, propellants, and other pyrotechnics, Picatinny embarked on a major diversification program after World War II. Starting with the 2.36-inch antitank rocket (known as the "bazooka") introduced during the war, researchers at Picatinny developed the 4.5-inch Folding Fin Light Artillery Rocket (designated the M8) and, in the late 1940s, began work on rocket boosters and assisted take-off units that were subsequently incorporated into the Martin *Matador*, the United States' first operational surface-to-surface cruise missile.

In 1950, the Army assigned the development of nuclear munitions to Picatinny Arsenal. Also that year, the arsenal, operating as a subcontractor to the Atomic Energy Commission, formally established the Atomic Applications Laboratory (AAL) to conduct R&D in this field, beginning with the development of a 280-millimeter atomic shell capable of being fired from a conventional artillery gun.[34] During the remainder of the decade, laboratory personnel focused

---

[32] See Richard G. Hewlett and Francis Duncan, *Atomic Shield, 1947–1952*, vol. 2 of *A History of the United States Atomic Energy Commission* (University Park: Pennsylvania State University Press, 1969); Richard G. Hewlett and Jack M. Holl, *Atoms for Peace and War, 1953–1961: Eisenhower and the Atomic Energy Commission*, vol. 3 of *A History of the United States Atomic Energy Commission* (Berkeley: University of California Press, 1989); and Richard G. Hewlett and Francis Duncan, *Nuclear Navy, 1946–1962* (Chicago: University of Chicago Press, 1974). Also useful are the individual laboratory histories. See, for example, Leland Johnson and Daniel Schaffer, *Oak Ridge National Laboratory: The First Fifty Years* (Knoxville: University of Tennessee Press, 1994); and Jack M. Holl, *Argonne National Laboratory, 1946–1996* (Urbana: University of Illinois Press, 1997).

[33] Redstone Arsenal in Alabama served as the headquarters for the Army Ballistic Missile Agency (ABMA). In 1959, the newly formed National Aeronautics and Space Administration (NASA) absorbed Redstone (which had merged with the nearby Huntsville Arsenal in 1950) and a significant portion of ABMA's staff and support functions. This transfer effectively ended the Army's role as a major participant in the Defense Department's military space program. One year earlier, the Army had transferred the Jet Propulsion Laboratory, operated under contract by the California Institute of Technology (Caltech), to NASA. The transfer of ABMA, however, did not preclude ongoing development and production of launch vehicles and related equipment for the Army's guided missile fleet. Much of this work, especially R&D and prototype production, was carried out in the manufacturing arsenals. On Army R&D at Caltech before the transfer to NASA, see I. Stone, "Caltech Eases Transfer of Air Research Burden," *Aviation Week* 66 (3 June 1957): 277–89. Also on the Jet Propulsion Laboratory during this period, see Clayton R. Koppes, *JPL and the American Space Program: A History of the Jet Propulsion Laboratory* (New Haven: Yale University Press, 1982). The transfer of Redstone Arsenal to NASA is discussed in Michael J. Neufeld, "The End of the Army Space Program: Interservice Rivalry and the Transfer of the Von Braun Group to NASA, 1958–1959," *Journal of Military History* 69 (July 2005): 737–58.

[34] Picatinny's atomic shell was successfully tested in 1952.

their efforts on mating nuclear warheads manufactured in the AEC's production facilities to the launch and delivery vehicles assigned to the Army's missile and rocket force. Researchers in AAL's Tactical Atomic Weapons Laboratory, for example, developed, in collaboration with industrial contractors, the atomic payload units for the *Honest John* ground-based mobile rocket and the *Corporal* surface-to-surface guided missile. AAL also conducted routine tests of atomic bomb-equipped rockets and missiles within a broad range of temperature, humidity, vibration, shock, and other environmental conditions to ensure proper operational performance of the fuse and detonation devices, electronic and propulsion systems, and other critical components.[35]

Wartime research and development in solid-state electronics and the invention of the transistor at the Bell Telephone Laboratories in 1947 prompted the military services to invest significant institutional resources in this rapidly expanding field of study.[36] Prior to World War II, most research and development in the arsenals had focused on physical, chemical, and metallurgical studies of metals and alloys, the constituent materials of all types of ordnance. This work, in which metallurgical investigations typically predominated, drew upon the empirical, engineering-based origins of solid-state physics, a field of study that was just beginning to assume professional identity as an independent academic discipline after the war. "The single outstanding trend which has become paramount during the past few years," wrote the head of ONR's metallurgy branch in 1957, "is the tremendous impact exerted by solid-state physics upon metallurgical research."[37] Application-driven studies of metals, however, did not necessarily preclude arsenal researchers from exploring more theoretical topics within solid-state physics, though that brand of research was increasingly contracted out to the universities through the Office of Ordnance Research. Despite the institutional constraints imposed on it by the growth of R&D outsourcing and the acute competition for resources within the federal research

---

[35] M. W. Kresge, "Research and Development, Military Explosives and Propellants," *Journal of Applied Physics* 16 (December 1945): 792–97; "Rockets at Picatinny Arsenal," *Jet Propulsion* 26 (February 1956): 114; P. P. Luellig Jr., "Arsenals," *Field Artillery Journal* 42 (March–April 1974): 51–52; W. Beller, "Army Research and Development in Missiles, Aviation, and Avionics," *Aero Digest* 73 (October 1956): 22–23; I. O. Drewry, "Army Ordnance Tackles Task of Marrying Atomics with Artillery," *Army Information Digest* 13 (December 1958): 12–16; Drewry, "Atomic Applications Laboratory: Newest Addition to Picatinny Arsenal," *Sperryscope* 14, no. 5 (1957): 20, 22–23.

[36] See, for example, Paul W. Henriksen, "Solid-State Physics Research at Purdue," *Osiris*, 2nd ser., 2 (1986): 237–60; Lillian Hoddeson, "The Roots of Solid-State Research at Bell Labs," *Physics Today* 30 (March 1977): 23–30; Hoddeson, "Research on Crystal Rectifiers during World War II and the Invention of the Transistor," *History and Technology* 11 (1994): 121–30; Hoddeson, "The Invention of the Point-Contact Transistor," *Historical Studies in the Physical Sciences* 12 (1981): 41–76; George Wise, "Science at General Electric," *Physics Today* 37 (December 1984): 52–61; and Ross Knox Bassett, *To the Digital Age: Research Labs, Start-Up Companies, and the Rise of MOS Technology* (Baltimore: Johns Hopkins University Press, 2002). Also useful, but highly technical, is the exhaustive multivolume history of industrial research in the Bell System written by the staff of the Bell Telephone Laboratories. See *A History of Engineering and Science in the Bell System*, 7 vols. (Murray Hill, N.J.: Bell Telephone Laboratories, 1975–1985).

[37] J. J. Harwood, "Some Aspects of Government-Sponsored Research in Metallurgy," *Journal of Metals* 9 (May 1957): 669. On the disciplinary origins of solid-state physics, see Lillian Hoddeson et al., *Out of the Crystal Maze: Chapters in the History of Solid-State Physics* (New York: Oxford University Press, 1992), esp. chap. 9.

establishment, the arsenal system maintained a diversified research program on metals and alloys throughout the postwar period.

All of the arsenals conducted some research on metals, but the Watertown and Frankford arsenals stood out as the major sources of expertise in this field. Postwar metals research at these two arsenals generally focused on ferrous (iron-rich) and nonferrous (iron-deficient) metallurgy. Researchers at Watertown explored the former while their colleagues at Frankford studied the latter. Established in 1880, the experimental and testing laboratory at Watertown Arsenal solved manufacturing problems related to the casting and forging of gun tubes. "The scientific staff of this laboratory," observed Watertown's commanding officer in 1940, "is constantly engaged in a search for cleaner metals, steels that will resist gun-firing erosion to the maximum degree, and tools that are capable of machining the tough steels produced." During World War II, the arsenal applied the laboratory's expertise in metalworking to the production of 90-millimeter antiaircraft guns, 16-inch seacoast guns, 240-millimeter shells, recoil mechanisms for 8-inch howitzers, and other weapons. Improvement of casting and forging techniques used to manufacture gun tubes and routine testing of metals continued at Watertown after the war, but work along all three lines progressed in step with studies that explored the underlying scientific principles of metallic behavior.[38] "The major problem in ferrous metallurgy," wrote the Ordnance Department's chief of research and development at the end of 1946, "is to develop an understanding of the plastic flow, rupture properties, and quench cracking susceptibility of steel, the alloying of steels, steel erosion, and the response of steels to complex thermal cycles and strains."[39] Increased understanding of solid-state materials aided Watertown's efforts to tackle this problem.

Like their counterparts at Watertown, researchers in the laboratory division at Frankford Arsenal engaged in similar work to improve manufacturing processes and cut production costs of ordnance fabricated from copper, bronze, and brass alloys and new classes of lightweight materials. Frankford also devoted much time and effort during and after the war to problems of ammunition preservation and storage. Although this research was clearly practical in origin, focusing, for example, on methods of dehumidification and rust prevention, some

---

[38] W. G. Gude, "Foundry Research at Watertown Arsenal," *Foundry* 73 (December 1945): 104–06, 186, 188; R. W. Case, "Manufacturing Preparedness at Watertown Arsenal," *Machinery* 46 (March 1940): 100–01 (quote). In 1945, the research laboratory at Watertown Arsenal consisted of three operating divisions: research, metallurgical engineering, and testing. The research division was responsible for "developing new knowledge and assembling basic information as to the factors affecting the behavior of metals and structural components used in ordnance construction." The metallurgical engineering division focused on more applied topics, such as welding and the melting and refining of steel. It was "largely occupied with development programs in connection with the improvements of standard weapons or the construction of new weapons and component items." As its name implies, the testing division performed "testing functions required by the Research and Metallurgical Engineering Divisions of the Laboratory and the Arsenal as a whole in connection with its production and procurement." N. A. Matthews, "Ferrous Metallurgical Research," *Journal of Applied Physics* 16 (December 1945): 780–81.

[39] A. Leggin, "Ordnance Department Research and Development," *Chemical and Engineering News* 24 (25 December 1946): 3351.

aspects of it emulated more speculative studies underway in universities and industrial laboratories on the fundamental behavior of crystalline materials.[40]

Among the many problems faced by researchers at the Frankford Arsenal was how to ensure with reasonable certainty that the small-arms ammunition and artillery shells turned out by the production lines would function properly on the battlefield. Maintaining high standards of quality control depended in part on a detailed understanding of the behavior of the metal components used in the manufacturing process. During World War II, laboratory research in this field focused on theoretical and experimental studies of the plastic deformation of metals. A metal changes shape when it is subjected to an external load, such as pressing, rolling, or forging. Depending on the arrangement of the atoms that make up its internal structure, the metal will either retain that new shape or return to its original dimensions. Plasticity is the mechanical property that determines the extent to which a metal maintains its shape following the application of an external force. Since the 1920s, physicists and metallurgists in the United States and Europe had constructed various theories to explain the mechanism by which metals deformed plastically. One explanation that gained acceptance during this period focused on the concept of the dislocation, a point defect or imperfection in the lattice structure of a metal. First introduced in 1934, dislocation theory suggested that atomic imperfections predisposed metals to deform and fracture at stress levels lower than those predicted for ideal crystals. It also provided some clues as to why plastically deformed metals exhibited increased resistance to further deformation, a phenomenon called work hardening. By the end of the decade, dislocation theory had emerged as one of the leading explanations of plastic deformation in metals, and it has continued to be an important subject of study in materials science.[41] Dislocation theory and the experimental studies that supported it had a significant impact on the development of ordnance materials at Frankford Arsenal, and within the arsenal system in general, during and after World War II.

Even though the existence of dislocations was not verified experimentally until 1955, physicists working in industrial and academic laboratories in the late 1930s had used dislocation theory to explain certain types of metallic behavior that turned out to be directly relevant to ordnance development and production in the arsenal system. Internal friction was one particularly important property that received widespread attention. The intensity of this phenomenon depends on the extent to which the vibrational energy absorbed by a metal from an external source is dissipated nonuniformly as it propagates from one atom to another in the crystal lattice. Energy loss is greatest where imperfections, or dislocations, exist in the atomic arrangement of the metal's internal structure. Before the war, a small team of physicists at the Westinghouse Electric and Manufacturing Company in Pittsburgh and the University of Pennsylvania in Philadelphia pioneered research on the internal friction of metals.

---

[40] See C. H. Greenall, "Non-Ferrous Metallurgical Research at Frankford Arsenal," *Journal of Applied Physics* 16 (December 1945): 787–92.

[41] Hoddeson et al., *Out of the Crystal Maze*, 317–33.

Although based heavily on empirical investigations, the research conducted by this group also benefited from theoretical insights drawn from quantum mechanics. Conceived in Europe in the mid-1920s and introduced to physicists in the United States at the end of the decade, this highly mathematical interpretation of classical electrodynamics revolutionized the study of atomic and molecular structure. Moreover, solid materials, especially metals, were ideally suited to quantum theoretical analyses.[42] In addition to publishing several seminal articles on internal friction that helped place the newly emerging discipline of solid-state physics on a firm theoretical footing, several members of the Pittsburgh-Philadelphia group transferred to the laboratory at Frankford Arsenal, where they continued their research on internal friction in metals to solve a very practical problem—season cracking in the brass casings of artillery shells and other ammunition.[43] During the war, investigations of copper, one of the primary constituent materials of brass, constituted the single largest field of nonferrous metallurgical research at Frankford.

The powder packed into artillery shells and ammunition cartridges normally gives off gases, especially ammonia. When shells and cartridges are stored for extended periods of time, the ammonia causes tiny cracks to appear in the brass casings. If left untreated, artillery shells weakened by season cracking might

---

[42] On the origins of quantum theoretical physics in the United States and the application of research in this field to industrial problems, see, for example, Stanley Coben, "The Scientific Establishment and the Transmission of Quantum Mechanics to the United States, 1919–32," *American Historical Review* 76 (April 1971): 442–66; S. S. Schweber, "The Empiricist Temper Regnant: Theoretical Physics in the United States, 1920–1950," *Historical Studies in the Physical and Biological Sciences* 17 (1986): 55–98; Katherine R. Sopka, *Quantum Physics in America, 1920–1935* (New York: Arno Press, 1980); Charles Weiner, "A New Site for the Seminar: The Refugees and American Physics in the Thirties," in *The Intellectual Migration: Europe and America, 1930–1960*, ed. Donald Fleming and Bernard Bailyn (Cambridge, Mass.: Belknap Press of Harvard University Press, 1969); Spencer R. Weart, "The Physics Business in America, 1919–1940: A Statistical Reconnaissance," in *The Sciences in the American Context: New Perspectives*, ed. Nathan Reingold (Washington, D.C.: Smithsonian Institution Press, 1979); Lillian Hoddeson, "The Entry of the Quantum Theory of Solids into the Bell Telephone Laboratories, 1925–40: A Case-Study of the Industrial Application of Fundamental Science," *Minerva* 18 (autumn 1980): 422–47; and Arturo Russo, "Fundamental Research at Bell Laboratories: The Discovery of Electron Diffraction," *Historical Studies in the Physical Sciences* 12 (1981): 117–60. For a detailed technical history of quantum mechanics, see Max Jammer, *The Conceptual Development of Quantum Mechanics* (New York: McGraw-Hill, 1966).

[43] Physicists Thomas Read and Frederick Seitz spearheaded research on the internal friction of metals at Westinghouse Electric and the University of Pennsylvania. Read, who received his training in theoretical physics at Columbia University, joined the solid-state group at Westinghouse in 1939. Seitz, a Princeton-trained theoretician, was a close friend of Read's boss, Edward Condon, associate director of the Westinghouse Research Laboratories and himself an accomplished and widely respected theoretical physicist. Seitz, who had been invited by Condon to Pittsburgh to work on solid-state problems, collaborated with Read to study the internal friction of metals during the summer of 1939 and again the following year. Their collaborative effort produced a series of four pioneering review articles on the plastic properties of solids published in the *Journal of Applied Physics* in 1941. These articles, Seitz later recalled, "attempted to describe, in a more or less systematic way, the roles that dislocations could play in affecting the various properties of crystalline materials." Read left Westinghouse in 1941 for a permanent research position at Frankford Arsenal. Although he remained at the University of Pennsylvania, Seitz consulted regularly with Read and his staff at Frankford. Hoddeson et al., *Out of the Crystal Maze*, 337–38, 348; Frederick Seitz, *On the Frontier: My Life in Science* (New York: AIP Press, 1994), 106–7, 134–35 (quote on 135). On solid-state research at Westinghouse during the 1930s, see Thomas C. Lassman, "From Quantum Revolution to Institutional Transformation: Edward U. Condon and the Dynamics of Pure Science in America, 1925–1951 (Ph.D. diss., Johns Hopkins University, 2000), chaps. 2–3.

explode prematurely during firing, causing catastrophic injury to gun crews. Joined by new wartime recruits, mostly from academia, the solid-state physics group at Frankford Arsenal designed and built testing apparatus to measure the internal friction of brass shell casings for the purpose of identifying cracks and other structural imperfections. One advantage of this experimental method was that it did not require invasive procedures. Researchers merely had to measure how much energy was absorbed and dissipated in the brass metal—that is, calculate the internal friction—rather than cut the shell apart, one of the standard practices at the time, to identify potential weaknesses caused by season cracking. Moreover, the technique was sensitive enough that cracks could be spotted early, allowing investigators to study how they formed and grew over time. Taking advantage of this new technique, employing other analytical methods, and working closely with universities and several metals-producing companies, the arsenal's manufacturing divisions quickly adjusted their production methods to turn out more reliable and structurally sound ordnance.[44]

Studies of plastic deformation and internal friction of metals continued at Frankford after the war. This research, like most of the other metallurgical investigations underway in the laboratory, remained focused, however, on the solution of problems related to ordnance production. In the early 1950s, metallurgical studies at Frankford were grouped into three categories: "basic metallurgical research," "process research," and "special problems." Basic metallurgical research included further work on dislocation theory and its application to the development of new alloys. The search for alloys also drew on advances in foundry research, another topic covered within this general category. Begun at the arsenal in 1943, foundry work focused on the refinement of methods to cast titanium, magnesium, and aluminum for use in the next generation of high-performance materials. Fabrication, welding, corrosion, and heat treatment of alloys engaged the efforts of technical staff working on process research. Special problems covered topics found in both the basic metallurgical and process research categories. Work ranged from ongoing studies of season cracking in ammunition to the development of substitute alloys to offset lingering shortages of zinc and copper used in the manufacture of brass gun cartridge cases.[45] That studies of dislocation theory and foundry processes were grouped together under the same category—"basic metallurgical research" suggests the extent to which they were directed toward the same goal—the solution of ordnance problems.

---

[44] Collaborating universities and industrial firms included the Case School of Applied Science in Cleveland, Lehigh University, the New Jersey Zinc Company, and the Aluminum Company of America. Greenall, "Non-Ferrous Metallurgical Research at Frankford Arsenal," 787–89; interview with Herbert I. Fusfeld by Thomas C. Lassman, April 2–3, 2005 (unedited transcript), Niels Bohr Library, Center for History of Physics, American Institute of Physics, College Park, Md., 14–15, 17–19, 20. Fusfeld joined Read's group at the Frankford Arsenal in December 1941, shortly after receiving his B.S. degree in physics from Brooklyn College. During the war, Fusfeld and Read collaborated on studies of internal friction in metals to find a solution to the problem of season cracking in artillery shell casings. Fusfeld received M.S. and Ph.D. degrees in physics from the University of Pennsylvania before resigning from the arsenal in 1953 to pursue an industrial career at the American Machine and Foundry Company.

[45] D. J. Murphy, "Metallurgical Activities at Frankford Arsenal," *Metal Progress* 62 (August 1952): 67–72.

Longer-term research unrelated to specific production needs, by contrast, was conducted in the universities and other private-sector institutions that received contracts from the Office of Ordnance Research.

A similar institutional strategy guided the innovation process at Watertown Arsenal, the other Army ordnance installation that supported an extensive metallurgical R&D program during the postwar period. Although the definitions assigned to different types of research at Watertown were not necessarily the same as those used at Frankford Arsenal, the content of the work was nevertheless directed toward the same outcome—the development of more effective and reliable weapons. Most of Watertown's metallurgical work, what was termed "supporting" and "applied" research, focused on finding solutions to problems encountered during ordnance development. There were some exceptions, however. Scientists working in Watertown's Materials Research Laboratory in the 1960s, for example, tackled problems known to their academic counterparts in the universities, such as research on interatomic bonding energies, electronic structures of materials, and impurities in solids. But most metallurgical studies along these lines, especially those that drew on recent advances in solid-state physics, were gradually transferred out of Watertown and the other arsenals. Funds for this work were distributed to civilian contractors by the Office of Ordnance Research.[46] That trend persisted especially after the production facilities at Watertown Arsenal shut down in 1967, and Frankford Arsenal closed ten years later.

Metals research in the arsenal system relied on insights drawn from empirical and theoretical investigations in metallurgy and solid-state physics. It also benefited from the analytical capabilities of sophisticated instrumentation. Ever since its introduction as a diagnostic tool early in the twentieth century, the X-ray tube had enabled academic and industrial researchers to accumulate detailed knowledge of the internal structures of a wide variety of materials, ranging from bones and internal organs in living organisms to metallic compounds. In the latter the penetrating power of X-ray radiation provided researchers in the arsenals with critical information to identify and correct structural weaknesses in the metal components of ordnance delivery systems, such as howitzers, antiaircraft guns, and other weapons.

---

[46] L. G. Klinker, "Metallurgical R&D in the Army," *Journal of Metals* 13 (February 1961): 129–31; "AMRA Goal: New Materials to Transform Ideas into Materiel," *Army Research and Development News Magazine* 6 (September 1965): 32–35. The contracts for metallurgical research awarded by the Office of Ordnance Research and other funding agencies in the military services were part of a much larger national materials research program established by the Defense Department's Advanced Research Projects Agency (ARPA) in 1960. That year, ARPA awarded grants to Cornell University, Northwestern University, and the University of Pennsylvania to build laboratories for interdisciplinary research and instruction in physics, chemistry, metallurgy, and other materials-related subjects. Two years later, the program had to expand to include eleven laboratories located at universities throughout the United States. In addition to expanding the Defense Department's contracting base for metallurgical research, this program also laid the institutional groundwork for the subsequent growth of *materials science* as an independent academic discipline. See C. F. Yost and E. C. Vicars, "Interdisciplinary Laboratory Program in Materials Science," *Journal of Metals* 14 (September 1962): 666–70. On the origins of the program, see Richard J. Barber Associates, *The Advanced Research Projects Agency, 1958–1974* (Washington, D.C.: Advanced research Projects Agency, December 1975).

X-rays consist of high-frequency electromagnetic radiation. They are produced when electrons are accelerated to high energies through a large voltage potential in an evacuated chamber. Until World War II, modified vacuum tubes were the most common X-ray sources, and they were widely used by medical practitioners in hospitals to diagnose and treat diseases. Operational ranges typically did not exceed two million electron volts. New types of particle accelerators capable of generating much higher voltages, both for scientific study and clinical use, began to appear in the 1930s, when nuclear physics began to capture the interest of the American scientific community. One of the first practical high-energy electron accelerators, known as the *betatron*, was invented at the University of Illinois in 1940, and it was transformed into a powerful X-ray source at the research laboratory of the General Electric Company during the war.[47] Conventional X-ray tubes and the far more powerful betatrons were employed extensively in the Army's arsenal system before and after the war. Unlike their counterparts in academia, who by and large used these instruments to study the structure and behavior of atoms and molecules, arsenal researchers conducted X-ray studies to solve urgent practical problems related to ordnance development and production.

Nestled on the upper Mississippi River between Iowa and Illinois, the Ordnance Department's Rock Island Arsenal served as a major center for applied X-ray research dating back to the 1930s. After World War II, the arsenal's primary products included mortars, light and medium artillery, gun carriages, and rocket and guided missile launchers. Rock Island also overhauled and rebuilt weapons already operating in the field. The research that supported these manufacturing and maintenance functions had always been and continued to be narrowly focused on production problems. Research for its own sake was not part of Rock Island's mission officially, nor that of any of the other Army arsenals. Rock Island engineers, for example, drafted the initial plans and specifications for the 3.5-inch rocket launcher (also known as the "super bazooka"), and the arsenal also turned out the first prototypes scheduled for testing and debugging prior to mass production by industrial contractors.[48] The first quantities of this new antitank weapon entered service with American combat forces shortly after the outbreak of hostilities in Korea. Similar procedures guided the development of other weapon systems, such as the Army's first mobile, large-caliber launcher for the *Honest John* rocket and a helicopter-mounted, single-rail rocket launcher for the *Little John* rocket.[49]

During the immediate postwar period, the bulk of research and development at Rock Island was scattered throughout the arsenal's manufacturing divisions.

---

[47] See J. L. Heilbron and Robert W. Seidel, *Lawrence and his Laboratory*, vol. 1 of *A History of the Lawrence Berkeley Laboratory* (Berkeley: University of California Press, 1989). On the origins of the betatron, see D. W. Kerst, "Historical Development of the Betatron," *Nature* 157 (26 January 1946): 90–95.

[48] Engineers at Picatinny Arsenal also contributed to the development of the 3.5-inch rocket launcher. See "Rockets at Picatinny Arsenal," 114.

[49] Rock Island Arsenal began producing rocket launchers in 1942. W. W. Warner, "Arsenals in Action," *Army Information Digest* 6 (September 1951): 39–40; M. S. Werngren, "Skills Spell Strength," *Army Information Digest* 17 (September 1962): 62; Neil M. Johnson and Leonard C. Weston, *Development and Production of Rocket Launchers at Rock Island Arsenal, 1945–1959* (Rock Island, Ill.: U.S. Army Weapons Command, 1962), 1, 8–9.

The Artillery Branch, for example, performed its own R&D on rocket launchers as well as conventional artillery. A separate laboratory division existed at the arsenal, but it provided technical support to the individual R&D operations in the manufacturing units. Management completed a major overhaul of the arsenal's organizational structure in 1953, resulting in the consolidation of all of Rock Island's scattered R&D functions into a new, centralized Office of Research and Engineering Activities. According to Rock Island's official history, the purpose of this realignment was to "produce a closer, more effective relationship between basic and applied research activities." Laboratories were built to accommodate new and expanded research programs on rust-preventive compounds, lubricants, finishes, packaging materials, all types of rubbers, and other nonmetallic materials used in the arsenal's major products. New inspection facilities supported X-ray analyses of critical components used in gun assemblies, while an experimental production facility fabricated and tested prototype materials. Periodically throughout the 1950s and 1960s, management made additional organizational adjustments to maintain the institutional integrity of this strong connection among research, development, and production.[50]

The origins of X-ray research at Rock Island Arsenal can be traced back to 1935, when a 500,000-volt X-ray machine was installed to inspect metal castings and other critical parts. During this period, arsenal researchers were particularly interested in detailed analysis of stressed points in gun carriages.[51] A major expansion of this work came after the war, when the arsenal installed a betatron to inspect the internal parts of gun assemblies without taking them apart. In addition to its manufacturing operations, the arsenal served as a storage depot for artillery recoil mechanisms used by combat forces in the field. In many cases, recoil mechanisms arrived at the arsenal for refurbishment and storage without service records, making it practically impossible to determine their repair status without complete disassembly. Using the betatron made this cumbersome and time-consuming task unnecessary. Unlike the conventional X-ray equipment that it replaced, the Rock Island betatron produced X-ray energies nearly ten times more powerful than those previously employed to analyze the constituent materials of new and stored carriage assemblies. High-energy electrons striking a small platinum target could produce X-rays with energies reaching 22 million electron volts, thereby allowing radiographic analysis of metal components that contained substantial quantities of iron.

In addition to providing greater penetrating power than low-intensity X-rays, high-energy X-rays produced secondary emissions that minimized scattering effects. Researchers at Rock Island found that the secondary emissions generated by the collision of X-rays with atoms in metals proceeded in the same direction as the incident X-rays that produced them in the first place. Low-voltage X-rays did not produce the same result; secondary scattering was

---

[50] *A History of Rock Island and Rock Island Arsenal from Earliest Times to 1954*, vol. 3 (1940–1954), (Rock Island, Ill.: Rock Island Arsenal, 1965): 513–15, 561, 711–12, 729, 764 (quote on 514); Warner, "Arsenals in Action," 43.

[51] "X-Ray in an Arsenal," *American Machinist* 84 (13 November 1940): 930–31.

a persistent problem that resulted in blurred or "foggy" images. The benefits of a high-energy source included fog-free radiographs, shorter exposure times, and improved ability to penetrate thicknesses of materials previously inaccessible to low-voltage X-rays. Given these advantages, the Rock Island betatron was able to detect very small defects in recoil assemblies and other metallic items stored and produced at the arsenal. Moreover, the efficiencies in operation prompted one observer to note that "betatron radiographs could be made in short periods of time, thus permitting production line inspection of sections of moderate thickness."[52]

Initially confined to the analysis of steel, the primary material used in gun recoil mechanisms, the Rock Island betatron was quickly adapted for the inspection of both low-density materials, such as aluminum, and very high-density "superalloys" used in the manufacture of jet engines, rockets, and other propulsion technologies that typically operated in extreme conditions.[52] High-energy X-ray analysis also spread to other arsenals. Researchers operating the betatron at Picatinny Arsenal in New Jersey, for example, focused their efforts on the inspection of powder charges in large-caliber artillery shells exceeding 240 millimeters in diameter. In this case, X-rays were used to identify cavities in the charge, the presence of which might cause a malfunction in the gun, or worse, a premature explosion during firing.[53] Though the methods of analysis were different, the practical requirements driving X-ray research at Rock Island and Picatinny arsenals matched very closely the short-term goals that guided studies of internal friction of metals at Frankford Arsenal.

Given that research and development in the arsenal system focused broadly on solving practical, ordnance-related problems, it is perhaps fitting to examine, if only briefly, how the types of R&D projects undertaken individually at Frankford, Watertown, Rock Island, and Picatinny arsenals also existed collectively in one location, namely at the Army's "big gun factory"—Watervliet Arsenal, situated on the Hudson River near Albany in upstate New York. After World War II, Watervliet gradually transformed itself from a large-scale production facility narrowly focused on a single technology—artillery—into a designer and builder of prototype weapon systems and components manufactured in large quantities by industrial contractors. By 1960, for example, a section of Watervliet's "Big Gun Shop," which had turned out the first 16-inch coastal cannon—the highly effective 155-millimeter artillery gun used in World War II—and more recently, the 280-millimeter atomic cannon, had been converted into a pilot production line that manufactured solid-propellant rocket motors for the *Nike-Hercules* surface-to-air missile.[54]

---

[52] G. Elwers, "Ordnance Using X-Rays to Inspect Complex Assemblies," *Iron Age* 168 (25 October 1951): 95–99 (quote on 97);

[53] Elwers, "Ordnance Using X-Rays to Inspect Complex Assemblies," 98–99; Harry E. Bawden, ed., *The Achievement of Rock Island Arsenal in World War II* (Davenport, Ia.: Bawden Brothers, 1948), 75.

[54] W. M. D. Tisdale, "It's Always Tomorrow," *Army Information Digest* 15 (December 1960): 29. The *Nike-Hercules* surface-to-air missile was produced in quantity by the Western Electric Company, the manufacturing arm of the Bell Telephone System.

This broad institutional transformation accompanied a major reorganization of the arsenal's R&D operations. In 1959, management centralized R&D under a new administrative structure—the Research and Engineering Division. The division split into three separate units: the Research Branch, the Design Engineering Branch, and the Industrial Engineering Branch. The following year, wrote one historian of the aresnal, a new group of laboratories opened "to increase the arsenal's ability to investigate the properties of metals, to seek new and improved coatings for gun tubes, and to study non-destructive testing techniques for all the U.S. arsenals and Ordnance Corps installations." A new research program in solid-state physics occupied one of these laboratories to complement expanded work on the mechanical and physical testing of ordnance materials. The arsenal also acquired modern instrumentation for studies in electron microscopy and X-ray diffraction.[55] "Here [in the Research Branch]," wrote Watervliet's commanding officer in 1960, "a hard core of 'old pro' ordnance experts combine the invaluable knowledge and craft of experience with the talents of scientific specialists imported from industry and educational institutions. Many of them—holders of Ph.D. and master's degrees in metallurgy, mechanics, physics, chemistry—have joined the team…."[56] By 1962, the arsenal's laboratories employed 11 Ph.D.s, 67 master's degree holders, and 251 college graduates with bachelor's degrees. Twelve years later, the number of Ph.D.s working in the Research and Engineering Division had quadrupled to forty-four.[57]

Like the other arsenals, Watervliet concentrated much of its R&D on the development and analysis of the materials used to produce cannon, howitzers, mortars, and recoilless rifles.[58] In the late 1960s, for example, scientists and engineers tapped Watervliet's long-standing tradition in metallurgical research to improve the firing life of the steel gun tube mounted on the 175-millimeter cannon, which at the time was one of the largest conventional field artillery pieces used by Army combat forces. As the firing ranges of large-diameter cannon like the 175 increased, the gun tubes had to withstand higher pressures, which resulted in a loss of a quality in the steel called "toughness." To eliminate this problem, scientists at Watervliet pre-stressed the steel during fabrication. By applying pressures of approximately 100,000 pounds per square inch to specific locations on the walls of the gun tubes, higher yields of stress were recorded without a corresponding loss of the original toughness in the steel. Using this process, known as *autofrettage*, researchers tripled the operational life of the standard gun tube mounted on the 175-millimeter cannon.[59]

---

[55] *A History of Watervliet Arsenal, 1813 to Modernization 1982*, 185–89 (quote on 189).

[56] Tisdale, "It's Always Tomorrow," 30.

[57] *A History of Watervliet Arsenal, 1813 to Modernization 1982*, 196; R. H. Sawyer, "Portrait of an Arsenal," *Army Logistician* 7 (January-February 1975): 25.

[58] R&D on recoilless rifles was transferred from Frankford Arsenal to Watervliet in the early 1960s. *A History of Watervliet Arsenal, 1813 to Modernization 1982*, 194–95.

[59] Ibid., 221. See also C. S. Maggio, "Since 1813, Watervliet Arsenal Has Pioneered the Logistics of Cannon Manufacture," *Army Logistician* 5 (September-October 1973): 18–23. Autofrettage was not a new process. This method of pretreating the constituent materials of gun tubes and other critical components had been used in the manufacturing arsenals for decades. See, for example, "Technical Developments in Ordnance Department," *American Machinist* 55 (22 December 1921): 1022a.

The continued diversification of Watervliet's Research and Engineering Division complemented this problem-oriented research on gun fabrication and performance. In 1969, the laboratories were modernized, and new facilities were built for research in experimental mechanics and thermodynamics, solid-state physics, electrochemistry, and physical chemistry. Moreover, Watervliet scientists also won high praise from the scientific community for their work on the theory of the mechanics of solids. A new research program in superconductivity arose out of this broad knowledge base in solid materials. A highly speculative field of investigation in which practical applications lay far in the future, superconductivity research at the arsenal in the 1970s and 1980s focused on exotic materials that exhibited unique magnetic and electrical properties.

Studies of superconductivity at Watervliet Arsenal originated in the laboratory facilities dedicated to high-pressure testing, normally in the range of 200 kilobars (200,000 times normal atmospheric pressure). In 1973, a separate research program was established, focusing on the production of significantly higher pressures, in the range of 500 to 1,000 kilobars. Using these extremely high pressures, arsenal scientists sought to create entirely new materials. Their efforts began to pay off by the end of the decade, when the laboratory produced two new phases of bismuth, exhibiting unusually high electrical conductivity. Metallic states of sodium chloride, gallium phosphide, and boron were also produced for the first time. The limited metastability of these materials—that is, the extent to which they remained structurally intact outside a high-pressure environment—was a recurring problem, however. Most specimens were too unstable, but one—cadmium sulfide—maintained its integrity as a metal under normal atmospheric conditions, and it also exhibited unique magnetic properties. Other work along this general line of investigation included a search for metallic hydrogen, which prompted further work on superconductivity.[60] Speculative as it was, this research represented only a small fraction of the overall R&D effort at Watervliet Arsenal. In 1981, the arsenal's research director confirmed the laboratory's primary function: "We furnish the engineering for the arsenal['s] products.... Our projects have led to better ways of making cannons."[61]

Decline of the Arsenal System

By the time scientists and engineers at Watervliet Arsenal immersed themselves in research on superconducting materials, the arsenal system as a whole had already undergone a significant contraction that left only three of the original, old-line arsenals in operation by 1980. Springfield and Frankford arsenals were permanently closed; their research, development, and production functions were either phased out entirely, transferred to the remaining arsenals, or shifted to industrial contractors. Manufacturing facilities at Watertown

---

[60] *A History of Watervliet Arsenal, 1813 to Modernization 1982,* 231; "Watervliet Arsenal Improves Laboratory Facilities," *Army Research and Development News Magazine* 10 (March 1969): 19.

[61] L. D. Kozaryn, "Watervliet Arsenal: Birthplace of the Army's Big Guns," *Soldiers* 36 (February 1981): 43.

Arsenal had also been shuttered. This outcome was prompted by the continued outsourcing of weapons R&D and production throughout the postwar period.[62] The sources of this trend were rooted in multiple and related causal events that evolved over time: the waning influence of the once-powerful and independent Army technical services; increasing centralization of weapons acquisition policies in the Office of the Secretary of Defense; steadily rising productivity of private industry after the war and the corresponding expansion and diversification of corporate research and development into weapons-related fields; and the establishment and growth of a permanent captured market for those defense industries that manufactured military technologies during the Cold War.

Perhaps the most significant causal event that signaled the demise of the arsenal system was the gradual centralization of decision-making authority within the Office of the Secretary of Defense, a process that began in 1947 and culminated in the elimination of the independent status of the Army technical services nearly two decades later.[63] Until that time, the Ordnance Department and the other six technical services operated as autonomous organizations under the direction of a relatively weak Army Staff. In 1962, however, institutional rigidity within the Army's procurement system prompted Secretary of Defense Robert McNamara to wrest control of the weapons acquisition process from the technical services and place it within a new centralized unit—the Army Materiel Command. The establishment of AMC did result in some organizational division of labor between R&D and production and procurement at the laboratory level, but this outcome may not have met the expectations originally envisioned by the civilian scientists, such as Vannevar Bush, and like-minded Army leaders who favored a more complete separation of these functions. Research and development in the Army remained intimately connected to weapons production and procurement throughout the Cold War.

High-level disagreements among civilian and military policymakers about the structure, function, and organization of research and development did not necessarily capture the operational realities of weapons innovation in the arsenals. A disjunction sometimes existed between the policies designed to manage innovation and the actual workings of that process in the arsenal system. The embrace of research, development, and production within the same institutional setting—exemplified in the metals research programs at Frankford and Watertown arsenals—proved to be highly successful during the postwar period. To be sure, this outcome also depended on the Army's established priorities and institutional patterns of funding and resource allocation. Much more historical

---

[62] In 1960, for example, the government financed nearly 60 percent of the research and development conducted in industry, largely through contracts awarded by the Department of Defense. Merton J. Peck and Frederic M. Scherer, *The Weapons Acquisition Process: An Economic Analysis* (Boston: Division of Research, Graduate School of Business Administration, Harvard University, 1962), 215. For additional quantitative data on Defense Department funding of industrial research after World War II, see Nathan Rosenberg and David C. Mowery, *Technology and the Pursuit of Economic Growth* (Cambridge: Cambridge University Press, 1989), chap. 6.

[63] See Roger R. Trask and Alfred Goldberg, *The Department of Defense, 1947–1997: Organization and Leaders* (Washington, D.C.: Historical Office, Office of the Secretary of Defense, 1997), 1–53, esp. 31–34.

research on this subject is needed, but the evidence presented in this chapter suggests that the commitment to the organizational separation of R&D from production, partially grounded in views expressed by Bush and other civilian and military policymakers, may have precluded a more nuanced evaluation of the limits of technological innovation within the arsenal system.

Whether such an evaluation would have altered perceptions and policies leading to a more active role for the arsenals during the later years of the Cold War is questionable, given the continued shift of weapons procurement from public to private-sector institutions. Defense Secretary McNamara's decision to centralize weapons acquisition policy within OSD was not based entirely on notions of administrative reform and institutional efficiency. To be sure, his prior experience as a senior executive at the Ford Motor Company had manifested itself in various policies to rationalize Defense Department operations along the lines adopted by business managers in large industrial corporations. Moreover, the controversy and embarrassment that surrounded the failure of the Springfield Armory to develop quickly a suitable replacement—the M14—for the existing M1 rifle then in service prompted a sequence of contemptuous responses from McNamara that ultimately resulted in the armory's closure in 1968.[64] Larger forces were also at work during this period. Big business had recovered much of its luster after languishing under the forces of economic instability during the 1930s, when critics charged that the government should intervene to compensate for industry's failings. The spectacular wartime success of the manufacturing sector and the corresponding postwar economic boom had helped to reverse this trend. So did a business-friendly political climate that favored private sector weapons procurement at the expense of those public-sector institutions—the arsenals—that had fulfilled that requirement for more than a century.[65]

The arsenal system's demise as the primary source of weapons innovation in the Army after World War II should not, however, suggest that it was merely the victim of institutional circumstances beyond its control. To some extent, and perhaps ironically, the decline was prompted by the successful execution of the arsenal mandate. During and after World War II, the arsenals

---

[64] It is unclear to what extent the organizational relationship between R&D and production at the Springfield Armory contributed to the problems that plagued the M14 rifle program. Much more research on this subject is needed. According to Edward Clinton Ezell, *The Great Rifle Controversy: Search for the Ultimate Infantry Weapon from World War II through Vietnam and Beyond* (Harrisburg, Pa.: Stackpole Books, 1984), which is considered to be the standard source on the subject, the program's difficulties can be attributed to several factors: the inherent conservatism of the line officers in the Ordnance Department who determined weapons requirements, and the tendency of engineers at the armory to favor efficient production of existing small arms rather than wholesale adoption of new designs and manufacturing methods. These explanations are convincing and well-documented. Ezell also identifies another cause—the Ordnance Department's failure to separate Springfield's R&D from its production functions. "Ordnance leaders did not learn," he writes, "that it was fatal to place a research department under a production-oriented organization" (p. xvi). Significantly, Ezell provides almost no evidence to show that the combination of R&D and production—which had persisted at Springfield Armory for more than a century—crippled the rifle program.

[65] See Aaron L. Friedberg, *In the Shadow of the Garrison State: America's Anti-Statism and Its Cold War Grand Strategy* (Princeton: Princeton University Press, 2000), 245–50, 265–77; and David M. Hart, *Forged Consensus: Science, Technology, and Economic Policy in the United States, 1921–1953* (Princeton: Princeton University Press, 1998), chaps. 6–7.

had, with some exceptions, met their mission requirements, transferring the technological know-how of weapons production to private industry. Over time, the continuous transmission of knowledge through this institutional connection and the ongoing expansion of America's defense industries during the Cold War helped manufacturing firms develop a similar in-house capability, thereby reducing their long-term dependence on the arsenal system. That the Army also depended on a rapidly growing number of industrial firms, not just to fill production quotas but also to engage in the development of entirely new weapon systems, further contributed to the declining operational status of the arsenals. Many of the same institutional constraints guided the postwar evolution of in-house research and development in the Navy and the Air Force.

CHAPTER THREE

Research and Development in the Navy

At the end of World War II, the United States operated the largest and most technologically sophisticated navy in the world. A massive interlocking network of public and private shipyards drove the wartime expansion of the American submarine and surface fleets. During the war, the federal government had invested more than $1 billion in this sprawling complex, while employment in the shipbuilding industry peaked at 1.7 million workers, up from 102,000 in 1940.[1] Like the Army's manufacturing arsenals, the Navy's shipyards handled all phases of ship construction, equipment installation, repair, overhaul, maintenance, and eventual retirement. A broad knowledge base in science and engineering supported these functions, which resided in the research and development (R&D) laboratories operated by the Navy's technical bureaus. After the war, however, the Navy's R&D and production infrastructure experienced many of the same institutional pressures that prompted the gradual decline of the Army's arsenal system. The Department of Defense shifted ship construction from the Navy's own plants to privately owned shipyards. A similar transition from public to private-sector institutions occurred within the Navy's R&D establishment after 1945.[2] This chapter examines how the evolution of the naval shore establishment during the Cold War altered the institutional landscape of the Navy's major in-house research and development laboratories.

What set the Navy apart from the Army in terms of their respective postwar R&D programs was the extent to which both services separated and institutionalized the categories of *research, development,* and *production*. Whereas the Army sought to disconnect R&D from production, the Navy had already taken an important step in that direction before the war. The origins of this strategy can be traced to the founding of the Naval Research Laboratory in 1923. Organizationally independent of the Navy's technical bureaus, this laboratory had been established to conduct long-term fundamental research in the physical sciences broadly related to naval applications. Although product-driven investigations—in electronics, rocketry, and materials testing and analysis, for example—were not uncommon, especially during wartime, development work that focused on specific weapons requirements was not part of the laboratory's mission; the technical bureaus handled that function.[3] The unique status accorded

---

[1] Philip Shiman, *Forging the Sword: Defense Production during the Cold War* (Champaign, Ill.: Construction Engineering Research Laboratories, U.S. Army Corps of Engineers, July 1997), 31.

[2] See Aaron L. Friedberg, *In the Shadow of the Garrison State: America's Anti-Statism and Its Cold War Grand Strategy* (Princeton: Princeton University Press, 2000), 250–64.

[3] A. H. Van Keuren, "The U.S. Naval Research Laboratory," *Journal of Applied Physics* 15 (March 1944): 221–26; B. M. Loring, "Nonferrous Foundry Research at the Naval Research Laboratory," *Foundry* 74 (February 1946): 98–101, 247–49; "Navy Believes Cost of R&D Can Be Cut," *Aviation Week* 66 (3

the Naval Research Laboratory within the Naval R&D establishment suggests that the remaining bureau laboratories, like their counterparts in the Army's arsenal system, maintained stronger institutional connections among research, development, and production.

In 1946, Congress enacted legislation establishing the Office of Naval Research (ONR). In addition to its mandate to coordinate R&D in the technical bureaus and take over administrative control of the Naval Research Laboratory from the Office of the Secretary of the Navy, ONR quickly emerged as one of the largest sources of government funding for academic research in the physical sciences.[4] ONR also provided substantial funds to the Naval Research Laboratory, thus securing the laboratory's position as the Navy's leading center for long-term exploratory research throughout the postwar period. Although the Army and the Air Force duplicated ONR's programmatic function—through the establishment of the Army Research Office and The Applied Research Section (later the Office of Air Research)—no single organization comparable to the Naval Research Laboratory existed in the Army or the Air Force to complement and support the weapons-oriented R&D underway in their arsenals and laboratories. It is partially for this reason that the Navy was able to maintain a diversified in-house research and development infrastructure after World War II, even as other policies and administrative measures were put in place by the Office of the Secretary of Defense (OSD) to divest the naval shore establishment of its major production facilities in favor of private-sector contractors.

At the end of World War II, responsibility for the Navy's research, development, and production functions resided in the Naval Research Laboratory and seven independent bureaus: ordnance, ships, aeronautics, supplies and accounts, naval personnel, medicine and surgery, and yards and docks. The bureaus of ordnance, ships, and aeronautics were collectively referred to as the "material bureaus," because they carried out the bulk of the Navy's R&D and provided the fleet with the vast majority of its weapons and associated delivery systems, either through direct manufacture or contracts with private industry.[5]

June 1957): 137; Booz Allen Hamilton Inc., *Review of Navy R&D Management, 1946–1973* (Washington, D.C.: Department of the Navy, June 1, 1976), 118. On the origins, growth, and diversification of the Naval Research Laboratory, see William M. McBride, "The 'Greatest Patron of Science'?: The Navy-Academia Alliance and U.S. Naval Research, 1896–1923," *Journal of Military History* 56 (January 1992): 7–33; David K. Van Keuren, "Science, Progressivism, and Military Preparedness: The Case of the Naval Research Laboratory, 1915–1923," *Technology and Culture* 33 (October 1992): 710–36; and Ivan Amato, *Pushing the Horizon: Seventy-Five Years of High-Stakes Science at the Naval Research Laboratory* (Washington, D.C.: Naval Research Laboratory, 1998).

[4] K. R. Spangenberg and W. E. Greene, "Basic Research Projects under ONR Contracts," *Electronics* 22 (June 1949): 66–69; "ONR Guides Navy Contract Research," *Aviation Week* 66 (3 June 1957): 351; Daniel J. Kevles, *The Physicists: The History of a Scientific Community in Modern America* (Cambridge, Mass.: Harvard University Press, 1987), 355. On the history of ONR, see Harvey M. Sapolsky, *Science and the Navy: The History of the Office of Naval Research* (Princeton: Princeton University Press, 1990); and S. S. Schweber, "The Mutual Embrace of Science and the Military: ONR and the Growth of Physics in the United States after World War II", in vol. 1 of *Science, Technology, and the Military*, ed. Everett Mendelsohn, Merritt Roe Smith, and Peter Weingart (Dordrecht, The Netherlands: Kluwer Academic Publishers, 1988).

[5] The four remaining bureaus also maintained in-house laboratories and, in some cases, R&D

The Navy fullfilled fleet requirements for equipment and supplies through a bilinear organization. The Chief of Naval Operations (CNO) exercised military control over the fleet, while the civilian assistant and undersecretaries of the Navy managed the shore establishment. This division of labor separated consumer logistics, the responsibility of the CNO's staff, from producer logistics, which resided in the bureaus. Although the CNO set the material requirements for the fleet, the bureaus controlled all phases of the procurement process. Bureau chiefs had direct access to the Secretary of the Navy, received their own appropriations from Congress, and maintained complete control over research, development, evaluation, procurement, and distribution of materials and facilities. The bureaus retained their independence throughout the immediate postwar period, but, by the late 1950s, the Secretary of the Navy and an expanded staff of assistant secretaries began to exercise more authority over their functions. In 1959, for example, the bureaus relinquished their longstanding control of R&D appropriations and the budgeting process to the newly appointed Assistant Secretary of the Navy for Research and Development. Shortly thereafter, the bureaus lost their coveted access to the Secretary of the Navy. In 1966, the Navy abolished the technical bureaus and the bilinear organization.

This persistent drive toward centralization at the expense of bureau autonomy was, in part, a response to the more sweeping postwar consolidation of decision-making authority within the Office of the Secretary of Defense. No longer serving as a site of service coordination—exemplified by the short-lived and largely ineffective Research and Development Board (RDB)—OSD gradually replaced coordination with direct control of the military departments through an expanded staff of permanent assistant secretaries to minimize interservice rivalries and avoid functional duplication and waste in the weapon system acquisition process.[6] At the same time, the introduction of new weapons technologies prompted Navy leaders to re-evaluate the roles and missions of the bureaus. In some cases, such as the development of guided missiles, the Navy established new organizations and R&D programs that cut across traditional bureau lines. Perhaps nowhere was the impact of this transformation more visible than in the material bureaus: ordnance, ships, and aeronautics.

Established in 1842, the Bureau of Ordnance had historically turned out a broad range of offensive and defensive weapons, including bombs, torpedoes, depth charges, mines, guns, rockets, projectiles, fuzes, armor, and fire control

---

programs through contracts with private-sector institutions. See W. B. Young, "Research in the Bureau of Supplies and Accounts," *Journal of Applied Physics* 15 (March 1944): 278; H. W. Smith, "Research in the Bureau of Medicine and Surgery of the U.S. Navy," *Journal of Applied Physics* 15 (March 1944): 279–88; L. E. Denfield, "Research Activities of the Bureau of Naval Personnel," *Journal of Applied Physics* 15 (March 1944): 289–90; and W. C. Wagner, "Navy Yard Laboratories, Bureau of Ships," *Journal of Applied Physics* 15 (March 1944): 243–48.

6 "Mobilization of Scientific Resources—IV, the U.S. Navy," *Journal of Applied Physics* 14 (March 1944): 203–08; J. A. Furer, "Research in the Navy," *Journal of Applied Physics* 15 (March 1944): 209–13; Booz Allen, *Review of Navy R&D Management*, 1–10, 35, 54–57, 75; David K. Allison, "U.S. Navy Research and Development since World War II," in *Military Enterprise and Technological Change: Perspectives on the American Experience*, ed. Merritt Roe Smith (Cambridge, Mass.: MIT Press, 1985), 290–312.

equipment.[7] The bureau also handled the production of the assemblies and mechanisms—such as gun turrets and mounts, bomb racks, and power drives—that enabled weapon systems to function effectively in the field. The bureau's Research and Development Division coordinated all technical work conducted in-house and in academic institutions and industrial firms. Before and during World War II, investigations of a long-term, fundamental nature were rarely conducted in the bureau's laboratories. Instead, researchers focused their talents on more immediate problems related to development and production, such as the design and standardization of ordnance materials and the testing and evaluation of equipment procured from industrial contractors.[8] After the war, however, many of the bureau's laboratories diversified into newer fields of science and technology. This institutional transformation was driven in large part by wartime advancements in weapons technology. The bureau's traditional output of guns and conventional ordnance gradually expanded to include missiles and rockets, nuclear power, and microwave electronics. These technological developments were exploited in myriad R&D organizations, ranging from large, centralized corporate laboratories to small engineering staffs assigned to the manufacturing operations of ammunition plants scattered throughout the United States. Representative examples to be discussed in this chapter include the Naval Ordnance Laboratory (White Oak, Maryland), Naval Proving Ground (Dahlgren, Virginia), Naval Ordnance Test Station (China Lake, California), and the Crane Naval Ammunition Depot (south central Indiana).

The Navy had established the Bureau of Construction and Repair in 1842 and the Bureau of Steam Engineering (renamed the Bureau of Engineering in 1920) twenty years later. Both bureaus merged in 1940 to form the Bureau of Ships. This new bureau managed the network of shipyards that designed and built vessels for the surface and submarine fleets and coordinated similar activities of private-sector shipbuilders. The Navy yards also maintained research and development laboratories to provide technical support for their manufacturing divisions. Work in this field proceeded along two separate but related lines. Testing and standardization laboratories evaluated and inspected materials and equipment provided by industrial contractors. They also helped the in-house production units solve chemical and metallurgical problems and offered specialized expertise in the analysis and testing of rubber, paints, and other critical materials.[9] Among the largest of these types of R&D facilities was the Naval Boiler and Turbine Laboratory located at the Philadelphia Navy Yard.[10]

---

[7] In 1862, the Navy transferred the bureau's hydrography division (part of the original Bureau of Ordnance and Hydrography that had been established two decades earlier) to the new Bureau of Navigation.

[8] Buford Rowland and William D. Boyd, *U.S. Navy Bureau of Ordnance in World War II* (Washington, D.C.: Bureau of Ordnance, Department of the Navy, 1953), 20–22.

[9] Wagner, "Navy Yard Laboratories, Bureau of Ships," 243; H. A. Ingram, "Research in the Bureau of Ships," *Journal of Applied Physics* 15 (March 1944): 215–20.

[10] The origins of the laboratory can be traced back to 1909, when the Bureau of Steam Engineering

Founded at the Washington Navy Yard in 1898, the David Taylor Model Basin moved to a larger, modern facility in nearby Carderock, Maryland, in 1940. Investigations at the model basin focused on the speed and powering of ships, launching stability, action in waves, maneuvering capabilities, propeller design, and resistance of ship structures to vibrations and shocks caused by explosions and other external forces.[11] Although practical requirements drove the bulk of this work, it spawned nonetheless a wealth of knowledge in more abstract scientific fields, such as hydrodynamics.[12] Long-term research in this and other related scientific disciplines constituted a significant share of the basin's R&D program after World War II. Meanwhile, recent developments, especially in microwave electronics, prompted the Bureau of Ships to institutionalize a new program in antisubmarine warfare and underwater detection. In 1945, the Office of Scientific Research and Development (OSRD) transferred its wartime contracts in these fields to the bureau, which subsequently consolidated and incorporated them into the new Naval Electronics Laboratory, located in San Diego. Perhaps nowhere was the impact of wartime science and technology on ship design and construction more acutely manifest than in the development of nuclear reactors to replace conventional power generation equipment and propulsion systems in submarines and surface ships. Work on nuclear technology originated at the Naval Research Laboratory in 1939, rapidly spread to the bureau's other in-house laboratories and shipyards after the war, and stimulated widespread participation among private contractors, especially the large electrical equipment manufacturers.

In 1921, the Navy established the Bureau of Aeronautics. The last of the three material bureaus to be examined in this chapter, it oversaw the design, production, and testing of aircraft and related equipment and materials (e.g., engines, communication devices, fuels, lubricants, and metal alloys). Because the domestic aircraft industry was in the early stages of its growth and already directed most of its limited output to the Army's air arm, the Navy had earlier founded its own in-house aircraft development and production facility—the

---

established the Fuel Oil Test Plant at the Philadelphia Navy Yard to mitigate the hazards of using fuel oil for steam generation in ships. The bureau added a refractory laboratory to the test plant in 1915, followed by a turbine testing laboratory in 1942. Expanded during the war, the newly named Naval Boiler and Turbine Laboratory served as the "sole source government agency in which full-sized boilers, turbines, and gears of marine designs are tested under simulated service conditions with the principle variables accurately controlled." C. A. Bonvillian, "Naval Boiler and Turbine Laboratory," *Journal of Applied Physics* 15 (March 1944): 236–39; E. Kranzfelder, "Naval Boiler and Turbine Laboratory," *Marine Engineering and Shipping Review* 52 (June 1947): 66–75 (quote on 66).

[11] H. S. Howard, "The David Taylor Model Basin," *Journal of Applied Physics* 15 (March 1944): 227.

[12] The introduction of the steam engine and screw propeller into naval operations in the nineteenth century had raised critical problems in ship design and performance; for example understanding the relationship among the resistance, speed, and engine power of ships. In the United States, naval engineers conducted performance tests using completed vessels, whereas their French and British counterparts followed a more economical and theoretically informed strategy, instead using scale models to predict, with considerable accuracy, water resistance and other operating parameters. Out of this work, historian Rodney Carlisle writes, "the science of ship hydrodynamics was born." See Rodney P. Carlisle, *Where the Fleet Begins: A History of the David Taylor Research Center, 1898–1998* (Washington, D.C.: Naval Historical Center, Department of the Navy, 1998), 24–25 (quote on 25).

Naval Aircraft Factory—at Philadelphia in 1917. During World War II, as the domestic industry rapidly expanded its production capacity, the Naval Aircraft Factory (renamed the Naval Air Material Center in 1943) scaled back production of complete aircraft in favor of research and development on prototype models, engines, flight instruments, catapults and arresting gear, and related aviation equipment. Other major facilities engaged in aircraft R&D included the Naval Air Station at Patuxent, Maryland, and the Naval Air Missile Test Center at Point Magu, California. This shift from production to research and development in the Bureau of Aeronautics persisted after the war as private airframe manufacturers expanded their internal R&D operations and assumed a greater role in military aircraft procurement. During the 1970s, in response to the continued growth and diversification of the aircraft industry and also as part of a general policy to streamline the Navy's shore operations, the Philadelphia facility was gradually phased out of existence, its remaining research and development functions shut down or transferred to naval installations located elsewhere.

Bureau of Ordnance

At the end of World War II, all R&D in the Bureau of Ordnance was coordinated by a separate research and development division organized into sections by functional specialization and type of ordnance material: engineering, ammunition, armor, bombs and projectiles, fire control, guns and mounts, and underwater ordnance.[13] The Bureau typically contracted out to academic institutions and industrial firms or conducted thwe work in-house.[14] The Naval Ordnance Laboratory (located north of Washington, D.C., in the Maryland suburb of White Oak) and the Naval Proving Ground at Dahlgren, Virginia (situated halfway between Washington and Richmond) ; carried out research, development, pilot production, inspection, testing, and evaluation of conventional ordnance materials. The Naval Ordnance Test Station at China Lake, located approximately 150 miles northeast of Los Angeles conducted the same type of work on missles and rockets. Ordnance production facilities built during the war were also included in this R&D network. Engineers at the Crane Naval Ammunition Depot in south central Indiana diversified their technical expertise beyond bombs, projectiles, and chemical agents to improve the operational performance of high-frequency

---

[13] The bureau included five other divisions, in addition to research and development, at the end of World War II: planning and progress, administrative, finance, production, and fleet maintenance. W. M. Moses, "Research in the Bureau of Ordnance," *Journal of Applied Physics* 15 (March 1944): 249–54.

[14] The Bureau of Ordanance managed many external R&D contracts , such as the one for underwater ordnance research at Pennsylvania State College near Harrisburg. In 1945, the bureau assumed responsibility for the Underwater Sound Laboratory at Harvard University, which had been set up in 1941 and managed by OSRD during the war. The bureau transfered the laboratory and its staff, along with two field testing stations in Rhode Island and Florida, from Harvard to Penn State and placed them under the direction of the School of Engineering. Continuing scientific studies in the laboratory focused on acoustics, electronics, applied mechanics, hydrodynamics, aerodynamics, and mathematics. See "Ordnance Research Laboratories at the Pennsylvania State College," *Science* 102 (3 August, 1945): 112; and E. A. Walker, "Ordnance Research Laboratory," *Journal of Applied Physics* 18 (March 1947): 263–67.

electron tubes, semiconductor materials, and missile guidance systems. This postwar expansion into high-technology R&D at Crane matched similar lines of work at White Oak, Dahlgren, and China Lake.

The origins of the Naval Ordnance Laboratory can be traced back to World War I, when the Navy's shipyards and other shore facilities experienced rapid expansion to meet urgent military requirements. Founded in 1800 as a major shipbuilding facility for the Continental Navy, the Navy Yard in Washington, D.C., gradually converted to gun production, and, in 1886, the Navy officially classified it as the primary manufacturer of heavy guns for the fleet.[15] This shift from ship to ordnance production expanded during World War I, and, late in 1917, the Navy erected a separate laboratory—called the Mine Building—at the yard and staffed it with a small group of engineers to develop mines for the North Atlantic sea blockade. Work on fuses was initiated at the Mine Building two years later, when a research group investigating new detonation methods moved to Washington from the nearby Naval Powder Factory at Indian Head, Maryland. The mine and fuse groups merged in 1929, and the new organization was formally designated the Naval Ordnance Laboratory. Ten years later, the laboratory was organizationally separated from the Navy Yard and reconstituted as an independent research and development facility within the Bureau of Ordnance. Although its primary wartime mission was to develop degaussing methods for ships to counter the recently introduced German magnetic mine, the laboratory also accumulated a diversified knowledge base in the scientific fields—terrestrial magnetism, underwater acoustics, and oceanography—associated with ongoing work on depth charges, torpedoes, projectiles, fuses, and bombs.[16]

In 1944, the bureau leadership began preparing plans to move the Naval Ordnance Laboratory to a new location outside Washington. The old facilities at the Navy Yard were no longer sufficient to house the laboratory's expanding technical programs.[17] The Navy broke ground for a new $40 million research campus in White Oak, Maryland, two years later, and it was completed and fully operational in 1950.[18] In addition to continuing work on bombs, torpedoes,

---

[15] In 1945, the Navy Yard was officially renamed the Naval Gun Factory. Paolo E. Coletta, ed., *United States Navy and Marine Corps Bases, Domestic* (Westport, Conn.: Greenwood Press, 1985), 183–87.

[16] R. D. Bennett, "Wartime History of the Naval Ordnance Laboratory," *Review of Scientific Instruments* 17 (August 1946): 293–95; Albert B. Christman, *Sailors, Scientists and Rockets: Origins of the Navy Rocket Program and of the Naval Ordnance Test Station, Inyokern,* vol. 1 of *History of the Naval Weapons Center, China Lake, California* (Washington, D.C.: Naval History Division, 1971), 4, 59–60; Joseph P. Smaldone, *History of the White Oak Laboratory, 1945–1975* (White Oak, Md.: Naval Surface Weapons Center, 1977), 167–69. Also on the wartime work of the Naval Ordnance Laboratory, especially the development of mines and countermeasures, see W. G. Schindler, "Research Activities of the Naval Ordnance Laboratory," *Journal of Applied Physics* 15 (March 1944): 255–61; and "NOL—Where the Arctic and Equator Meet," *All Hands,* no. 437 (July 1953): 12–13.

[17] Between January 1941 and July 1942, the size of the laboratory staff had increased more than tenfold, from sixty to eight hundred. By the end of the war, it had more than doubled again to nearly two thousand employees. The workforce continued to expand during the Cold War. Total employment reached three thousand by 1970. Schindler, "Research Activities of the Naval Ordnance Laboratory," 261; Bennett, "Wartime History of the Naval Ordnance Laboratory," 295–96; G. K. Hartmann, "Naval Ordnance Laboratory: From Concept to Hardware," *Defense Industry Bulletin* 6 (December 1970): 9.

[18] When completed, the White Oak campus comprised a total of sixty-nine laboratories, testing ranges,

projectiles, and other conventional ordnance materials, new complementary R&D programs the bureau established that helped set the stage for the laboratory's long-term growth. High-speed aerodynamic and ballistics studies, for example, were carried out in the captured and reconstructed supersonic wind tunnels used by German rocket engineers in Kochel, Bavaria, during the war to develop the V–1 flying bomb and the larger V–2 ballistic missile. Similarly, the persistent problems of detection, localization, and classification of airborne and underwater targets prompted ordnance researchers to push the frontiers of electronics technology to understand the generation, propagation, and processing of electromagnetic and acoustic signals. Research on semiconductors, alloys, ferrites, and other classes of magnetic materials proved vital to the development of more sensitive variable-time fuzes, homing torpedoes, and mine firing devices that were subsequently incorporated into fleet operations.[19]

Organizationally, the postwar Naval Ordnance Laboratory maintained an institutional division between R&D and production. Although laboratory personnel often manufactured "breadboard" models, or prototypes, for testing and inspection, mass production of new weapons was routinely turned over to industrial contractors.[20] This functional separation guided work on the MK56 and MK57 mines, which at the Naval Ordnance Laboratory developed in 1947 but ultimately shifted to private industry for full-scale production. Similarly in 1958, the laboratory began developing a nuclear-armed submarine-to-submarine missile, designated *SUBROC* (from *SUB*marine *ROC*ket). Improved sonar (*sound navigation and ranging*) technology had enabled modern attack submarines to extend the detection range of enemy vessels far beyond the engagement range of conventional torpedoes. SUBROC was designed to redress this tactical disparity between undersea detection and engagement. Launched like a torpedo, SUBROC traveled at high speed through the air before re-entering the water to strike a submerged target. Early in the program, the Goodyear Aerospace Corporation, the defense subsidiary of the Goodyear Tire and Rubber Company, served as the prime contractor to handle system integration and large-scale production. The first generation of SUBROC missiles entered service in the submarine fleet in 1965.[21]

---

and support facilities. It was also the larger of two identically named ordnance R&D installations owned and managed by the Navy after the war. In 1951, the National Bureau of Standards transferred its wartime guided missile program to surplus Navy facilities in Corona, California. Also called the Naval Ordnance Laboratory, the Corona site was formally transferred from the Bureau of Standards to the Navy in 1953. In 1967, the laboratory merged with the Naval Ordnance Test Station at China Lake to form the Naval Weapons Center. Four years later, the Navy permanently closed Corona and relocated its personnel and functions were relocated to China Lake. "Naval Weapons Center," *Sea Technology* 30 (November 1989): 66.

[19] W. E. Scanlon and G. Lieberman, "Naval Ordnance and Electronics Research," *Proceedings of the IRE* 47 (May 1959): 910; "The Naval Research Laboratory, White Oak, Maryland," *Science* 104 (13 September 1946): 237.

[20] "Navy Research Helps Industrial Progress," *Business Week* (30 October 1948): 48 (quote), 50, 52, 54.

[21] Booz Allen, *Review of Navy R&D Management*, 349; Hartmann, "Naval Ordnance Laboratory: From Concept to Hardware," 29; Norman Friedman, *U.S. Naval Weapons: Every Gun, Missile, Mine, and Torpedo Used by the U.S. Navy from 1883 to the Present Day* (Annapolis, Md.: Naval Institute Press, 1982), 129–30; Bernard Blake, ed., *Jane's Weapon Systems, 1987–88*, 18th ed. (London: Jane's Publishing, 1987), 572.

The separation of R&D from production—clearly delineated in the MK56, MK57, and SUBROC programs—mirrored a similar institutional division of labor between research and development, and testing. Separate departments for research, engineering, and testing had been established at the Naval Ordnance Laboratory before the new campus at White Oak opened in 1950. Sections in the research department, which "look[ed] into fundamental principles that might be applied," were generally grouped by scientific discipline: electricity and magnetism, acoustics, mechanics, explosive phenomena, and physical optics. The engineering department, by contrast, was responsible for hardware development. Sections in this department were, by and large, identified by specific ordnance items: ammunition, mines and depth charges, torpedoes, fuses, and plastics. The test department evaluated the electrical and mechanical performance of ordnance prototypes in controlled test facilities and in the field.[22] While the laboratory divisions periodically created, abolished, and shifted between departments and new programs, this organizational division of labor remained essentially intact at White Oak well into the 1970s.[23] Functional separation did not preclude collaboration among the laboratory's staff of scientists and engineers. Nor did it prevent cross-fertilization between the laboratory and industrial contractors. The Naval Ordnance Laboratory, *Business Week* reported in 1948, "helps [contractors] set up the jobs and get the 'bugs' out of the mass-production line [and it] sends out researchers and engineers to lend a helping hand."[24]

Unlike the Naval Ordnance Laboratory, which had been born and reared within the Navy establishment, the Naval Ordnance Test Station at China Lake descended directly from of the wartime rocket development program, which the Army Air Corps (Army Air Forces after 1941) established under contract at the California Institute of Technology (Caltech) in nearby Pasadena. Prior to 1940, rocket technology had received scant attention from the military services. Most rocket R&D was centered in civilian institutions. During the war, however, physicist Charles Lauritsen, a respected expert in high-voltage nuclear physics, and his research group at Caltech laid much of the groundwork for the Navy's wartime rocket program at China Lake.[25]

---

[22] "Naval Ordnance Laboratory, White Oak, Maryland," 237–38; R. B. Dittmar, "Development of Physical Facilities for Research," *Proceedings of the Institute of Radio Engineers* 37 (April 1949): 425–26; "Ordnance Test Facilities Greatly Expanded at NOL," *Product Engineering* 21 (April 1950): 152; D. S. Muzzey, "How the Project Manager System Works at the Naval Ordnance Lab," *Armed Forces Management* 4 (August 1958): 29.

[23] In 1975, the Secretary of Defense directed the Navy and the Air Force to turn over to the Army all in-house procurement, production, and distribution of ammunition and related ordnance. Transfer of the Navy's production facilities was completed in 1978. Shiman, *Forging the Sword*, 81. The Naval Ordnance Laboratory permanently closed in 1997.

[24] "Navy Research Helps Industrial Progress," 48, 50 (quote).

[25] Caltech's rocket program was split between Lauritsen's group, which coordinated testing and evaluation activities at China Lake, and the group headed by aerodynamicist Theodore von Kármán. At the end of the war, the rocket work under von Kármán's direction shifted to the newly established Jet Propulsion Laboratory, operated by Caltech under contract for the Army. J. D. Gerrard-Gough and Albert B. Christman, *The Grand Experiment at Inyokern*, vol. 2 of *History of the Naval Weapons Center, China Lake, California* (Washington, D.C.: Department of the Navy, Naval Historical Division, 1978), 280; Clayton R. Koppes, *JPL and the American Space Program: A History of the Jet Propulsion Laboratory* (New Haven: Yale University Press, 1982), chaps. 1–2.

Lauritsen also played a major role in site selection and facilities planning at China Lake. This sprawling installation, which covered more than one thousand square miles by the mid-1950s, was conceived in 1943 to test and evaluate the aircraft rockets, propellants, and launchers produced by his staff back in Pasadena. Two years later, as rocket work rapidly shifted from development to mass production, Lauritsen and his military counterparts prepared to transfer the China Lake test facility from Caltech to the Navy and expand its mission to include a broad program of research and development.[26] During the postwar period, the station operated as a full-service weapons development installation, turning out home-grown rockets, guided missiles, torpedoes, and aircraft fire-control systems.[27] A diverse R&D infrastructure with specialized expertise in many scientific and engineering disciplines—physics, chemistry, mathematics and computing, metallurgy, ceramics, electronics, optics, aerodynamics, ballistics, and chemical, mechanical, and electrical engineering—supported these and other weapons programs. Taken together, this broad range of multidisciplinary activities made the Naval Ordnance Test Station the largest in-house R&D installation operated by the Navy after World War II. Its rapid growth also signaled the emergence of rockets and guided missiles as permanent additions to the Navy's postwar arsenal.[28]

The centerpiece of the research and development effort at the Naval Ordnance Test Station was the Michelson Laboratory, a vast, six-wing building completed in 1948 at a cost of nearly $10 million.[29] This state-of-the-art facility consolidated the station's previously scattered R&D functions, and it also occupied a central role in rocket and missile development.[30] Physically, it incorporated the latest features of modern laboratory design and function. While the laboratory was still on the drawing board, senior staff in the Bureau of Ordnance consulted leading industrial firms for advice and guidance during the planning stages. Ordnance officials visited both the venerable Bell Telephone Laboratories, which had recently moved from their original location in New York City to a state-of-the-art facility in Murray Hill, New Jersey, as well as the new research campus that electronics giant Radio Corporation of America had built in nearby Princeton. The tour also included such well-known private research institutions as the Mellon Institute of Industrial Research and the laboratories of the Gulf

---

[26] "China Lake: Navy in the Desert Is Guided Missile Laboratory," *All Hands*, no. 469 (March 1956): 60–61; Christman, *Sailors, Scientists, and Rockets*, 243; Gerrard-Gough and Christman, *The Grand Experiment at Inyokern*, 2–3.

[27] Like the Naval Ordnance Laboratory, the Naval Ordnance Test Station did not operate manufacturing facilities beyond the pilot production stage. After the war, industrial contractors, such as Philco and the General Tire and Rubber Company mass produced the missiles and rockets developed at China Lake.

[28] The transition from conventional ordnance to missiles and rockets was already underway during the war. In 1944, for example, the Army spent more than $150 million on rocket procurement. The Navy's expenditures were much higher, reaching $100 million per month in 1945. Gerrard-Gough and Christman, *The Grand Experiment at Inyokern*, 194.

[29] The laboratory was named after physicist Albert A. Michelson, a Naval Academy graduate and the first American to win the Nobel Prize for physics (1907).

[30] When it opened, the laboratory had consumed approximately 10 percent of the $100 million investment in new facilities and staff made by the Bureau of Ordnance at China Lake. F. G. Sawyer, "Rocket Chemistry at Inyokern," *Chemical and Engineering News* 27 (18 July 1949): 2067.

Oil Corporation, both located in Pittsburgh, and the Battelle Memorial Institute in Columbus, Ohio.[31]

Researchers in the Michelson Laboratory gradually assumed control of the management, content, and scope of internal R&D programs.[32] Special attention focused on pursuing a broad program of fundamental research to support the short-term work on weapons development underway in the engineering and testing laboratories. Concerned about the imbalance between these two categories of research, the laboratory's research director told the station commander in 1947, "It is considered of great importance that a certain amount of fundamental research which offers promise of support for development programs of the future, be sponsored by this station.... The benefits to be derived from close association with work of this kind are very great from the standpoint of the stimulation of the applied research and development programs."[33]

One outcome of this dialogue between the civilian technical staff and the naval officers that managed the site on behalf of the Bureau of Ordnance was the establishment in 1948 of a special discretionary fund for undirected scientific research. This fund was to be distributed among the laboratory's six major divisions (chemistry, metals, electronics, photography, aerodynamics, and physics and optics) as overhead on specific development projects. Initially set at 3 percent of the budget for each individual R&D project, the fund later increased to 5 percent and became a permanent line item in the station's annual appropriation. By the early 1950s, a similar discretionary research program had been set up at the Naval Ordnance Laboratory, as well as other Navy R&D facilities operated by the three material bureaus.[34]

The expansion of fundamental research under civilian rather than military control at China Lake and other Navy laboratories also aided efforts to recruit first-rate scientists and engineers who otherwise might have been tempted to pursue more lucrative—and in some cases intellectually challenging—careers in academia and industry. "The Research Department [at China Lake]," *Civil Engineering* reported in 1948, "pursues fundamental research studies, not only in the interests of scientific objectives, but also to attract and retain outstanding scientists . . . and to enhance the prestige of the station and the Navy in the scientific world."[35] Like the Army arsenals, the Navy laboratories experienced recruitment shortfalls and high attrition rates among its most talented

---

[31] Gerrard-Gough and Christman, *The Grand Experiment at Inyokern*, 34–36.

[32] Control of the R&D program at China Lake became a contentious issue between civilian scientists and engineers, who worked in the laboratory, and the military personnel, who managed the station for the Bureau of Ordnance. Civilian R&D managers maintained that the programmatic functions of the laboratory should be independent of the military command structure. Otherwise efforts to recruit first-rate scientists would suffer. See Gerrard-Gough and Christman, *The Grand Experiment at Inyokern*, 255–64, 269.

[33] Gerrard-Gough and Christman, *The Grand Experiment at Inyokern*, 244–45, 305–6 (quote), 305–06.

[34] Ibid., 244–45, 305–6 (quote), 328–29.

[35] "Navy Dedicates New Research Laboratory at Inyokern, Calif.," *Civil Engineering* 18 (June 1948): 88. On the disparity between industrial and government pay scales, see, for example, "Federal Labs Lose Key Men," *Chemical and Engineering News* 37 (11 May 1959): 42–43.

researchers.[36] One important exception was the Naval Research Laboratory, the direct beneficiary of ample funding from ONR and a clear mission statement that emphasized fundamental research rather than weapons development.[37] Other in-house laboratories, however, did not always share the same institutional advantages. Despite its growth as a major computing facility in the 1950s and 1960s, the Naval Proving Ground at Dahlgren experienced difficulties hiring qualified technical personnel. Low salaries at the David Taylor Model Basin and the Naval Ordnance Laboratory had the same effect.[38] In 1954, for example, Ralph Bennett, an accomplished electrical engineer and physicist and a former engineering professor at the Massachusetts Institute of Technology, resigned his position as director of the Naval Ordnance Laboratory to accept a more lucrative offer as manager of the technical department at General Electric's (GE) Knolls Atomic Power Laboratory in Schenectady, New York. Already excited about "the chance to learn a new technology [at GE]," Bennett was especially attracted to the substantial increase in salary; it jumped nearly 70 percent, from $15,000 to $25,000.[39]

Just as it did at the Naval Ordnance Laboratory in Maryland, a clear organizational division existed between R&D and production at the Naval Ordnance Test Station. The station engaged in prototype assembly and pilot manufacturing of rockets and missiles, but weapon systems cleared for operational use after testing and evaluation were turned over to industrial contractors for quantity production. Similarly, research was, by and large, organizationally separate from engineering and other development activities. In 1957, for example, the bureau split into departments by functional specialization and type of ordnance: rockets and missiles, aviation ordnance, underwater ordnance,

---

[36] To help alleviate this chronic problem in the service laboratories, Congress passed Public Law 313 in 1947. This law (and subsequent amendments) authorized the creation of special employment grades (and salaries) beyond the limits set by civil service requirements. The Salary Reform Act of 1962 established professional "supergrades" for personnel attached to RDT&E (Research, Development, Testing, and Evaluation) functions in the Department of Defense. Unlike previous legislation this act placed no limits on the number of supergrades available. Booz Allen, *Review of Navy R&D Management*, 124–25, 143. Regarding civil service pay scales and recruitment difficulties in government laboratories after World War II, see also Margaret W. Rossiter, "Setting Federal Salaries in the Space Age," *Osiris* 2, 2nd ser. (1992): 218–37; Clarence H. Danhof, *Government Contracting and Technological Change* (Washington, D.C.: Brookings Institution, 1968), 409–16; and Thomas C. Lassman, "Government Science in Postwar America: Henry A. Wallace, Edward U. Condon, and the Transformation of the National Bureau of Standards, 1945–1951," *Isis* 96 (March 2005): 25–51.

[37] In 1962, for example, the budget of the Naval Research Laboratory ($41,319,000) ranked second behind that of the Naval Ordnance Test Station ($54,659,000). Following in a distant third place was the budget of the Naval Ordnance Laboratory at White Oak ($29,928,000). "The Far-Flung Navy Research Network," *Missiles and Rockets* 10 (1 January 1962): 16.

[38] Kenneth G. McCollum, ed., *Dahlgren* (Dahlgren, Va.: Naval Surface Weapons Center, 1977), 15, 87–89; Carlisle, *Where the Fleet Begins*, 312.

[39] Bennett quoted in Smaldone, *A History of the White Oak Laboratory*, 23. Bennett's experience was not unique. Similar problems hampered efforts to replace technical division heads who had retired from the laboratory after the war. As late as the 1950s, for example, the solid-state and physical properties of materials divisions were leaderless. The internal candidates identified to fill the vacant management positions preferred "to devote their full energies to research rather than administrative matters, [and] outsiders of caliber [were] unwilling to make the financial sacrifice entailed." Prompted by this staffing shortage and the likelihood of ongoing recruitment shortfalls, the chief of the laboratory's physics program merged both divisions into a single organizational unit in 1961. Ibid., 95 (quote), 169–70.

explosives and propellants, research (including the Michelson Laboratory), engineering, testing, and weapons planning. Functional separation of research and engineering did not, in itself, prohibit collaboration across organizational boundaries. Interdepartmental cooperation was expected in cases when the station received weapons requirements from the Chief of Naval Operations. In a 1957 article reviewing the station's weapons development process, *Aviation Week* reported that teams drawn from the functional departments "will assist [the rockets and missiles department] in design studies which ultimately lead to development of a finished prototype." This cooperative strategy was perhaps most effectively institutionalized in the development of the Sidewinder, a highly successful air-to-air missile that entered fleet service in 1956. All phases of technical development incorporating the efforts of scientists and engineers— structural design, aerodynamic configuration, infrared guidance, propulsion, launching arrangement—were completed at China Lake.[40] A similar process guided in-house development of the Mighty Mouse, a small-caliber, air-to-surface missile that began rolling off assembly lines in 1951. Also during this period, the station turned out the first prototypes of the Shrike antiradar missile and the Walleye television-guided glide bomb, both of which entered service in the mid-1960s.[41]

In addition to developing new missiles and rockets from scratch, the Naval Ordnance Test Station also improved weapons that had been effectively used during World War II. First introduced into service in the Army Air Forces in 1944, the high-velocity aircraft rocket (HVAR), unofficially dubbed Holy Moses, was the first Caltech-designed aircraft rocket tested for operational performance at China Lake. Like other aircraft rockets, Holy Moses was fitted with fixed fins to maintain aerodynamic stability during flight. Meanwhile, researchers at Caltech had been experimenting with several designs and configurations to improve the performance of Holy Moses and other rockets. In the field of ballistics, for example, it was well established that projectile rotation during firing—in rifles and artillery, for example—improved stability and accuracy. Using the same principle for surface-to-air applications, Caltech researchers introduced a design for a finless, tube-launched rotating rocket that compared favorably with its fin-stabilized equivalent.

Launching a spinning rocket from the air rather than the ground, however, proved to be more problematic. The presence of fixed tubular launchers on the wings of high-performance aircraft, especially jet aircraft, reduced airspeed and impaired maneuverability. Moreover, the stability of a rocket fired during flight

---

[40] "NOTS Converts Ideas into Missiles," *Aviation Week* 66 (3 June 1957): 148. Philco, a diversified radio and electronics manufacturer based in Philadelphia, was selected by the Navy in 1954 to be the prime contractor for Sidewinder. Other firms, such as Raytheon and the Loral Corporation, joined Philco as major contractors as the program expanded and new versions of the missile were introduced into service. For an introduction to the history of the Sidewinder program, see Ron Strum, *Sidewinder: Creative Missile Development at China Lake* (Annapolis, Md.: Naval Institute Press, 1999).

[41] Gerrard-Gough and Christman, *The Grand Experiment at Inyokern*, 296; K. F. Mordoff, "China Lake Facilities Dedicated to Diverse Weapons Tasks," *Aviation Week and Space Technology* 124 (20 January 1986): 56; D. B. Young, "Integrated Research," *Ordnance* 40 (July-August 1955): 56.

dropped sharply after it exited the launch tube (due to the large disparity between initial spinning and high aircraft velocity). Slow recovery of the rocket during flight typically resulted in wide variation in trajectory and poor tracking to the target. Researchers at China Lake adapted a folding-fin mechanism originally developed in the Army to improve the stability and accuracy of air-launched spinning rockets. The folding fins remained closed around the rocket during firing, but, once the rocket cleared the launch tube, they extended into a full, fixed-fin position through the operation of a pressure-actuated piston assembly. The improved folding-fin design developed at the Naval Ordnance Test Station was quickly adapted to the new, multipurpose, air-launched Zuni rocket, which replaced the original fixed-fin Holy Moses in the early 1950s.[42]

Throughout the 1960s and well into the 1970s, China Lake continuously served as the Navy's primary source of missile and rocket technology. By the 1980s, however, the mission of the Naval Ordnance Test Station—renamed the Naval Weapons Center in 1967—had begun to change to reflect the realities of the Defense Department's growing reliance on industrial contractors and other private-sector institutions for weapons R&D and production. "Weapons Center personnel," observed *Aviation Week and Space Technology* in 1986, "now spend more time managing technology with defense contractors involved with the design and manufacture of a weapon system, rather than in earlier times, when a need would arise and the center would design, build, test, and deliver to the fleet a weapon to meet the requirement in record time."[43] China Lake still maintained extensive R&D, pilot production, and testing and evaluation facilities, but much of the work on weapons focused on system support, upgrades, and other services for industrial contractors.[44] The propulsion laboratory, for example, operated R&D, pilot production, and test facilities to support work on explosives, solid and liquid propellants, warheads, and rocket motors. These facilities were also used "to study and find solutions to industry production problems and . . . serve as a production source to meet surge requirements for a few months during a crisis." The center's electronics manufacturing productivity laboratory carried out similar functions, with a mission to "upgrade production facilities in the [United States], reduce costs, improve product quality, and reduce production times."[45]

As scientists and engineers at the Naval Ordnance Test Station evaluated the performance of missiles and rockets, their East Coast counterparts at the Naval Proving Ground in Dahlgren, Virginia, conducted similar testing work on conventional ordnance—bombs, guns, and projectiles—prior to full-scale industrial production. Unlike China Lake, however, Dahlgren did

---

[42] Gerrard-Gough and Christman, *The Grand Experiment at Inyokern*, 84, 294–97.

[43] D. M. North, "Navy Center Expands Mission to Include Technology Management," *Aviation Week and Space Technology* 124 (20 January 1986): 46.

[44] In the 1980s, the Michelson Laboratory maintained its long-standing tradition in fundamental research, but it also supported work on fuzes, guidance systems, propellants, and explosives. Researchers in other laboratories at the Naval Weapons Center studied lasers, optical systems, radar, electromagnetic interference, and microelectronics technology. See Mordoff, "China Lake Facilities Dedicated to Diverse Weapons Tasks," 40.

[45] Mordoff, "China Lake Facilities Dedicated to Diverse Weapons Tasks," 55–56.

not conceptualize and develop its own weapon systems but instead received materials for testing and evaluation from other service facilities, such as the Naval Ordnance Laboratory, or from industrial contractors. This tradition of ordnance proofing and testing can be traced back to 1872, when the Navy established its first proving ground in Annapolis, Maryland. In 1890, the proving ground transferred from Annapolis to Indian Head, Maryland, located next to the Naval Powder Factory on the shores of the Potomac River about twenty miles south of Washington, D.C.[46] All types of naval guns, bombs, gunpowder, projectiles, armor, fuzes, and cartridge cases were tested at Indian Head until the end of World War I, when space limitations prompted the Bureau of Ordnance to search for a larger location. The testing requirements for newer long-range guns and the continuous expansion of the powder factory made such a move especially urgent. Construction of facilities at Dahlgren began in the spring of 1918, and, by 1923, the new proving ground was in full operation.

Shortly after Dahlgren opened, management established an experimental department, headed by a civilian Ph.D. physicist, to conduct routine testing of ordnance materials.[47] Tight budgets during the interwar period precluded a major expansion of the department, but diversification of the testing program continued, albeit slowly. In 1936, the experimental department became the experimental laboratory, and its major functions focused on bomb calibration, exterior ballistics, velocity measurements, and armament tests. Four years later, Dahlgren set up a separate armor and projectile laboratory to support additional testing functions and also to conduct metallurgical research. Technical investigations expanded at both laboratories during World War II along two separate but related lines: (1) routine acceptance testing of materials and development of new testing and evaluation procedures, and (2) prosecution of R&D to improve the performance of weapons and armor.[48]

After World War II, Dahlgren's traditional testing and proofing activities continued, often expanding during major conflicts, such as the Korean and Vietnam wars, and then contracting in peacetime. Although this cyclical behavior often caused anxiety among administrators, who feared that closure of the installation was imminent, a crucial reprieve came in the 1950s in the form of a major expansion into electronics and high-speed computing to support the Navy's new fleet ballistic missile program. The aggressive move into electronic computing was by no means arbitrary. Rather, it complemented Dahlgren's long-standing expertise in ballistics testing and evaluation, and it also tracked the larger postwar transformation of naval weapons technology from conventional ordnance to missiles and rockets, jet aircraft, and nuclear weapons. The transition from proofing to R&D manifested itself in the establishment of new programs to explore the latest developments in fire control, electronics, optics, ballistics, and

---

[46] On the Naval Powder Factory, see Rodney P. Carlisle, *Powder and Propellants: Energetic Materials at Indian Head, Maryland, 1890–2001*, 2d ed. (Denton: University of North Texas Press, 2002).

[47] The first director of the experimental department was Louis Thompson, a ballistics expert who had received his Ph.D. in physics from Clark University in 1917.

[48] D. I. Hedrick, "Research and Experimental Activities of the U.S. Naval Proving Ground," *Journal of Applied Physics* 15 (March 1944): 262; Christman, *Sailors, Scientists, and Rockets*, 4–5, 55, 63–64.

guidance. In 1967, for example, researchers at Dahlgren began experimenting with guided projectiles fired from naval guns. This work continued into the 1970s, when the first laser-guided projectiles were introduced into the fleet.

Until the mid-1950s, Dahlgren's computing capabilities relied on the punched-card machines that the staff had installed during World War II to produce bombing, rocket, and projectile tables. In 1955, Dahlgren acquired the Naval Ordnance Research Calculator (NORAC). Designed and built under contract by the International Business Machines Corporation, NORAC was more than one hundred times faster than the computing equipment already in operation at the proving ground. In addition to carrying out routine ballistics calculations, NORAC was also used for war gaming exercises, and, in 1959, it was put to work computing trajectories and other operational parameters for the Navy's new fleet ballistic missile program. Three years later, a $2 million computation facility was added to supplement NORAC's work on missile and space systems. This expansion in computational analysis and the continued diversification of Dahlgren's mission prompted the Navy leadership to rename the proving ground the Naval Weapons Laboratory in 1959. In 1974, Dahlgren merged with the Naval Ordnance Laboratory at White Oak to form the Naval Surface Weapons Center.[49]

Dahlgren's diversification beyond proofing and evaluation of ordnance into electronics and computers matched a similar institutional transformation within the ammunition manufacturing plants owned and operated by the Bureau of Ordnance. Like Dahlgren and the bureau's other large corporate laboratories, the engineering support functions attached to the Navy's ordnance factories tackled and solved major technical problems in electronics, optics, and missile guidance and fire control. One important source of this effort outside the perimeter of the Navy's laboratory establishment was the Crane Naval Weapons Support Center, located in south central Indiana.[50] Founded as a weapons depot in 1940 to help meet the Navy's rapidly growing wartime material needs, Crane stored smokeless powder and poison gas, loaded gun projectiles and ammunition cartridges for small arms, and manufactured all sizes of shells, bombs, depth charges, and other ordnance materials. After 1945, Crane continued to function as a storage and production facility, but it also moved into technical fields beyond those directly relevant to its wartime mission.

During the war, Crane engineers tested and evaluated the ordnance materials produced by the depot's own manufacturing divisions and industrial contractors. In 1947, this testing function was centralized in a new department called the Quality Evaluation Laboratory. The laboratory also set standards for munitions safety and quality control. Within a decade, however, the laboratory's technical capabilities had expanded to provide evaluation protocols for the new electronics technologies that were rapidly replacing mechanical assemblies in firing mechanisms, guidance controls, fuzes, and other critical ordnance components.

---

[49] McCollum, *Dahlgren*, 13–17, 123, 128–29; Coletta, *United States Navy and Marine Corps Bases*, 164.
[50] The depot was named after Commodore William Montgomery Crane, the first chief of the Navy's Bureau of Ordnance and Hydrography (renamed the Bureau of Ordnance in 1862).

In 1955, the Secretary of the Navy set up the Special Projects Office outside bureau jurisdiction to develop Polaris, the Navy's first submarine-launched ballistic missile capable of delivering a nuclear warhead to a distant target. The Quality Evaluation Laboratory diversified its technological capabilities even further through this organizational unit.

Crane did not simply graft a new R&D program onto its testing and evaluation functions. Nor did it replace altogether the engineering staff with newly minted Ph.D. scientists. Rather, the technological shift from conventional ordnance to advanced missile systems like Polaris was a complementary process in which diversification remained grounded in Crane's long-standing engineering tradition. Semiconductors, for example, were used in the fire control, navigation, guidance, and other subsystems on Polaris. Crane engineers and the new cadre of academically trained scientists that joined them during this period acquired extensive expertise in solid-state electronics to develop new testing, screening, and evaluation procedures to ensure peak operational performance of semiconductors, microwave tubes, and other precision electronic devices. In response to this technological shift, Crane management set up the Fleet Logistics Support Department (separate from the Quality Evaluation Laboratory) in 1970 to handle electronics work on the Polaris and Terrier missile systems.[51] Functional specialization at Crane continued throughout the remainder of the Cold War as more advanced ballistic missiles—Poseidon and Trident—were introduced into fleet service. By the early 1990s, what began as the Quality Evaluation Laboratory had evolved into the following individual product divisions: microelectronics technology, electronic module test and repair, microwave components, electromechanical power systems, electronic warfare, conventional ammunition engineering, small arms, and acoustic sensors. Work in these fields combined a broad knowledge base in electronics technology with a continuing focus on product testing and evaluation and technical oversight of manufacturing processes carried out in industry.[52]

Bureau of Aeronautics

Like the Bureau of Ordnance, the Bureau of Aeronautics owned and operated an institutionally diverse technological infrastructure that included research and development laboratories, testing and inspection facilities, and aircraft manufacturing plants. This network of laboratories and factories remained largely intact until the early years of the Cold War, when the military services began shifting the bulk of their resources for aircraft R&D and procurement to private-sector contractors.[53] Rapid demobilization of the armed forces after World War II had precipitated a massive restructuring of the domestic aircraft

---

[51] The Quality Evaluation Laboratory continued "to concentrate on munitions testing." Robert L. Reid and Thomas E. Rodgers, *A Good Neighbor: The First Fifty Years at Crane, 1941–1991* (Evansville: Historic Southern Indiana Project, University of Southern Indiana, 1991), 88.

[52] Ibid., 51, 81, 85–91, 103–5.

[53] Booz Allen, *Review of Navy R&D Management*, 122; Christman, *Sailors, Scientists, and Rockets*, 176.

industry. Manufacturers shed excess capacity to offset sharp declines in military procurement. The establishment of an independent air force in 1947 and the subsequent onset of the Cold War, however, helped reverse this trend as the firms that survived the immediate postwar shakeout acquired lucrative development and production contracts from the newest military service. Significantly, this institutional relationship helped the largest planemakers turn out, in close collaboration with the military services, successive generations of advanced tactical and strategic aircraft and the sophisticated electronics technologies that maintained their operational superiority during the Cold War.[54] In addition to encountering competition from private airframe manufacturers, the Bureau of Aeronautics also continued to lose institutional stability as it engaged in a fierce struggle with the Bureau of Ordnance over control of the Navy's rapidly expanding rocket and guided missile programs. Despite the imposition of temporary measures designed to alleviate this jurisdictional conflict—for example, the establishment of the Special Projects Office in 1955 to manage and coordinate the Polaris ballistic missile program and the creation of the Lead Bureau Concept two years later the ongoing battle over missile cognizance and the growing significance of weapon systems integration prompted the Navy leadership to merge the bureaus of Aeronautics and Ordnance into the new Bureau of Naval Weapons in 1959.[55]

The Bureau of Aeronautics and its successor organization—the Bureau of Naval Weapons—did not simply relinquish control of the large in-house R&D infrastructure that had served the Navy's aeronautical interests since World War I. The process was gradual and varied. Some facilities closed, whereas others merged into new organizations. The Navy's experience with aircraft development began in 1915, when Congress enacted legislation establishing the National Advisory Committee for Aeronautics (NACA) to support and coordinate a broad program of research on behalf of both civilian and military aviation. Subsequently, NACA established a network of in-house laboratories and testing facilities to develop a diverse knowledge base in the aeronautical sciences.[56] The Navy adopted a similar strategy to connect NACA's research capabilities to military aircraft requirements. This strategic mission was effectively institutionalized in the new

---

[54] In 1948, the Air Force controlled half of the $300 million allocated by all federal agencies for aeronautical research and development. R. McLarren, "Largest Aero Research Program," *Aviation Week* 48 (23 February 1948): 42.

[55] On the *Polaris* program, see Harvey M. Sapolsky, *The Polaris System Development: Bureaucratic and Programmatic Success in Government* (Cambridge, Mass.: Harvard University Press, 1972). The Lead Bureau Concept institutionalized the mechanisms used by the Special Projects Office to develop the *Polaris* missile system. In exceptional cases and depending on the weapon requirement, one bureau would be selected to manage the technical prosecution of a designated project. It would also coordinate the activities of other participating bureaus. Although it tended to dilute the authority and independence of the individual bureaus and cut across organizational lines, the Lead Bureau Concept helped solve the immediate problem of cognizance that had caused territorial skirmishes and inflamed relations between the former bureaus of Ordnance and Aeronautics. Booz Allen, *Review of Navy R&D Management,* 46.

[56] L. C. Stevens, "Research in the Bureau of Aeronautics," *Journal of Applied Physics* 15 (March 1944): 271–72; McLarren, "Largest Aero Research Program," 44–46. On the history of NACA, see Alex Roland, *Model Research: The National Advisory Committee for Aeronautics, 1915–1958,* 2 vols. (Washington, D.C.: National Aeronautics and Space Administration, 1985).

Naval Aircraft Factory, established at Philadelphia in 1917. Initially set up for the sole purpose of producing aircraft, such as seaplanes (flying boats) for patrol and reconnaissance operations, the factory also manufactured engines, catapult and arresting gear, parachutes, and other aviation equipment.[57] R&D functions were subsequently added to carry out studies of engines, electronic equipment, flight instruments, fuels, lubricants, and structural materials for airframes. Diversification of R&D along these lines continued after the Navy established the Bureau of Aeronautics in 1921. Perhaps most important, the Naval Aircraft Factory set the limits of technological innovation within the Navy's in-house aviation program during the post–World War II period.

When the factory first opened, research—at least to the extent that it supported the manufacturing operations—focused primarily on inspection and quality control of completed aircraft and modification of existing designs that originated in industry. Related studies of the physical properties of constituent materials—primarily wood, fabrics, and metals—were carried out as well. In 1920, all materials work was consolidated into the new Physical Testing Laboratory. Eight years later, as aircraft manufacturers shifted from wood to metal construction, the laboratory diversified and split into two divisions: one concentrating on materials, the other on airframe structures. Researchers in the structural division conducted static and dynamic studies of wings, tail surfaces, and fuselages, as well as investigations of vibration effects. Their counterparts in the materials division worked on corrosion resistance and protection and developed improved paints, finishes, and other coatings. Division personnel drafted and published reports based on this work, which they then distributed to civilian airframe manufacturers. In the aeronautical engineering laboratory, which moved to Philadelphia from the Washington Navy Yard in 1924, similar studies took place on liquid- and air-cooled aircraft engines, fuels, lubricants, carburetion and electrical systems, and other power plant components. This type of R&D, ranging from materials research on plastics and metal alloys to reliability testing of aircraft engines in simulated flight conditions, continued at the Naval Aircraft Factory during the 1920s and 1930s and throughout World War II.[58]

In 1943, the factory, laboratories, and all other support functions at Philadelphia the bureau into four separate commands under an umbrella organization called the Naval Air Material Center (NAMC). Although it was still an important production facility, the Naval Aircraft Factory began to concentrate more of its resources on prototype development and small-scale manufacturing of improved airframe models. The Naval Aircraft Modification Unit adapted standard Navy aircraft currently in service for special functions, while the Naval Air Experiment Station coordinated all in-house R&D on materials, radio and electronic equipment, engines and accessories, and flight

---

[57] J. W. Meader, "The Naval Air Material Center, Philadelphia, Pennsylvania," *Journal of Applied Physics* 15 (March 1944): 273.

[58] William F. Trimble, *Wings for the Navy: A History of the Naval Aircraft Factory, 1917–1956* (Annapolis, Md.: Naval Institute Press, 1990), 105–06.

instruments.[59] The Naval Auxiliary Air Station conducted local flight operations and tested aircraft arresting gear for flight deck operations aboard the Navy's aircraft carriers. "The Naval Air Material Center," wrote an NAMC technical consultant in 1944, "functions as a completely self-contained development group, intimately associated with the design and development of experimental aircraft."[60]

In 1946, the Bureau of Aeronautics established new testing and evaluation facilities to support the development of jet aircraft and guided missiles—two wartime technologies already poised to replace piston-engine airplanes and conventional ordnance in fleet operations. Complete testing of Navy jets was located at the Naval Air Test Station on the Patuxent River in Maryland. The laboratories, ground facilities, and sea range at the Naval Air Missile Test Center at Point Magu, California, supported testing and evaluation of missiles, launchers, and auxiliary equipment. In 1955, engine development work, which had originated at Philadelphia, expanded into new facilities at Trenton, New Jersey. The Naval Air Turbine Test Station and the Aeronautical Turbine Laboratory tested and evaluated gas turbines, turbojets, ramjets, and other types of advanced aircraft power plants designed and built by commercial engine manufacturers, such as Westinghouse Electric, Pratt & Whitney, Curtiss-Wright, General Electric, and the Allison Division of General Motors.[61] In 1967, the Navy transferred all engine R&D underway at Philadelphia to Trenton and merged it into the Naval Air Propulsion Test Center, successor organization to the Naval Air Turbine Test Station and the Aeronautical Turbine Laboratory.[62]

Several major innovations emerged from the Naval Air Material Center after World War II. Since the late 1930s, engineers in the Naval Aircraft Factory had been working on the development, manufacture, and installation of aircraft catapults and arresting gear for aircraft carriers. By the late 1940s, conventional hydraulic catapults had reached their operational limits, especially as jet aircraft replaced their piston-engine counterparts. Inefficient at low speeds, jet aircraft required more powerful catapults for carrier-based launches. The solution was the steam catapult, introduced into service aboard the fleet's Essex-class aircraft carriers in 1954.[63] Four years earlier, the Aeronautical Instruments Laboratory, a division of the Naval Air Experiment Station, developed and tested the first helicopter autopilot. Meanwhile, in 1946, the station's aeronautical materials laboratory began investigating the properties and behavior of titanium, a lightweight, heat-resistant alloy that manifested many of the same strength,

---

[59] The Naval Experiment Station originally included four laboratories: Aeronautical Materials Laboratory, Radio and Electrical Laboratory, Aeronautical Engine Laboratory, and the Instrument Development Laboratory. Other laboratories were established, merged, renamed, and dismantled in subsequent years. In 1948, for example, the station set up the Aeronautical Medical Equipment Laboratory was set up to study the effects of altitude, temperature, vibration, and acceleration on humans. Ibid., 322.

[60] Meader, "The Naval Air Material Center, Philadelphia, Pennsylvania," 273–74 (quote on 274).

[61] I. Stone, "Air Test Center Speeds Navy's Missiles to Fleet Use," *Aviation Week* 66 (3 June 1957): 140–45; G. L. Christian, "NATTS Is World's Top Jet Test Facility," *Aviation Week* 66 (3 June 1957): 16–62.

[62] Trimble, *Wings for the Navy*, xiii, 326, 329.

[63] Work on the steam catapult began in Britain before further improvements were completed at the Naval Air Material Center. Ibid., 318–19.

corrosion-resistant, and tensile-strength properties of heavier metals, such as stainless steel.[64] Like aluminum and other lightweight metal alloys, titanium also showed promise as a component material in turbojet engines. The laboratory also established a polymers division in 1952 to study and develop high-strength synthetic rubber, plastics, and textiles for use in cockpit canopies, windows, and other aircraft components.[65]

Research and development in these and other fields continued throughout the postwar period until the 1970s, when a series of major reorganizations at the local and regional levels and within the Bureau of Aeronautics culminated in the rapid decline of naval aviation at Philadelphia. In 1956, the Naval Aircraft Factory became the Naval Air Engineering Facility (NAEF), and its major functions officially shifted from aircraft production to research, development, prototyping, and maintenance of aircraft and guided-missile launching and recovery equipment.[66] The following year, the bureau granted independent status to the laboratories previously assigned to the wartime Naval Air Experiment Station. In 1962, NAEF adopted a new name—the Naval Air Engineering Center (NAEC)—and the Naval Aircraft Factory became the Naval Air Engineering Laboratory, bringing to five the total number of R&D laboratories operating alongside NAEC.[67] By the mid-1970s, however, efforts underway since the 1950s to streamline the Navy's shore establishment and shift more in-house R&D operations to private-sector contractors prompted a sharp reduction of aviation activities in Philadelphia as facilities were closed, merged, or transferred to other Navy installations.[68]

Bureau of Ships

At the end of the World War II, the Bureau of Ships relied on private shipyards and its own shipyards to design, fabricate, and assemble the hulls and superstructures required for destroyers, cruisers, battleships, aircraft carriers, and submarines. The Bureau of Ordnance supplied guns, depth charges, torpedoes, and other weapons, while industrial contractors typically provided operating

---

[64] Research on high-strength alloys was also supported by ONR, which established and coordinated with the material bureaus a major titanium R&D program in 1952. See J. J. Harwood, "Metallurgy Research Program of the Office of Naval Research," *Journal of Metals* 9 (May 1957): 673.

[65] Trimble, *Wings for the Navy*, 321–22, 329–30.

[66] When the Naval Aircraft Factory officially lost its production status in 1956, the Navy was already in the process of reorganizing its aviation programs in the Philadelphia area. Two years earlier, the Naval Air Development and Material Center had been established at Johnsville, Pennsylvania. This new organizational unit administered the Naval Air Development Center at Johnsville, the Naval Air Material Center at Philadelphia, the Naval Air Turbine Test Center (moved from Philadelphia to Trenton in 1955), and the Naval Air Test Facility at the Naval Air Station in Lakehurst, New Jersey. In 1959, the Naval Air Development and Material Center became the headquarters organization for the Naval Air Research and Development Activities Command.

[67] The other laboratories (Aeronautical Engine Laboratory, Aeronautical Structures Laboratory, Aeronautical Materials Laboratory, and the Air Crew Equipment Laboratory) were the direct organizational descendents of the four laboratories grouped together in the Naval Experiment Station in 1943.

[68] Trimble, *Wings for the Navy*, 323–324, 329–30.

equipment—ranging from nuclear-powered propulsion systems to sophisticated electronics technologies for communications and countermeasures. A broad and diversified knowledge base in the scientific and engineering disciplines supported these procurement functions.[69] Like the bureaus of Ordnance and Aeronautics, R&D in the Bureau of Ships was institutionally and functionally specialized. The Engineering Experiment Station in Annapolis inspected, tested, evaluated, and set production and performance standards for equipment manufactured in industry. Located just outside of Washington, D.C., the David Taylor Model Basin, by contrast, focused on more fundamental studies in hydrodynamics, nuclear propulsion, and other scientific fields to develop new and more efficient hull and propeller designs for submarines and surface ships. The burgeoning field of microwave electronics claimed equal institutional status in the Bureau of Ships during this period. Developments in electronics heavily influenced ship design, construction, and operation during the Cold War. In 1945, the bureau assumed control of the antisubmarine warfare program (Division 6) established by the wartime Office of Scientific Research and Development. The bureau centralized major R&D programs at the Naval Electronics Laboratory in San Diego and at the Underwater Sound Laboratory in New London, Connecticut.

Wartime innovations in electronics, ranging from the vacuum tube amplifiers that powered microwave radar sets to the attendant growth of semiconductor science and technology, revolutionized the design and function of the computer, communication, navigation, and fire control systems that came to have an increasingly prevalent role in ship operation and performance during the Cold War. By the 1960s, electronic systems accounted for more than one-third of the cost of naval ship construction.[70] Through its in-house electronics R&D programs, the Navy expanded its technical knowledge of ship navigation and detection. Much of this work had originated during World War II, when the Navy initiated a major effort to improve sonar technologies for antisubmarine warfare. Essentially the underwater equivalent of radar, sonar employed sound waves rather than electromagnetic radiation to detect enemy targets and map out the ocean environment to improve navigation. To improve sonar technologies required more detailed study of the properties and behavior of the transmission medium itself—in this case, sea water. Thus a corresponding expansion of oceanography research accompanied further work on sonar technology.

Although wartime research on sonar and antisubmarine warfare was conducted in many different academic, industrial, and government institutions, three coastal laboratories handled the bulk of the Navy's in-house program. The Navy Radio and Sound Laboratory in San Diego expanded under contract to the University of California, while Columbia University operated a new laboratory

---

[69] Booz Allen, *Review of Navy R&D Management,* 7–8, 121.

[70] Shiman, *Forging the Sword,* 61. On the history of the wartime microwave radar program and the postwar electronics boom that followed it, see Henry E. Guerlac, *Radar in World War II,* vol. 8 of *The History of Modern Physics, 1900–1950* (New York: Tomash Publishers and the American Institute of Physics, 1987); Robert Buderi, *The Invention That Changed the World: How a Small Group of Radar Pioneers Won the Second World War and Launched a Technological Revolution* (New York: Simon and Schuster, 1996); and Louis Brown, *A Radar History of World War II: Technical and Military Imperatives* (London: Taylor and Francis, 1999).

located in New London, Connecticut.[71] Late in 1941, the Bureau of Ordnance set up a third R&D facility—the Underwater Sound Laboratory—at Harvard University. At the San Diego laboratory, scientists and engineers in the sonar data division conducted fundamental research on acoustic propagation phenomena, while their counterparts in the sonar devices division built prototype devices for specific combat requirements handed down by the Navy. The technical staff at San Diego also handled a third function, personnel training in sonar technology and operation. Similar R&D programs were set up at New London and Harvard. In 1944, when OSRD began preparing to shut down its operations, the Navy agreed to take over the wartime antisubmarine warfare program. On 1 March 1945, the Bureau of Ships assumed control of the San Diego facility and renamed it the Naval Electronics Laboratory. The New London facility also reverted to the bureau, but the Harvard laboratory was transferred to the School of Engineering at Pennsylvania State College.[72] Two years later, the University of California, under contract with the Office of Naval Research, established the Marine Physics Laboratory at San Diego to study ocean acoustics and related geophysical phenomena.

By the 1960s, academic institutions and contractor-operated facilities, such as the Marine Physics Laboratory conducted most of the oceanography research for the Navy. The Navy also closely coordinated this work with studies underway at the Naval Electronics Laboratory. Unlike their diesel-powered predecessors, nuclear submarinescould travel much longer distances at greater depths. , which prompted the Navy to expand deep-sea research and ongoing development of sonar and other antisubmarine warfare technologies. "Development of such systems," wrote the Chief of Naval Research in 1963, "is enormously complicated by the fact that sound transmission is distorted, reflected, scattered, and absorbed not only by temperature differences but also by the chemical properties of the sea, marine life ranging from whales to microscopic plankton, sea surface conditions, and the nature of the sea floor. In order to overcome and bypass these obstacles, naval research is attempting to learn about ocean currents from the surface to the bottom, the daily variations in the temperature structure of the ocean, the formation and breakup of polar ice, and gravity and magnetic conditions at sea." To understand these complex ocean environments, scientists and engineers at the Naval Electronics Laboratory had initiated in the late 1950s a new program to develop, build, and operate a series of manned research vehicles for deep-sea studies.[73] Meanwhile, the laboratory developed and produced many prototype

---

[71] H. C. Mason, "Navy's Electronics Laboratory," *Sperryscope* 16, no. 6, (1963): 11; P. H. Hammond, "The U.S. Navy Radio and Sound Laboratory," *Journal of Applied Physics* 15 (March 1944): 240–42.

[72] On the transfer of the Harvard laboratory to the Pennsylvania State College, see footnote 14, above.

[73] F. N. D. Kurie and G. P. Harnwell, "The Wartime Activities of the San Diego Laboratory of the University of California Division of War Research," *Review of Scientific Instruments* 18 (April 1947): 207–12, 218; L. D. Coates, "Chief of Naval Research Details Program," *Data* 8 (September 1963): 10. Also on the Navy's role in oceanography research during the Cold War, see Jacob Darwin Hamblin, "The Navy's 'Sophisticated' Pursuit of Science: Undersea Warfare, the Limits of Internationalism, and the Utility of Basic Research, 1945–1956," *Isis* 93 (March 2002): 1–27; Hamblin, *Oceanographers and the Cold War: Disciples of Marine Science* (Seattle: University of Washington Press, 2005); and Gary E. Weir, *An Ocean in Common: American Naval Officers, Scientists, and the Ocean Environment* (College Station: Texas A&M University Press, 2001).

sonar devices, including huge, shipboard units installed on submarines for precision navigation through polar ice regions. Laboratory researchers also refined radar-detection techniques, pushed the frontiers of communication engineering with new antenna designs, and developed shipboard command and control systems. The first all-purpose digital computer system—the Naval Tactical Data System—entered fleet service in 1962.[74]

The advances in submarine design, construction, and propulsion that helped drive sonar development at the Naval Electronics Laboratory after World War II were concentrated in two major R&D institutions owned and operated by the Navy—the Engineering Experiment Station and the David Taylor Model Basin. Founded at the turn of the century to assist in the adaptation of the steam engine and the screw propeller to modern naval tactics and strategy, the experiment station and the model basin developed, tested, and evaluated the superstructures of submarines and surface ships, improved industrial designs of conventional and nuclear-powered propulsion systems and related equipment, and extended the Navy's knowledge base in hydrodynamics and materials science and engineering.

The Engineering Experiment Station opened in Annapolis, Maryland, in 1908 under the direction of the Bureau of Steam Engineering. Originally set up to improve and develop commercially manufactured ship engines, the station shifted to more routine testing and inspection of engines and other shipboard equipment to meet the Navy's growing requirements for material and equipment specifications and production and performance standards. Engineers analyzed a broad range of machinery components and materials, including heat transmission apparatus; boiler, pump, engine, and pipe fittings; lubricants; packings and gaskets; metals; and coal. Tonnage restrictions imposed on the Navy by a series of treaties after World War I prompted the station to augment its testing functions with organized R&D on lightweight diesel engines as ships exchanged structural weight for increased firepower. This type of development work, in which incremental improvements and new innovations were sometimes forthcoming, remained subordinate to testing throughout the interwar period and during World War II.

After 1945, the station gradually assumed a more active role in organized research and development, though much of its work remained focused on commodity testing of aviation gasoline, greases, bearings, pressure gauges, underwater cutting tools, welding and packing materials, boiler compounds, and polishes. In 1959, the Bureau of Ships officially extended the station's mission "from testing and determination of the suitability of certain steam machinery for use in naval vessels" to the "conduct of applied research, development, investigations, evaluations, and tests in the fields of physics, chemistry, metallurgy, and electricity."[75] Station managers had anticipated this change of goals the previous year when they reorganized the operating units along disciplinary

---

[74] Mason, "Navy's Electronics Laboratory," 12–13. See also, H. C. Mason, "Navy Electronics Lab Serves BuShips," *Data* 8 (September 1963): 54–59.

[75] Carlisle, *Where the Fleet Begins*, 61–62, 66, 70–73, 89–90, 106–08, 178–79, 488 (quote).

rather than product lines: chemistry, mechanical engineering, applied physics, and metallurgy. By the 1970s, for example, the station (renamed the Marine Engineering Laboratory in 1963) had introduced, in collaboration with commercial engine manufacturers, a new generation of nickel- and cobalt-based superalloys for use in the blade assemblies of marine gas turbines operating in corrosive saltwater environments, and it had also compiled an impressive record of achievement in the fields of machinery silencing and vibration dampening. In the atomic power field, station engineers had made significant contributions to the improvement of shaft bearings, auxiliary diesel engines, reactor piping, and fire-resistant hydraulic fluids used in the propulsion systems of nuclear submarines.[76]

The Engineering Experiment Station cultivated a broad and diversified knowledge base in ship propulsion technology that supported rather than fulfilled the Navy's ambitions for shipboard atomic power. The David Taylor Model Basin, by contrast, played a larger and more direct role in the development of America's Cold War nuclear submarine fleet, albeit on a smaller scale than the participating industrial firms contracted by the Bureau of Ships. The private sector completed the bulk of the R&D and production for the nuclear navy.[77] Nevertheless, submarine development at the model basin proceeded along several different but related lines. The basin's long-standing expertise in hydrodynamics and related scientific disciplines and expanding computational capability after World War II enabled researchers to develop revolutionary submarine hull designs that significantly improved speed and maneuverability and reduced underwater noise effects. The same technical resources were tapped to improve the nuclear reactor technologies originally conceptualized, developed, and manufactured by private firms.

Named after its first director, the David Taylor Model Basin was set up by the Bureau of Construction and Repair at the Washington Navy Yard in 1898. After decades of steady growth that matched the Navy's rapid expansion, the Navy built a larger and more modern model basin in nearby Carderock, Maryland. Construction of the towing tanks, test and evaluation laboratories, and other support facilities began in 1937, and the site became fully operational in 1940.[78] Throughout this period, engineers and scientists at the basin applied

---

[76] Ibid., 217–19, 222, 256–57, 492. The development of auxiliary components for submarine drive assemblies was all that remained of what had been an extensive propulsion program that began at the station in 1946. That year, engineers began working on a closed-cycle submarine power plant fueled by hydrogen peroxide. For nearly a decade, development of improved versions of the "Walters" engine (named for its German inventor) moved forward, but, advanced as this technology was, it could not compete with nuclear power. In 1954, just before the first nuclear-powered submarine, the Nautilus, began sea trials, the bureau permanently shut down Engineering Experiment Station's engine development program. Ibid., 241, 250–54.

[77] Although they played a steadily diminishing role in new ship construction after World War II, the Navy's shipyards actively participated in the shift from conventional to nuclear propulsion. The Electric Boat Division of the General Dynamics Corporation manufactured most of the Navy's nuclear submarines, but the Navy built ten, beginning with the Swordfish in 1957, were built at the Portsmouth Naval Shipyard in New Hampshire. By the early 1960s, Portsmouth had become a fully integrated nuclear submarine shipyard, capable of performing construction, overhauls, and repairs. Shiman, Forging the Sword, 62.

[78] Howard, "The David Taylor Model Basin," 227.

their working knowledge of hydrodynamics to problems in hull design, and, during World War II, they diversified into similar studies of mines, torpedoes, and other types of underwater ordnance. Although practical investigations persisted in such fields as propeller quieting and acoustic countermeasures to ward off homing torpedoes and shipborne sonar, studies of a more fundamental nature flourished after the war. They included research on nonuniform bodies through a fluid, vortex formation and interactions, turbulence, and interfaces among different fluids.[79] In 1958, one year before it released a similar statement on behalf of the Engineering Experiment Station, the Bureau of Ships revised the model basin's mission to include "fundamental and applied research in the fields of hydromechanics, aerodynamics, structural mechanics, mathematics, acoustics, and related fields of science."[80] Work in these fields during and after the war played a pivotal role in the transformation of the submarine fleet from diesel-electric to nuclear power.

At the Kaiser Wilhelm Institute for Chemistry in Berlin at the end of 1938, chemists Otto Hahn and Fritz Strassman obtained experimental evidence of uranium fission. News of this groundbreaking discovery quickly spread to the United States early in 1939, where it immediately caught the attention of Rear Adm. Harold Bowen, chief of the Bureau of Engineering and soon-to-be director of the Naval Research Laboratory. Bowen and other like-minded naval officers had been searching for new techniques to improve submarine propulsion and performance, which at the time relied on a cumbersome combination of diesel engines for surface operations and electric storage batteries for undersea maneuvers. Bowen set up a new research program at the Naval Research Laboratory to investigate the power potential of uranium fission, but this work was quickly absorbed into the much larger effort undertaken by the National Defense Research Committee (and subsequently OSRD and the Army Corps of Engineers) to develop the atomic bomb.[81]

The Navy's interest in nuclear propulsion resumed at the end of the war but not under the guidance of Admiral Bowen. In his place was Capt. Hyman Rickover, who had distinguished himself during the war in the electrical section of the Bureau of Ships. Although he lacked Bowen's position and rank, the hard-driving Rickover was still able to create, almost single-handedly, the Navy's nuclear submarine fleet through a well-established network of personal and professional relationships in the bureau system and private industry.

For decades, the Navy's propulsion requirements had been met by industrial contractors. Large firms, such as GE, Westinghouse Electric, Babcock and Wilcox, and the Allis-Chalmers Manufacturing Company, designed and built

---

[79] Carlisle, *Where the Fleet Begins*, 185–86.

[80] Ibid., 487.

[81] Richard G. Hewlett and Oscar E. Anderson Jr., *The New World, 1939–1946*, vol. 1 of *A History of the United States Atomic Energy Commission* (University Park: Pennsylvania State University Press, 1962), 10–11, 15. See also Joseph-James Ahern, "'We Had the Hose Turned on Us!': Ross Gunn and the Naval Research Laboratory's Early Research into Nuclear Propulsion, 1939–1946," *Historical Studies in the Physical and Biological Sciences* 33 (2003): 217–36. On the wartime Manhattan Project, see Richard Rhodes, *The Making of the Atomic Bomb* (New York: Simon and Schuster, 1986).

the engines, boilers, steam turbines, drive assemblies, and electrical equipment that formed the power plants of modern surface ships and submarines. Through his contacts with engineers and executives at these and other manufacturing firms during the war, Rickover fashioned an integrated research, development, and production program that directly linked prior technical expertise in conventional power-generation technology to the latest advances in atomic energy. His efforts along this line culminated in the establishment of the Bettis Atomic Power Laboratory near Pittsburgh in 1948. Operated by Westinghouse under contract to the Navy, scientists and engineers at Bettis collaborated to design and build the pressurized water reactor installed on the *Nautilus*, the world's first nuclear-powered submarine. The early success of the *Nautilus* helped establish Westinghouse's pressurized water reactor (and subsequent versions of it) as the standard propulsion unit for the nuclear fleet in the decades that followed. General Electric established a similar, though less successful, reactor development program during the same period. In 1946, the newly formed Atomic Energy Commission (the civilian successor to the wartime Manhattan Project) had granted a contract to GE to set up the Knolls Atomic Power Laboratory near the company's primary R&D and manufacturing operations in Schenectady, New York. Originally established to develop reactors for civilian electric power production, the laboratory received a contract from the Navy in 1950 to develop atomic power plants for submarines. Two years later, the Navy instructed the Knolls laboratory to design and build a reactor, using a sodium liquid metal cooling system, for the SSN–575 *Seawolf*, the second nuclear submarine after the *Nautilus* to enter fleet service.[82]

Although it did not fill the same central role as industry in the development and production of atomic reactors, the David Taylor Model Basin still played an important role in the postwar growth of nuclear power technology for naval applications. In 1952, a new applied mathematics laboratory was established at the Carderock complex. Equipped with a UNIVAC computer system, one of the first mainframe computers, the laboratory focused on theory and analysis, planning and programming, and engineering and development. A major effort was undertaken to determine the operating lifetimes of the nuclear reactors installed in the Navy's first generation of atomic-powered submarines. Technical staff wrote new computer programs to generate the first practical mathematical models of reactor-core behavior. Computation of core geometry and composition, for example, enabled accurate determination of the diffusion rates of neutrons (which caused uranium fission), while simulation studies revealed the depletion patterns of uranium fuel and the accumulation of fission by-products. Taken as a whole, these computer analyses enabled engineers working at the Bettis and Knolls Atomic Power Laboratories and other private and public R&D facilities to predict the power-producing

---

[82] For a detailed examination of these events, see Richard G. Hewlett and Francis Duncan, *Nuclear Navy, 1946–1962* (Chicago: University of Chicago Press, 1974). Also on Rickover, see Francis Duncan, *Rickover and the Nuclear Navy: The Discipline of Technology* (Annapolis, Md.: Naval Institute Press, 1990); Normal Polmar and Thomas B. Allen, *Rickover and the Nuclear Navy* (New York: Simon and Schuster, 1982).

capabilities of various reactor designs. Refueling projections were also forthcoming, and they were incorporated into the reactor designs for the *Skate* and *Skipjack* classes of nuclear submarines and the atomic-powered aircraft carrier *Enterprise*, as well as the replacement cores for the original reactors installed on the *Nautilus* and *Seawolf*.[83]

Postwar developments in reactor design at the model basin were matched by major advances in submarine hydrodynamics and architecture. Until nuclear propulsion was perfected to the point where it could safely extend the underwater range and speed of submersible vessels, the Navy had to rely on incremental improvements to its vintage wartime submarine fleet. Immediately after the war,the navy set up the GUPPY (Greater Underwater Propulsive Power) program to retrofit World War II—era submarines to achieve higher speeds and to run quieter under water. Removal of deck guns, changes in the shapes of sterns and bows, and development of new conning tower configurations were some of the many adjustments made to the different classes and types of submarines assigned to the GUPPY program. Although these changes led to improvements in speed and performance, drag effects and propeller and engine noise still imposed serious limits on further development of a quiet and fast conventional submarine fleet. Beginning in 1950, however, researchers at the model basin began experimenting with new hull forms. Three years later, they unveiled the design for the research vessel *Albacore*. Incorporating a revolutionary new "tear-drop" shape, *Albacore* exhibited more hydrodynamic stability and ran much quieter and faster than the retrofitted submarines in the GUPPY fleet. *Albacore's* shape also marked a major improvement over the hull designs adopted for the *Nautilus, Seawolf,* and *Skate* classes of nuclear-powered submarines. Commissioned in 1959, the SSN–585 *Skipjack* was the first completely redesigned submarine that incorporated both the optimal design of the *Albacore* and the latest advances in shipboard nuclear reactor technology. This basic platform, which emerged from the close institutional partnership between private industry and the Navy's in-house R&D laboratories, guided the development of the attack and ballistic missile submarine fleet for decades.[84]

From Bureaus and Laboratories to System Commands and Research Centers

In 1959, the same year that the Navy commissioned the *Skipjack*, the bureaus of Ordnance and Ships merged to form the Bureau of Naval Weapons.

---

[83] Carlisle, *Where the Fleet Begins*, 223–24.

[84] Ibid., 243–49, 254–56. See also Gary E. Weir, *Forged in War: The Naval-Industrial Complex and American Submarine Construction, 1940–1961* (Washington, D.C.: Naval Historical Center, 1993), chaps. 5–6. Attempts were made to develop new propulsion technologies, but none displaced the nuclear reactor as the primary source of power for submarines. In the 1980s, for example, a new R&D program on superconducting motors for surface ships the Navy established at the David Taylor Naval Ship Research and Development Center (created in 1967 when the model basin in Carderock merged with the Marine Engineering Laboratory in Annapolis). Several successful prototypes were built, but they were not produced in quantity or incorporated into the fleet. See Carlisle, *Where the Fleet Begins*, 379–84.

Although the merger resolved jurisdictional tensions over missile development, it created difficulties with regard to managerial organization and effectiveness. Massive and unwieldy, the new bureau controlled 60 percent of the assets of the Naval Material Support Establishment, itself founded in 1963 through a merger of the bureaus of Yards and Docks, Supplies and Accounts, and Ships. To avoid the likelihood of future jurisdictional conflicts arising from the development of new weapon systems, the Navy leadership reorganized the bureau structure in 1965 into six separate functional commands administered by a new umbrella organization—the Naval Material Command (headed by the Chief of Naval Material). Each command was based on an integrated systems approach (for ships, air, ordnance, electronics, facilities engineering, and supply) that cut across the once-rigid institutional boundaries that had defined the old bureau system.

The Navy reorganized the in-house laboratories in response to the formation of the Naval Material Command. In line with this transformation, the Navy established late in 1965 the dual position of Director of Naval Laboratories (reporting to the Assistant Secretary of the Navy for Research and Development) and Director of Laboratory Programs (reporting to the Chief of Naval Material) to coordinate the programs and functions of the laboratories managed by the new command structure. This realignment placed direct management of the laboratories and technical programs under the control of a civilian scientist, who no longer reported to the individual bureau chiefs. Like the bureaus, several of the in-house laboratories were reorganized into major centers along functional lines. In 1967, the Navy established the first center—the Naval Ship Research and Development Center—followed by the Naval Weapons Center, Naval Undersea Research and Development Center, Navy Electronics Laboratory Center, and the Naval Air Development Center.[85]

The transformation of the independent bureaus into centralized system commands illustrates the extent to which the introduction of new weapons technologies upset traditional roles and missions. The Special Projects Office, Lead Bureau Concept, and other ad hoc measures initially eased jurisdictional tensions between the bureaus, but naval leaders sought a better and more lasting

---

[85] Booz Allen, *Review of Navy R&D Management,* 85–90. The Naval Ship Research and Development Center comprised the David Taylor Model Basin, Marine Engineering Laboratory, and the former Mine Defense Laboratory (Panama City, Florida). The Naval Ordnance Test Station at China Lake and the Naval Ordnance Laboratory (Corona) merged to form the Naval Weapons Center. The Pasadena annex of the Naval Ordnance Test Station and the Undersea Technology Directorate of the Naval Electronics Laboratory combined to form the Naval Undersea Research and Development Center (San Diego). The Naval Air Development Center at Johnsville, Pennsylvania, acquired the Aerospace Crew Equipment Department, the Aeronautical Materials Department, and the Aeronautical Structures Department previously assigned to the Naval Air Engineering Station at Philadelphia. The Naval Electronics Laboratory Center (San Diego), Naval Weapons Laboratory (formerly the Naval Proving Ground at Dahlgren), and the Naval Ordnance Laboratory (White Oak) remained intact. In addition to the major weapons centers and laboratories, several smaller R&D facilities were either established outright or reorganized through mergers and divestitures: the Naval Underwater Weapons Research and Engineering Station (formerly the Naval Torpedo Station; Newport, Rhode Island); the Underwater Sound Laboratory (New London); Naval Applied Science Laboratory (Brooklyn); Naval Radiological Defense Laboratory (San Francisco); and the Naval Civil Engineering Laboratory (Port Huenene, California). "R&D Centers/Laboratories," *Armed Forces Journal* 106 (17 May 1969): 30–31; "Navy Establishes R&D Center," *Journal of the Armed Forces* 104 (8 April 1967): 2.

solution. The new system command structure was largely a response to this organizational and technological dilemma. It was also a direct result of measures taken by leaders in the Pentagon to centralize control of the weapons acquisition process in the Office of the Secretary of Defense.

During this period of transition from material bureaus to system commands, the organizational division of labor among research, development, and production remained largely intact. Although a programmatic separation of research from development had been one of the hallmarks of postwar naval policy since the early 1920s, it failed to capture the scope of the weapons innovation process in many of the Navy's own laboratories. Except for the Naval Research Laboratory and the establishment of the discretionary funding program in the Bureau of Ordnance in 1948, the Navy's laboratories, like those in the Army's arsenals, thrived on the multidirectional interactions among research, development, testing, and prototype weapons production.

By the end of the Cold War, the Navy bureaus and their organizational descendents, joined by the Naval Research Laboratory and the Office of Naval Research, had developed a wide range of sophisticated and highly effective weapon systems, ranging from the Sidewinder air-to-air missile to the nuclear propulsion systems that powered the fleet's attack and ballistic missile submarines. These and other technological successes may well have represented the pinnacle of Navy R&D during the postwar period. After the collapse of the Soviet Union and the Eastern Bloc countries in the late 1980s and early 1990s, the Navy was left without a set of clearly stated goals or a coherent mission to achieve them. Consequently, policymakers in the Navy, Department of Defense, and the Executive Branch struggled with the difficult problem of how to adjust the Navy's R&D establishment to the realities of a radically different geopolitical environment in which traditional Cold War rivalries no longer persisted. More historical research on this subject is needed, but the pace at which the Navy divested its internal R&D functions quickened during the 1990s as military budgets dropped and the Defense Department enacted sweeping measures to reduce the size and scope of its force structure.[86]

---

[86] See Rodney P. Carlisle, *Navy RDT&E Planning in an Age of Transition: A Survey Guide to Contemporary Literature* (Washington, D.C.: Navy Laboratory / Center Coordinating Group and the Naval Historical Center, 1997); and Philip L. Shiman, "Defense Acquisition in an Uncertain World: The Post–Cold War Era, 1990–2000," in *Providing the Means of War: Historical Perspectives on Defense Acquisition, 1945–2000*, ed., Shannon A. Brown (Washington, D.C.: U.S. Army Center of Military History and Industrial College of the Armed Forces, 2005).

CHAPTER FOUR

Research and Development in the Air Force

The use of atomic weapons against Japan in August 1945 marked the end of World War II and the culmination of the Manhattan Project—arguably the United States Army's most technologically challenging wartime research, development, and production program.[1] The destruction of Hiroshima and Nagasaki also signaled the beginning of a new era in aerial warfare, one in which the strategic and tactical imperatives of an expanding nuclear arsenal would place increasing technical demands on the operational capabilities of American air power. In 1947, Congress passed the National Security Act, which established an independent air force to oversee the military aviation functions previously assigned to the Army.[2] In its new capacity as a separate service equivalent to the Army and the Navy, the Air Force quickly put policies in place to absorb the latest breakthroughs in jet propulsion, rocketry, solid-state electronics, and other state-of-the-art technologies introduced during the war. Such policies were shaped throughout the Cold War by a recurring tension between those Air Force leaders, who believed that technological superiority depended upon the organizational separation of research and development (R&D) from weapons production, and those who argued that these functions must remain combined within a single organization to ensure successful weapons innovation. Like the Army and the Navy, the Air Force enacted policies and created new organizational structures to maintain the separation of R&D from production. In many cases, however, research strategies and practices at the laboratory level were driven more by changing weapons requirements than by sweeping management directives handed down by the Air Staff.

Before World War II, the Air Force—then known as the Army Air Corps—maintained most of its research, development, and testing operations at Wright Field in Dayton, Ohio. R&D at Wright focused on the development of aircraft

---

[1] On the Army's role in the Manhattan Project, see Vincent C. Jones, *Manhattan, The Army and the Atomic Bomb,* in *United States Army in World War II, Special Studies* (Washington, D.C.: U.S. Army Center of Military History, 1985); and Richard G. Hewlett and Oscar E. Anderson Jr., *The New World, 1939–1946,* vol. 1 of *A History of the United States Atomic Energy Commission* (University Park: Pennsylvania State University Press, 1962).

[2] Roger R. Trask and Alfred Goldberg, *The Department of Defense, 1947–1997: Organization and Leaders* (Washington, D.C.: Historical Office, Office of the Secretary of Defense, 1997), 6–11. On Army aviation after the establishment of the Air Force, see, for example, Richard P. Weinert Jr., *A History of Army Aviation, 1950–1962* (Fort Monroe, Va.: Office of the Command Historian, U.S. Army Training and Doctrine Command, 1991); Frederic A. Bergerson, *The Army Gets an Air Force: Tactics of Insurgent Bureaucratic Politics* (Baltimore: Johns Hopkins University Press, 1980); Christopher C. S. Cheng, "United States Army Aviation and the Air Mobility Innovation, 1942–1965" (Ph.D. diss., University of London, 1992); and Matthew Allen, *Military Helicopter Doctrines of the Major Powers, 1945–1992: Making Decisions about Air-Land Warfare* (Westport, Conn.: Greenwood Press, 1993), chap. 1.

specifications and standards; testing and evaluation of aircraft production models; improvement of engines, fuels, armament, airframes, and other critical materials; aeromedicine; and the management and coordination of research contracts with private industry. Longer-term fundamental studies in such fields as aerodynamics were typically carried out in academic institutions and in the government research laboratories operated by the National Advisory Committee for Aeronautics and the National Bureau of Standards.[3] But many technological innovations had also originated in the private sector and not in government-owned manufacturing facilities of the type that had historically turned out new weapons for the Army and the Navy. Without a similar institutional legacy of its own, the Air Force relied more heavily on the domestic aircraft industry to design, build, and equip the next generation of aerial weapons. Consequently, the Air Force's in-house R&D operations, which did undergo a major expansion after 1945, focused primarily, but not exclusively, on the testing, evaluation, and improvement of aircraft and other weapon systems produced by industrial contractors rather than on the accumulation of the requisite knowledge needed to develop those technologies internally.

The origins of military aviation in the United States can be traced back to 1907, four years after the Wright Brothers successfully demonstrated powered, heavier-than-air flight at Kitty Hawk, North Carolina. Initially, modern aircraft were expected to be of direct benefit to military reconnaissance and observation during field operations, which prompted the Army leadership to establish a separate Aeronautical Division in the Office of the Chief Signal Officer.[4] At the end of World War I, the War Department transferred the expanding aviation arm out of the Signal Corps and granted it independent status as the Army Air Service. In 1926, the Air Service became the Army Air Corps and then, in 1941, the Army Air Forces (AAF). Throughout this period, the Army's air arm continued to develop and improve its tactical pursuit, close air support, and strategic bombing functions, all of which dated back to World War I. Employed with devastating effects during World War II, strategic bombing became increasingly important as the Air Force adopted offensive nuclear capabilities in the early years of the Cold War.[5] Moreover, the advent of nuclear weapons, jet propulsion, and guided missiles prompted the leaders of the Army Air Forces to confront the seemingly intractable problem of how to achieve technological superiority at a time when aircraft production took precedence to achieve maximum effectiveness against military targets in Germany and Japan. Even before the war ended, however, disagreement within the Army's senior ranks

---

[3] Lawrence R. Benson, *Acquisition Management in the United States Air Force and Its Predecessors* (Washington, D.C.: Air Force History and Museums Program, 1997), 7.

[4] *Splendid Vision, Unswerving Purpose: Developing Air Power for the United States Air Force During the First Century of Powered Flight* (Wright-Patterson Air Force Base, Oh.: Air Force History and Museums Program, 2002), 199–200.

[5] On the Army Air Corps before and during World War II, see Maurer Maurer, *Aviation in the U.S. Army, 1919–1939* (Washington, D.C.: Office of Air Force History, 1987); Bernard C. Nalty, ed., *Winged Shield, Winged Sword: A History of the United States Air Force*, vol. 1 (Washington, D.C.: Air Force History and Museums Program, 1997), chaps. 1–3, 6–10; and Edgar F. Raines Jr., *Eyes of Artillery: The Origins of Modern U.S. Army Aviation in World War II* (Washington, D.C.: U.S. Army Center of Military History, 2000).

had hardened. Proponents of quantity production of serviceable aircraft to maintain a ready force in the event of another war squared off against advocates of a more technologically advanced air arm, which would incorporate the latest developments in science and engineering. Perhaps nowhere was this ongoing conflict between a "force-in-being" and a "force-of-the-future" more clearly visible than in the effort to incorporate a diversified research and development program into the Army's existing aircraft procurement system and the one that replaced it after 1947.

Like their counterparts in the Army and the Navy, Air Force leaders considered the extent to which research and development should be connected to production. In some cases, they copied institutional mechanisms put in place by the Army and the Navy to secure scientific knowledge from private-sector research institutions. In 1948, for example, the Air Staff established the Applied Research Section (renamed the Office of Air Research [OAR] in 1949) as the organizational equivalent of the Office of Naval Research (ONR) to award contracts to universities and industrial laboratories for longer-range fundamental studies unrelated to immediate weapons requirements but broadly correlated to Air Force interests.[6] OAR also coordinated basic research underway in the in-house service laboratories operated by the newly created Air Research and Development Command (ARDC). Established in 1950, ARDC managed the R&D facilities previously assigned to the Air Force's procurement arm—the Air Materiel Command (AMC).[7] Wright Field and the remaining ARDC laboratories also supported significant R&D programs in electronics, metallurgy, physics, and other scientific and engineering disciplines. Even in these cases, however, the content and scope of the work still focused on Air Force requirements.

The division between fundamental research outsourced to the private sector and the more focused, application-oriented studies handled by the Air Force's own laboratories remained largely intact, with some modest adjustments, during the Cold War. What did undergo a major transformation, however, was the extent to which the Air Staff coordinated the functions of the in-house R&D laboratories with the procurement of aircraft and other weapons from industrial contractors. Before World War II, military aircraft were typically assembled using off-the-shelf components produced in industry and in the Army's technical

---

[6] See, for example, R. G. Gibbs, "Chemistry Division of New Air Force Research and Development Command Will Emphasize Basic Research," *Chemical and Engineering News* 30 (3 March 1952): 854–55; and C. F. Yost, "Metallurgy Program of the Air Force Office of Scientific Research," *Journal of Metals* 9 (May 1957): 671.

[7] The Applied Research Section was originally assigned to the Air Materiel Command's Engineering Division at Wright Field. The Office of Air Research was renamed the Office of Scientific Research (OSR) in 1951. Four years later, after the establishment of the Air Research and Development Command, OSR became the Air Force Office of Scientific Research (AFOSR) and was assigned independent status equivalent to ARDC's other in-house R&D centers (e.g., Wright Air Development Center, Arnold Engineering Development Center). In 1961, after the Air Materiel Command and the Air Research and Development Command merged to form the new Air Force Systems Command, AFOSR became the Office of Aerospace Research (OAR). "OSR: Keystone of Basic Research," *Aviation Week* 59 (17 August 1953): 87; Nick A. Komons, *Science and the Air Force: A History of the Air Force Office of Scientific Research* (Arlington, Va.: Historical Division, Office of Information, Office of Aerospace Research, 1966): 65; *Splendid Vision, Unswerving Purpose*, 368.

services. Private firms delivered engines and airframes, for example, while the Army Ordnance Department provided armaments and munitions and the Signal Corps supplied communications equipment.[8] Moreover, development and procurement of aircraft proceeded in sequential order, from R&D through prototype construction and testing to full-scale production.

Prompted by the urgency of wartime requirements for more technologically advanced weapons during the Cold War, aircraft manufacturers began to overlap these sequential functions to accelerate the procurement process, a concept known as *concurrency*. They also began to use a related strategy, that came to be known as the *weapon system concept*. Contractors no longer conceived of aircraft as agglomerations of interchangeable parts assembled sequentially but rather as complex, fully integrated systems in which all constituent components were designed, built, maintained, and operated according to precise specifications and rigorous performance requirements.[9] Faced with the increasing complexity of military aircraft, the rapid pace of innovation in electronics and propulsion technologies after the war, and changing strategic considerations, Air Force leaders increasingly employed both concurrency and the weapon system concept in the weapons acquisition process.[10]

The transition from sequential development to systems integration and concurrency had a major impact on the Air Research and Development Command, the umbrella organization established in 1950 to manage the Air Force's network of in-house laboratories. In 1961, ARDC's laboratories and testing installations merged, once again, with the procurement functions of the Air Materiel Command to form the Air Force Systems Command (AFSC). The Air Staff realigned the ARDC laboratories to provide technical support to AFSC's four major weapons divisions (ballistic systems, space systems, aeronautical systems, and electronic systems), while the Air Force Office of Scientific Research (AFOSR) merged into a new and diversified Office of Aerospace Research (OAR) to manage and coordinate both in-house R&D and extramural research in universities and industrial laboratories. This reorganization simultaneously consolidated and decentralized the entire Air Force acquisition process, placing responsibility for research, development, and procurement squarely within the divisions. Although centralization of decision-making authority in the Office of the Secretary of Defense (OSD) in the 1960s limited its operational flexibility, a

---

[8] See, for example, G. C. Gentry, "Aircraft Armament," *Journal of Applied Physics* 16 (December 1945): 771–73.

[9] During World War II, Consolidated Aircraft, Boeing, and the Glenn L. Martin Company all used concurrency to produce the B–24, B–26, and B–29 bombers. Boeing also employed the nascent weapon system concept on the B–29 program but only for some of the aircraft's major components. Convair's F–102 interceptor was the first postwar military aircraft whose development and procurement cycles were guided at the outset by concurrency and the weapon system concept.

[10] Michael E. Brown, *Flying Blind: The Politics of the U.S. Strategic Bomber Program* (Ithaca, N.Y.: Cornell University Press, 1992), 17–27; Elliott V. Converse, "The Air Force and Acquisition, 1945–1953," October 2003, 40–48 (unpublished manuscript), U.S. Army Center of Military History, Fort Lesley J. McNair, Washington, D.C. I am indebted to Dr. Converse for sharing an early version of this manuscript with me.

trend that was reversed in the 1980s, the Air Force System Command remained largely intact throughout the Cold War.[11]

Following a brief discussion of the origins of R&D in the Army's air arm before and during World War II, this chapter examines in detail some of the major ARDC and AFSC installations that supported significant research, development, testing, and evaluation functions for the Air Force after 1945. Because Wright Field, which remained the Air Force's primary in-house R&D facility throughout the Cold War, lacked suitable wind tunnels and related experimental facilities for jet engines, rocket motors, and other high-speed propulsion systems, the Air Materiel Command established a new test facility for this purpose in southeastern Tennessee. In 1946, planning began for the new Air Engineering Development Division (later renamed the Arnold Engineering Development Center [AEDC], after Army Air Forces General Henry Arnold). Construction commenced in 1950, and the facility was formally dedicated the following year. In addition to overseeing routine testing and evaluation functions, AEDC scientists and engineers worked closely with their counterparts at NACA (after 1958, the National Aeronautics and Space Administration [NASA]) and also with industrial contractors. Together they extended AEDC's knowledge base in propulsion-related subjects, including fluid dynamics in near-ground and space environments, thermodynamics, electronics, fuels, propellants, and the structure and behavior of materials.

Major advances in solid-state electronics matched similar developments in propulsion, airframe, and materials technologies. Established in Boston in 1945, the Air Force Cambridge Research Center spearheaded electronics R&D, focusing on radio and radar technology and new classes of semiconductor materials used in aircraft avionics systems. Cambridge also managed large research and development programs in geophysics, optics, and plasma and space physics. The Rome Air Development Center, founded at Griffiss Air Force Base near Syracuse, New York, in 1950, managed, through industrial contracts and in-house R&D, the development of hardware for ground-based navigation and communication systems.

Although the Air Force operated an extensive network of support facilities, a handful of installations held primary responsibility for the testing and evaluation of new aircraft, missiles, and other major weapon systems manufactured by industrial contractors. Moreover, these functions were often carried out with the assistance of in-house laboratories operating on-site. The Air Force established the Air Force Armaments Center at Eglin Air Force Base near Pensacola, Florida, in 1949 to test all nonnuclear weapons—bombs, rockets, and missiles—fired from aircraft. It also compiled firing and bombing tables. The nuclear weapons developed by the civilian-controlled Atomic Energy Commission (AEC), by contrast, were mated to advanced delivery systems at the Special Weapons Center at Kirtland Air Force Base in New Mexico. In the 1960s, Kirtland's R&D

---

[11] OAR reported directly to the Air Staff, not to the weapons divisions. Michael H. Gorn, *Vulcan's Forge: The Making of an Air Force Command for Weapons Acquisition, 1950–1985*, 4th pr., vol. 1 (Andrews Air Force Base, Md.: Office of History, Air Force Systems Command, September 1989), 73, 76, 118.

capabilities expanded into the development of high-energy laser, microwave, and particle-beam weapons. The Air Force Flight Test Center at Edwards Air Force Base in California carried out flight testing of complete weapon systems (the combination of airframe, avionics, and ordnance). Edwards also static-tested the propulsion units for ballistic missiles, while Patrick and Holloman Air Force Bases in Florida and New Mexico, respectively, conducted test firings of short- and long-range missile delivery systems. These bases and their functions remained largely intact throughout the postwar period, albeit with a few exceptions. As concurrency and the weapon systems concept became more fully integrated into the Air Force's acquisition process, some research laboratories and test facilities closed, merged into new organizations, or transferred to other locations.

From Army Air Corps to United States Air Force, 1907–1950

Before World War II, research and development in the Army Air Corps was subordinated to procurement and production. R&D was essentially a support function in a larger program to expand the air arm through close coordination with the domestic aircraft industry. This relationship grew stronger after 1940. As demand grew for military aircraft, so did pressure on airframe manufacturers and the engineering departments in the Air Corps to favor quantity over quality. Production of proven designs took precedence over the massive R&D investments required to generate wholesale improvements in quality.[12] To be sure, the preference for quantity over quality did not preclude the introduction of important breakthroughs in design and construction, materials performance, and propulsion technologies during this period. A broad range of new innovations emerged from private industry and government laboratories. Nonetheless, it was not until 1945 that the Air Staff and a small group of civilian scientists began crafting a comprehensive R&D policy to strike what they believed should be a more even balance between production levels and technological superiority. The ensuing struggle, however, did not focus on this issue alone. The differences of opinion also involved an attempt to sort out the extent to which any new service-wide R&D program should be separated from the Army's traditional procurement functions. Some members of the War Department General Staff favored a close connection between R&D and procurement, whereas others, including many influential civilian experts, argued that full separation of the management of the two functions was a necessary prerequisite to successful weapons innovation. Although disagreements along this line resurfaced routinely throughout the postwar period, the advocates of separation won a crucial victory in 1950, when the Air Research and Development Command was fashioned

---

[12] Donald R. Baucom, "Air Force Images of Research and Development and Their Reflections in Organizational Structures and Management Policies" (Ph.D. diss., University of Oklahoma, 1976): 7; Amy E. Slaton, "Aeronautical Engineering at Wright-Patterson Air Force Base: A Historical Overview," in *The Engineering of Flight: Aeronautical Engineering Facilities of Area B, Wright-Patterson Air Force Base, Ohio,* ed. Emma J. H. Dyson, Dean A. Herrin, and Amy E. Slaton (Washington, D.C.: HABS/HAER, National Park Service, 1993), 25.

from the institutional remnants of the wartime R&D program in the Army Air Forces. But the transition to an independent R&D establishment—ARDC—was gradual. Any explanation of its origins and evolution must begin with a brief discussion of prior institutional developments and technological advances in Army aviation dating back to the end of World War I.

In October 1917, ten years after it had institutionalized aerial operations in the Aeronautical Division, the Army Signal Corps established the Airplane Engineering Department at McCook Field in Dayton, Ohio, to conduct experimental investigations in support of aircraft development and procurement. Army engineers at McCook built upon and applied the knowledge created in other laboratories—such as the National Bureau of Standards and the new research facilities operated by the National Advisory Committee for Aeronautics—to test airframes, engines, and other critical components; develop aircraft specifications; and improve materials. At the end of World War I, the War Department assumed control of the aviation functions previously assigned to the Signal Corps and consolidated them into the new Army Air Service. Under this sweeping administrative reorganization, the Airplane Engineering Department at McCook Field became the Airplane Engineering Division. Although the new division maintained elaborate chemical, metallurgical, and electrical laboratories, the content of the work undertaken in these and other facilities remained essentially the same—to support the development of aircraft produced in industry.

In 1926, Congress passed the Air Corps Act, which mandated a five-year aviation expansion program for the Army Air Service. The newly named Army Air Corps consolidated the existing functions of engineering, procurement, and supply in a separate organization—the Materiel Division. The old Airplane Engineering Division became the Experimental Engineering Section, composed of six product-oriented branches: airplane, lighter-than-air craft (dirigibles and observation balloons), power plant, equipment, materials, and armament. This organizational rationalization was accompanied by the transfer of the Materiel Division and all aircraft procurement functions from overcrowded buildings at McCook Field to adjacent facilities at the newly acquired Wright Field.[13] Resumption of routine activities at Wright Field included the inspection, testing, analysis, standardization, and improvement of engine fuels and coolants, propellers, lubricants, rubber, glass, metals and fabrics, and other essential materials used in aircraft construction. Some materials, such as aluminum and magnesium alloys, were developed from scratch. Others were tested under simulated operating conditions and analyzed chemically to determine strength

---

[13] In addition to the Experimental Engineering Section, the Materiel Division managed separate sections for administration, procurement, repair and maintenance, field services, and industrial war planning. Slaton, "Aeronautical Engineering at Wright-Patterson Air Force Base," 3–6, 8; *Splendid Vision, Unswerving Purpose*, 24–35, 44–64, 78–83. The Aircraft Radio Laboratory, which had been established by the Signal Corps at McCook Field shortly after World War I to develop new radio applications for aircraft communication, also moved to Wright Field. The laboratory's mission expanded in 1935 to include work on radio navigation. J. H. Gardner, "Aircraft Radio Labs," *Radio News* 27 (February 1942): 8; W. L. Bayer, "The Signal Corps Aircraft Radio Laboratory," *Journal of Applied Physics* 16 (April 1945): 248–49.

and performance characteristics. Meanwhile, testing and refinement of gun mounts; bomb sites, racks, and release mechanisms; and landing gear were carried out to simplify installation on aircraft and improve operational reliability.[14]

Important breakthroughs also came out of Wright Field during this period. In the aircraft (formerly airplane) branch's structures development and test laboratory, for example, researchers introduced the first practical, all-metal monocoque airframe.[15] Unlike conventional airframes, in which the internal (initially wood) framework or truss supported the entire weight-bearing load, the monocoque design eliminated this requirement by shifting the load to the external skin, thereby reducing the overall weight of the aircraft. Other major innovations to come out of Wright Field—through collaboration with the aircraft industry—included retractable landing gear, night-flying instruments, oxygen equipment and cabin pressurization for high-altitude flight, and the automatic pilot.[16]

The onset of World War II prompted a massive expansion of the domestic aircraft industry. During the interwar period, the Army Air Corps had maintained a fleet of less than one thousand serviceable aircraft. Between 1939 and 1945, however, production of aircraft, three-fourths of which were acquired by the Army Air Forces, soared to more than three hundred thousand units.[17] Administrative reorganization matched this sharp increase in aircraft production. In 1942, the Materiel Division at Wright Field became an independent command, which comprised four major divisions: procurement, production, inspection, and engineering.[18] Together these divisions managed a network of public and private-sector institutions in which more than 26,000 individual contractors turned out, at any given time, almost half a million different aircraft parts and essential supplies. The Engineering Division rendered technical assistance on major aircraft components through its four sections (service engineering, aircraft and physical requirements, propulsion

---

[14] W. E. Gillmore, "Work of the Materiel Division of the Army Air Corps," *S. A. E. Journal* 25 (September 1929): 233–34; L. H. Engel, "U.S. Air Center Speeds Research," *Science News Letter* 36 (8 July 1939): 27; G. H. Brett, "Materiel Division of the U.S. Army Air Corps," *Aero Digest* 35 (August 1939): 48–51.

[15] The aircraft branch had been established in 1932 through the merger of the airplane and lighter-than-air branches. The following year, the Experimental Engineering Section absorbed the Materiel Division's Procurement Section. In 1935, this added function was renamed the engineering procurement branch. *Splendid Vision, Unswerving Purpose*, 67, 72.

[16] A. McSurely, "Wright Field Tests New Air Weapons," *Aviation News* 1 (20 March 1944): 12; Slaton, "Aeronautical Engineering at Wright-Patterson Air Force Base," 15; *Splendid Vision, Unswerving Purpose*, 67–77.

[17] Benson, *Acquisition Management in the United States Air Force and Its Predecessors*, 13. On aircraft acquisition in the Army Air Forces during World War II, see Irving Brinton Holley Jr., *Buying Aircraft: Materiel Procurement for the Army Air Forces*, in *United States Army in World War II, Special Studies* (Washington, D.C.: Office of the Chief of Military History, Department of the Army, 1964).

[18] All logistics functions previously assigned to the Materiel Division transferred to the new Air Service Command at nearby Patterson Field in 1941. In 1944, the Air Service Command and the Materiel Command (the former Materiel Division) merged to form the Air Technical Services Command (ATSC), located at Wright Field. Two years later, ATSC was renamed the Air Materiel Command. In 1945, Wright and Patterson fields merged administratively, and the combined operation was christened the Wright-Patterson Air Force Base in 1948. Benson, *Acquisition Management in the United States Air Force and Its Predecessors*, 16–17; *Splendid Vision, Unswerving Purpose*, 87–88.

and accessories, and radio and radar) and ten in-house laboratories (aircraft, power plant, propeller, equipment, materiel, armament, photographic, aeromedical, engineering shops, and aircraft radio).[19] Scientists and engineers working in the section laboratories conducted much of the same type of testing, inspection, and, when necessary, research and development on materials and components that had been carried out at Wright Field and its predecessor, McCook Field, during the interwar period. Representative examples included wind-tunnel testing of airframe structures for performance, stability, and control; conservation of scarce materials and the development of suitable replacements; enhancement of engine power through higher horsepower ratings; development of high-octane aviation fuels; and improvements to optical equipment for aerial reconnaissance.[20]

The bulk of the R&D funds assigned to the Army Air Corps during the war was either distributed to laboratories in universities and industrial firms through the Office of Scientific Research and Development (OSRD) or absorbed directly as development costs in the production contracts awarded to the major aircraft manufacturers.[21] Consequently, the sharp decline in aircraft procurement and the anticipated closure of OSRD prompted the Air Staff to articulate a new R&D policy for the postwar period. "The large production contracts that have carried a considerable part of the development load are no longer with us," wrote Brig. Gen. Laurence Craigie, chief of the Engineering Division at Wright Field, in the October 1945 issue of the *Aeronautical Engineering Review*.[22] "The result," Craigie continued, "is that research and development must be prepared to stand on its own feet. [This] . . . can only be provided through adequate appropriations and the provision of adequate personnel and facilities."[23] Although Craigie presided over the cancellation of projects in the Engineering Division that "dealt with development of equipment for immediate use in combat" in favor of "longer range research," a far more

---

[19] In 1944, a fifth section—engineering control—was added to the Engineering Division. F. O. Carroll, "Research and Development at Wright Field," *Journal of Applied Physics* 16 (April 1945): 201.

[20] "For the Technical Superiority of Our Weapons," *Aero Digest* 45 (1 June 1944): 52–54; Slaton, "Aeronautical Engineering at Wright-Patterson Air Force Base," 30.

[21] "Debugging" of aircraft, for example, was one development cost typically amortized over the course of a production contract. According to Gorn, *Vulcan's Forge*, xviii, the Army Air Corps allocated $3.5 million for research and development in 1939. When aircraft production in the United States peaked in 1944, R&D expenditures exceeded $120 million.

[22] In the same article, Craigie summarized the Engineering Division's wartime role. Following the precedent established at McCook Field three decades earlier, the division focused primarily on testing and evaluation of aircraft and related equipment manufactured in industry: "Within the Engineering Division are twelve individual laboratories working on the design, development, and test of aircraft and aircraft equipment. These laboratories are divided functionally between three subdivisions—namely, Aircraft and Physical Requirements, Propulsion and Accessories, and Radio and Radar. In these laboratories, every piece of Air Force equipment is tested and tested again. Here the products of industry are matched against the most exacting specifications."

[23] L. C. Craigie, "Research and the Army Air Forces," *Aeronautical Engineering Review* 4 (October 1945): 7–8. Like the Navy and the Army's other technical departments, the Air Corps faced competition from the private sector for qualified scientists and engineers, a problem highlighted by Craigie in 1947: "The limitations on compensation for Civil Service employees makes it difficult for us to compete with industry in acquiring high caliber scientists and engineers." L. C. Craigie, "AAF Plans for Engineering and Research," *S. A. E. Journal* 55 (March 1947): 19.

comprehensive and influential evaluation of civilian and military aeronautics was already in progress under the direction of Gen. Henry Arnold, the Army Air Forces' chief of staff.[24]

In November 1944, one year before Craigie commented on the anticipated institutional restructuring of R&D in the postwar Army Air Forces, General Arnold met briefly with Theodore von Kármán, a widely respected aerodynamicist and head of the Daniel Guggenheim Aeronautical Laboratory at the California Institute of Technology (Caltech). Arnold asked von Kármán, who was also intimately involved in Caltech's wartime rocket R&D program, to investigate the current status of aeronautical research and make recommendations for the application of new scientific knowledge in the field to the long-term development of American air power.[25] As the head of Arnold's newly formed Scientific Advisory Group (SAG), von Kármán led a handful of academic and industrial scientists and engineers overseas the following spring. They concentrated their efforts in war-torn Germany, making a systematic survey of the sophisticated research and development facilities that had turned out the world's first operational jet aircraft and long-range rockets.

In addition to making recommendations for the transfer of sensitive German documentation and personnel to the United States, the advisory group compiled a set of preliminary findings, which von Kármán summarized in "Where We Stand," the first report he submitted to Arnold on behalf of the SAG membership in August 1945. Von Kármán predicted a new era in aerial warfare, one in which supersonic aircraft would be able to strike distant targets with electronically controlled, high-velocity missiles. Radar-guided communication and navigation systems would enable precise coordination of offensive and defensive air operations regardless of poor visibility and inclement weather. In December, the Scientific Advisory Group submitted the multivolume study *Toward New Horizons*, which not only reiterated the findings of "Where We Stand" but also included detailed discussions of key technical fields—aerodynamics, aircraft propulsion, guided missiles, radar—that required additional exploration because of their anticipated military value to future air operations.

In the opening volume, *Science, The Key to Air Supremacy*, von Kármán laid out his institutional vision for technological superiority in the Air Force of the future. His recommendations centered on the infusion of civilian scientific

---

[24] "ATSC Review and Long-Range Air-Research Program," *Aeronautical Engineering Review* 5 (February 1946): 73.

[25] Arnold also played a leading role in the establishment of Project RAND at the Douglas Aircraft Company in 1946. Created to develop a science of strategic warfare for the Air Force, RAND separated from Douglas two years later and reorganized as an independent, nonprofit corporation. RAND was the first of the new breed of "think tanks" that originated during the early years of the Cold War to provide expert advice to the Department of Defense and the military services on many facets of science and technology planning. On the origins of RAND, see David A. Hounshell, "The Medium Is the Message, or How Context Matters: The RAND Corporation Builds an Economics of Innovation, 1946–1962," in *Systems, Experts, and Computers: The Systems Approach in Management and Engineering, World War II and After*, ed. Agatha C. Hughes and Thomas P. Hughes (Cambridge, Mass.: MIT Press, 2000); and Martin J. Collins, *Cold War Laboratory: RAND, the Air Force, and the American State, 1945–1950* (Washington, D.C.: Smithsonian Institution Press, 2002).

expertise into the Army Air Forces through a combination of institution building at the laboratory and management levels. To facilitate what he believed would be more productive collaborations among universities, industry, and the AAF's in-house laboratories, von Kármán recommended that the management of research and development be completely separated from aircraft production and procurement. He also sought to have permanent lines of communication established between the civilian scientific community and the major AAF staff functions at headquarters.

Although the Air Staff endorsed von Kármán's recommendations, plans drawn up for their full implementation were shelved because of congressional budget cuts that placed strict limits on defense spending throughout the remainder of the decade. Nonetheless, von Kármán did manage to transform the Scientific Advisory Group into a permanent organization—the Scientific Advisory Board (SAB)—with direct access to the AAF Chief of Staff. In a similar move to establish a formal liaison between the SAB and the Air Staff and also to expand the role of R&D at the policymaking level, he encouraged Arnold to appoint a new Deputy Chief of Air Staff for Research and Development.[26] To fill this position, Arnold hand-picked Maj. Gen. Curtis LeMay, who had distinguished himself leading strategic bombing operations in Europe and Japan during the war. But LeMay lacked broad powers of supervision and was unable to coordinate effectively the AAF's sundry R&D activities. When the Air Force separated from the Army and became an independent military service in 1947, LeMay's position was eliminated altogether, its function transferred to the Deputy Chief of Staff for Materiel on the Air Staff.[27]

The demise of the Deputy Chief of Air Staff for Research and Development reflected a larger and more pervasive conflict between advocates of a separate R&D organization in the Air Force and those who favored the current institutional status of this function alongside logistics and procurement in the Air Materiel Command. At the time, one only had to look as far as the Navy to see how effectively that service had institutionalized prevailing wartime attitudes about the value of science to weapons innovation. The result had been the Office of Naval Research, founded in 1946 to exploit on behalf of the Navy the most recent advances in science and technology.[28] One observer of this transformation in Navy R&D was Theodore von Kármán, who recommended to the Air Staff in 1947 that the Air Force set up a similar organization to fund long-term extramural research in colleges and universities. Lt. Gen. Benjamin Chidlaw, commanding general of the Air Materiel Command, endorsed von

[26] Gorn, *Vulcan's Forge*, 1–5; Thomas A. Sturm, *The USAF Scientific Advisory Board: Its First Twenty Years, 1944–1964*, repr. ed., (Washington, D.C.: Office of Air Force History, 1986): 4–17; Michael H. Gorn, *Harnessing the Genie: Science and Technology Forecasting for the Air Force, 1944–1986* (Washington, D.C.: Office of Air Force History, 1986), chap. 1. Previously, management of R&D had been assigned to the AMC procurement and supply division. See A. Leggin, "Army Air Forces Research and Development," *Chemical and Engineering News* 24 (10 November 1946): 2914.

[27] Converse, "The Air Force and Acquisition, 1945–1953," 16–18.

[28] On the history of the Office of Naval Research, see Harvey M. Sapolsky, *Science and the Navy: The History of the Office of Naval Research* (Princeton: Princeton University Press, 1990).

Kármán's recommendation, but he added one important caveat: The proposed organization should be managed by AMC and located on-site at Wright Field, the hub of Air Force R&D and procurement.

Chidlaw's opinions were shared by other Air Staff officers, such as Lt. Gen. Kenneth Wolfe, deputy chief of staff for materiel, who believed that R&D functions should be intimately connected to the aircraft procurement process. In their view, such a connection guaranteed the most effective use of technical expertise to solve problems arising in all stages of aircraft development and production. Von Kármán and other civilian experts, by contrast, believed that maintaining a direct link between R&D and procurement would sacrifice research on the scientific frontier—the anticipated source of major innovations—in favor of work on short-term production problems, thereby limiting the development of a technologically advanced Air Force. Early in 1948, the Applied Research Section (renamed the Office of Air Research the following year) was set up in the Engineering Division of the Air Materiel Command. Although it was transferred out of the Engineering Division in 1949 and assigned the same organizational status as its parent, the new Office of Air Research did not operate as a wholly independent unit reporting directly to the Air Staff, as von Kármán and the Scientific Advisory Board had envisioned.[29]

OAR's existence in the Air Materiel Command was short-lived, however. Von Kármán's aborted attempts to institutionalize all of the recommendations listed in *Science, The Key to Air Supremacy* were recast by Brig. Gen. Donald Putt, who in September 1948 became director of research and development in the Office of the Deputy Chief of Staff for Materiel at Air Force headquarters in Washington, D.C. Prior to taking this position, Putt had earned a master of science degree in aeronautical engineering under von Kármán at Caltech and had risen through the engineering ranks of the Air Materiel Command. In consultation with Gen. Muir Fairchild, vice chief of staff, Putt asked the Scientific Advisory Board to assemble a committee of experts to review the status of Air Force R&D and recommend policies for long-term programming. The committee, under the direction of physicist Louis Ridenour, dean of the graduate school at the University of Illinois, submitted its report to Gen. Hoyt Vandenberg, Air Force chief of staff, in September 1949. The Ridenour Report, as it came to be known, reiterated prior recommendations made by von Kármán and the Scientific Advisory Group back in 1945. It also included some sweeping changes. In addition to appointing a new deputy chief of staff for research and development at Air Force Headquarters (to coordinate planning and policy) and maintaining a contracting arm—the Office of Air Research—to support basic research in academic and industrial laboratories, the report called for a new

---

[29] OAR did not have a separate budget line. AMC controlled its funding. Komons, *Science and the Air Force*, 16; Stephen B. Johnson, *The United States Air Force and the Culture of Innovation, 1945–1965* (Washington, D.C.: Air Force History and Museum Program, 2002): 34–35; Robert Sigethy, "The Air Force Organization for Basic Research, 1945–1970: A Study in Change" (Ph.D. diss., American University, 1980): 25; Sturm, "The USAF Scientific Advisory Board," 31; "Research Command Starts to Function," *Aviation Week* 55 (2 July 1951): 14; D. L. Putt, "Air Force Research and Development," *Aeronautical Engineering Review* 9 (March 1950): 41.

R&D command, separate from the Air Materiel Command. Endorsed by Putt, Arnold, Fairchild, and Vandenberg, the Ridenour Report served as the founding document for the new Air Research and Development Command, established in January 1950. Putt became director of R&D under Maj. Gen. Gordon Saville, whom Vandenberg appointed to serve as the first deputy chief of staff, development. Ridenour, meanwhile, agreed to serve as chief science advisor.[30]

Although organizationally independent of the Air Materiel Command, the new Air Research and Development Command was not as autonomous as it may have appeared to outside observers. Initially, AMC controlled ARDC's budget, and it also managed research and development contracts with private-sector institutions.[31] Moreover, the founding of ARDC underscored the long-standing difficulties of trying to set clear boundaries between *research* and *development* and the institutional environments in which they were expected to flourish. Shortly after ARDC was established, the Air Staff began the process of separating the R&D functions previously assigned to the Air Materiel Command. Brig. Gen. Donald Keirn, ARDC's deputy chief of staff for research, suggested that all in-house research in the new command be combined into one centralized laboratory. Ridenour rejected Keirn's proposal outright on ideological and practical grounds. Expecting to cover all of the technical fields of interest to the Air Force in a single laboratory was simply unrealistic. Far better to accumulate a broad knowledge base in science and engineering from private-sector R&D institutions through contracting agencies such as the Office of Air Research. Ridenour also argued that in-house research should be limited to work that the Air Force was uniquely qualified to handle—testing and evaluation of aircraft and other weapon systems. Moreover, he believed that "a good government laboratory is usually inferior to its civilian equivalent," a view that was not uncommon among other scientists whose professional standards often reflected the academic elitism of the university.[32] To be sure, all of these views and opinions were gradually incorporated into ARDC's internal laboratory structure, that is to say Ridenour's support for contracting through the growth and diversification of OAR and its organizational descendent—the Office of Scientific Research—and Keirn's predilection for in-house R&D facilities as evidenced by the expansion of several Air Force laboratories dedicated to electronics and materials research.

To some extent, however, historians have incorporated the differing views of Keirn, Ridenour, and other participants into their own interpretations and analyses of events, culminating in the formation of the Air Research and

---

[30] "Deputy Chief of Staff, Development" was the new name assigned to the position previously titled "Deputy Chief of Staff for Research and Development" given in the Ridenour Report. Johnson, *The United States Air Force and the Culture of Innovation*, 38, 43; Gorn, *Vulcan's Forge*, 5–9, 12–17.

[31] "R&D Command: New AF Group at Dayton Indicates Greater Stress on Basic Research," *Aviation Week* 53 (6 November 1950): 15; Johnson, *The United States Air Force and the Culture of Innovation*, 192; Gorn, *Vulcan's Forge*, 63–66.

[32] Ridenour quoted in Sigethy, "The Air Force Organization for Basic Research," 44; Komons, *Science and the Air Force*, 22–23. On academic perceptions of government science during this period, see, for example, Thomas C. Lassman, "Government Science in Postwar America: Henry A. Wallace, Edward U. Condon, and the Transformation of the National Bureau of Standards, 1945–1951," *Isis* 96 (March 2005): 25–51.

Development Command. Several studies, for example, have examined the motives behind ARDC's separation from AMC in terms of a protracted conflict between enlightened officers tuned to the potential benefits of an independent R&D command by forward-looking civilian experts and conservative, risk-averse officers who sacrificed technological superiority in favor of short-term production goals to maintain a ready force structure.[33] Although such a division may have existed at the management level, this argument is nevertheless misleading, because it assumes by consequence that R&D was most effective as a separate function, independent of production.[34] The evidence presented in this chapter, however, shows that the division of research and development from production was not always clearly visible in the laboratories. More historical research on this subject is needed, but it is perhaps just as likely that, managerial separation notwithstanding, the Air Force accumulated innovative capabilities precisely because each of these functions—research, development, and production— remained mutually dependent in the postwar period.

A similar disjunction between policy and practice was evident in ARDC's contracting programs. An executive order issued in 1954 obligated the Office of Scientific Research to limit its funding of unrestricted scientific research in favor of investigations expected to yield practical results directly relevant to Air Force requirements, but program managers quietly manipulated the language of the R&D funding categories to maintain OSR's institutional commitment to the accumulation of fundamental knowledge.[35] Like their counterparts in the Army and the Navy, the in-house Air Force laboratories and contracting units did not always operate according to the procedures and guidelines set down by the Air Staff and the civilian and military leaders who set broad policies in the Office of the Secretary of Defense.

Growth and Diversification: The Air Research and Development Command, 1950–1961

"The [Army] Air Forces are delving into every nook and corner of scientific endeavor. Projects are now underway to study atomic power, jet propulsion, physics of the higher atmospheres, radioactive explosives, electronics, guided missiles, and the use of new metals and ceramics," *Chemical and Engineering News* reported in 1946. The AAF spent two-thirds of the Army's $280 million R&D budget that year, mostly through contracts awarded to universities and industrial firms. In 1948, after it had been separated from the Army, the new Air Force managed a research and development budget nearly twice the size ($145 million) of the one assigned to the next largest consumer of government

---

[33] See, for example, Johnson, *The United States Air Force and the Culture of Innovation*; Gorn, *Vulcan's Forge*; and Baucom, "Air Force Images of Research and Development and Their Reflections in Organizational Structures and Management Policies."

[34] Converse, "The Air Force and Acquisition, 1945–1953," 24, also argues that the claims made by the historians cited in footnote 34, above, are overdrawn. I am grateful to Dr. Converse for bringing this point to my attention.

[35] See Komons, *Science and the Air Force*, chap. 5.

funds for aeronautical R&D, the Navy's Bureau of Aeronautics.[36] This massive technical effort was managed and coordinated through the directorate of research and development in the Air Materiel Command, located at the newly named Wright-Patterson Air Force Base in Dayton, Ohio.[37] When the Air Research and Development Command was established in 1950, however, AMC's R&D functions shifted to more narrow pursuits—trouble-shooting problems and making appropriate modifications to new aircraft, a process AMC managers called "support engineering." This type of work had a long history at AMC—"That is what AMC's research and development people have been doing for some time," *Aviation Week* observed in 1950.[38] As the new hub of research and development for the Air Force, ARDC's institutional growth and diversification proceeded along two separate but related trajectories. Internal expansion of the laboratories and testing facilities previously operated by the Air Materiel Command was matched by a major increase in R&D outsourcing to industry and academia. In 1953, for example, nearly 90 percent of ARDC's research and development budget was distributed through external contracts to 1,520 industrial firms and 160 colleges, universities, and other nonprofit R&D organizations.[39]

The Air Materiel Command's largest in-house R&D facility, comprising more than a dozen separate laboratories in three divisions (engineering, flight testing, and all-weather flying), was located at Wright-Patterson Air Force Base (renamed Wright Air Development Center [WADC] after the transfer of operations to ARDC). The Air Force consolidated electronics research,

---

[36] Leggin, "Army Air Forces Research and Development," 2914. Next in line after the Navy Bureau of Aeronautics ($75 million) were the following agencies and departments: National Advisory Committee for Aeronautics ($43.5 million), Navy Bureau of Ordnance ($21.5 million), Army Ordnance Department ($11 million), Office of Naval Research ($5 million), Civil Aeronautics Administration ($1.6 million), and the Weather Bureau ($630,000). Total federal expenditures for R&D in aeronautics and related fields that year exceeded $300 million. R. McLarren, "Largest Aero Research Program," *Aviation Week* 48 (23 February 1948): 45.

[37] The mission requirements of the directorate of research and development were met by the laboratories and testing facilities managed by the engineering division at Wright-Patterson and the all-weather flying division, located at the Clinton County Air Force Base in Wilmington, Ohio. In addition to research and development, AMC managed two other directorates: procurement and industrial mobilization planning; and supply and maintenance. B. W. Chidlaw, "New Weapons for Air Supremacy," *Aero Digest* 57 (September 1948): 51.

[38] "R&D Command: New AF Group at Dayton Indicates Greater Stress on Basic Research," *Aviation Week* 53 (6 November 1950): 15.

[39] T. S. Power, "The Air Research and Development Team," *Aeronautical Engineering Review* 14 (April 1955): 40. The annual budget of the Office of Scientific Research doubled in 1956 to fund expanded programs in hypersonics, propulsion methods and fuels, high-temperature studies, and solid-state physics. See R. Hotz, "USAF Expands Basic Research Program," *Aviation Week* 63 (18 July 1955): 12–13. The rapid growth of the defense establishment in the 1950s prompted many industrial firms to diversify into lucrative military markets, whereas others merely expanded the output of in-house production units originally established during World War II to manufacture weapons and other critical materials for the armed services. Strategic considerations also played a role in this transformation. Businesses turned to defense production as a hedge against cyclical downturns in civilian markets. "Munitions: A Permanent U.S. Industry," *Business Week* (27 September 1952): 27–28; "The Pentagon's Top Hands," *Business Week* (20 September 1958): 39. See also A. M. Smythe, "The 25 Biggest Defense Suppliers: Part One," *Magazine of Wall Street* 99 (29 September 1956): 12–14, 51–52; and Smythe, "The 25 Biggest Defense Suppliers: Part Two," *Magazine of Wall Street* 99 (13 October 1956): 65–67, 100.

dispersed across laboratories in Georgia, Ohio, Massachusetts, New Jersey, and New York, at two locations—the Air Force Cambridge Research Center in Boston and the Rome Air Development Center (RADC) at Griffiss Air Force Base near Syracuse, New York. AMC also ceded control of the huge wind tunnel and propulsion testing facilities—among the largest of their kind in the United States—at the newly established Arnold Engineering Development Center in Tennessee. The Special Weapons Center at Kirtland Air Force Base in New Mexico and the Armament Center at Eglin Air Force Base in Florida tested and evaluated delivery systems for atomic and nonnuclear weapons. The Flight Test Center at Edwards Air Force Base in California tested aircraft in the prototype and production stages, while the missile test centers at Patrick Air Force Base in Florida and Holloman Air Force Base in New Mexico carried out similar work on all types of short- and medium-range and intercontinental ballistic missiles.[40]

The headquarters operation of the Air Research and Development Command was originally located on-site at Wright Air Development Center but moved to Baltimore in 1951 (and later to Andrews Air Force Base outside Washington). In addition to managing the command's in-house facilities, the headquarters staff also coordinated the activities of other functions specific to ARDC's mission. The Office of Scientific Research, established in 1951 to take over the functions of the Office of Air Research, awarded research contracts to universities and industrial firms and coordinated basic research in the ARDC laboratories. "By basic research," wrote OSR's chief in 1953, "we mean fundamental investigations which are supported because of their probable contribution to advancement of scientific knowledge when we have no specific Air Force problem or application in mind."[41] Meanwhile, the Office of the Assistant for Operational Readiness dispatched teams of experts to maintain close liaison between the headquarters staff and the operational commands that used the weapons and other systems developed in ARDC laboratories and test facilities.[42] The job of each team was to tune the requirements of the commands to ARDC's R&D programming and "to keep the user commands conversant with the 'state-of-the-art' in their particular fields of interest." In the early 1950s, ARDC's technical program split into seven directorates: aeronautics and propulsion, armament, electronics, equipment, geophysics, human factors, and nuclear applications.[43]

All of these fields, except geophysics, were investigated to some extent at the Wright Air Development Center in the 1950s, either in-house or through contracts awarded to private-sector institutions. The newly introduced weapon systems concept, which redefined the institutional mechanisms by which the

---

[40] Leggin, "Army Air Forces Research and Development," 2915; Chidlaw, "New Weapons for Air Supremacy," 51; "Research Command Starts to Function," 14; "A New Command Is Born," *Flying* 48 (May 1951): 87; "R&D Pattern Taking Form," *Aviation Week* 54 (7 May 1951): 13.

[41] O. G. Haywood Jr., "The Air Research and Development Program," *Journal of Engineering Education* 43 (March 1953): 375.

[42] The operational commands: Strategic Air Command, Tactical Air Command, Air Defense Command, Air Training Command, and Military Air Transport Service.

[43] "ARDC Molds U.S. Air Development," *Aviation Week* 59 (17 August 1953): 79–80 (quote on 79); "Research Command Starts to Function," 14.

Air Force acquired aircraft, missiles, and other military hardware also guided this technical effort. "We can no longer afford to order an airframe and then try to stuff it with government furnished equipment developed separately under separate contracts," observed the chief of WADC's Weapons Systems Division. "From now on," he continued, "the faster aircraft go, the more exactly we must tailor our power, aerodynamics, guidance, and firepower to fit each other in a single airframe package."[44] Lending urgency to these technological considerations was the Air Staff's concern about recent advances in Soviet air power and the perceived threat that they posed to American security. Both factors—one technological, the other strategic—prompted ARDC managers and their subordinates at the Wright Air Development Center to rely on industry and the scientific community for major breakthroughs. Such reliance, however, was not to be sought at the complete expense of the in-house R&D programs that already maintained a vital link between the laboratory and the factory floor.[45] Representative examples to be discussed briefly below include the center's role in the development of the Convair B–58 *Hustler*, the first supersonic bomber, and the R&D activities underway in the center's aircraft and power plant laboratories.

Development of the delta wing B–58 began in the early 1950s, when the Air Force selected the Convair Division of the General Dynamics Corporation to serve as the program's prime contractor. In this capacity—a defining feature of the weapon systems concept—Convair managed all phases of the B–58's development, from the airframe produced in-house to the weapon subsystems (for bombing and navigation, autopilot and controls, offensive and defensive armament, communications, reconnaissance, cooling, and ground support) designed and built by other firms under contract.[46] Convair also handled the complete integration of all subsystems into a fully functional, combat-ready aircraft. ARDC monitored, evaluated, and supervised the overall development program, and, in collaboration with the Air Materiel Command, recommended and selected the contractor—in this case Convair—most qualified to complete the project. The Wright Air Development Center provided technical support.[47]

---

[44] "Weapon System Plan Spurs Development," *Aviation Week* 59 (17 August 1953): 83.

[45] ARDC put several procedural changes in place to accelerate weapon systems development. In 1955, for example, competitive bidding based on paper design studies was eliminated in favor of direct selection of contractors equipped with the expertise to meet specific service requirements. ARDC also made proprietary knowledge of weapons requirements available to a larger pool of contractors to boost industry participation in the procurement process, especially through the expansion of in-house corporate R&D. C. Witze, "Speed R&D, USAF Orders Industry," *Aviation Week* 63 (22 August 1955): 12–13; "USAF Urges Aircraft Industry to Use Own Funds for Research," *Aviation Week* 63 (5 September 1955): 14–15; "ARDC Trades Secrets for Progress," *Aviation Week Buyer's Guide* 63 (Mid-December 1955): 11; "Progress Proves ARDC's Mission Vital," *Aviation Week* 65 (6 August 1956): 76–77; C. Witze, "Industry Role in New Weapons Increased," *Aviation Week* 65 (6 August 1956): 86–88; "How ARDC 'Buys' Scientific Ideas," *Aviation Week* 66 (3 June 1957): 358.

[46] Convair did not manage development and production of the propulsion system. The high development cost prompted the Air Staff to assign those functions directly to ARDC.

[47] Other ARDC facilities also provided technical support. Air and ground tests on the B–58's weapon systems were conducted at Holloman Air Force Base in 1956. See I. Stone, "Holloman Evaluates Missile Systems," *Aviation Week* 65 (6 August 1956): 133.

WADC engineers collaborated with Convair to establish performance specifications for the major subsystems on the B–58. The Wright laboratories handled a related function, which also applied to other weapons programs, namely the development of engineering and production standards for interchangeable parts—fasteners, bearings, vacuum tubes, and other equipment—previously obtained as government-furnished equipment but now procured directly through subcontractors.[48]

"We do only enough research and development work in ARDC laboratories and centers to maintain a technical competency in our required fields and to tackle problems that are so specialized for USAF requirements that there is no outside interest in handling them," observed Lt. Gen. Thomas Power, ARDC's commander, in 1956.[49] Power's comments accurately described R&D policy at the Wright Air Development Center in the 1950s, where more than 85 percent of the funds earmarked for research and development were distributed to academic and industrial laboratories and other private-sector R&D organizations. The outsourcing of R&D was not necessarily carried out at the expense of Wright's own in-house functions, which included a combination of undirected studies in broadly defined fields of science and technology and focused investigations on specific weapons applications. Work along both lines proceeded in two of the center's six directorates: laboratories and research.[50] General research problems were investigated in the research directorate's aeromedical, aeronautical research, and materials laboratories, while studies that focused on aircraft hardware were concentrated in the nine commodities laboratories managed by the laboratories directorate: aircraft, aircraft radiation, armament, communications and navigation, electronic components, equipment, photo reconnaissance, power plants, and propellers.[51]

Engineers in the aircraft laboratory's wind tunnel and structures branches tested complete airframes and applied new aerodynamic knowledge to improve flight characteristics, such as lift, drag, stability, and range. They also synthesized test and performance data into specifications and design standards for use by aircraft and component manufacturers. Other work in these two branches focused on static-load testing of wings, tail surfaces, and complete airframes, such as the huge, six-engine Convair B–36 heavy bomber. The mechanical branch carried out similar studies on wheels, brakes, and tire assemblies at simulated speeds,

---

[48] "Weapon System Plan Spurs Development," 84–85; "ARDC Molds U.S. Air Development," 78. Convair employed the weapon system concept and concurrency to develop the B–58, but the results were not encouraging. Cost overruns, scheduling delays, and performance shortfalls plagued the program. See Brown, *Flying Blind*, chap. 5.

[49] Power quoted in "Progress Proves ARDC's Mission Vital," 76.

[50] In addition to laboratories and research, Wright managed four other directorates: flight and all-weather testing, engineering standards, procurement, and support.

[51] Among the R&D programs managed by the research directorate, a major effort in metallurgical research was supported by the aeronautical research and materials laboratories. Much of the work in the aeronautical research laboratory, for example, focused on the internal structure and physical and electrical properties of ceramics, semiconductors, and other magnetic and electronic materials required for avionics applications in jet aircraft. See J. W. Poynter, "Metallurgy Research Program of the Aeronautical Research Laboratory," *Journal of Metals* 9 (May 1957): 675–76.

while engineers in the special projects branch examined the friction, oxidation, and heating properties of alloy steel and ceramic bearings used in aircraft engines and flight control assemblies. Meanwhile, the power plant laboratory operated testing and calibration equipment to evaluate the operational performance of aircraft engines produced by commercial manufacturers. Types ranged from conventional piston engines to ramjets. In all cases, *Aviation Week* reported in 1953, "The [power plant] laboratory . . . reserves to itself the task of guiding and evaluating the manufacturers' development efforts and [the] solution of power plant problems developing in field operations."[52]

Although it had been a center of power plant development and testing before and during the war, the Wright Air Development Center was unable to fulfill these functions as Air Force planners abandoned propeller-driven, reciprocating engines in favor of much faster jet propulsion technologies. Consequently, Wright ceded control of high-speed engine testing and evaluation to the Arnold Engineering Development Center.[53] At this new facility in Tennessee—located next to the town of Tullahoma, seventy-five miles southeast of Nashville—the Air Force tested airframes, aircraft materials, and propulsion technologies capable of operating at higher speeds, temperatures, and altitudes than their wartime counterparts. "The emphasis on supersonic flight, guided missiles . . . and electronic equipment has established requirements for a whole new set of test facilities," wrote General Craigie in March 1947. Beyond the sound barrier (breached for the first time later that year), the air surrounding an airplane begins to exhibit fluid-like characteristics. "The design of an aircraft that will fly in such media," Craigie predicted, "becomes quite an assignment."[54] It was this and other unknowns in aircraft performance that guided technical programming at the Arnold Engineering Development Center during the 1950s.

The origins of the Tullahoma facility can be traced back to 1945, when Theodore von Kármán and the Scientific Advisory Group conducted their survey of the R&D laboratories that turned out jet engines, rocket motors, and other advanced propulsion technologies for the German aircraft industry. Prompted by von Kármán's recommendation that similar R&D facilities should be built in the United States, the AAF dismantled, shipped stateside, and reassembled at Tullahoma the propulsion laboratory constructed by the Bayerischen Motoren Werke in Munich in 1943 to develop jet engines for military aircraft. Also accompanying the equipment were some of the German scientists who had operated it during the

---

[52] A. McSurely, "WADC: $200-Million Research Key," *Aviation Week* 59 (17 August 1953): 99, 102, 107–8 (quote on 108).

[53] Putt, "Air Force Research and Development," 42; Leggin, "Army Air Forces Research and Development," 2914. In 1948, the Wright Air Development Center's largest wind tunnel operated at a maximum sustained speed of 400 miles per hour, well below the speed necessary to break the sound barrier. The power ratings of the tunnels at Wright did not exceed 40,000 horsepower. The wind tunnels planned for the Air Engineering Development Division (later Arnold Engineering Development Center), by contrast, were expected to operate at nearly four times that rating—150,000 horsepower. McLarren, "Largest Aero Research Program," 43; M. Dobert, "Home of the Impossible," *Flying* 40 (March 1947): 34.

[54] Craigie, "AAF Plans for Engineering and Research," 20; Leggin, "Army Air Forces Research and Development," 2915.

war.[55] This state-of-the-art laboratory served as the centerpiece of AEDC's new engine test facility, which conducted full-scale tests and evaluations of all types of jet engines operating under controlled temperature and humidity conditions at simulated altitudes reaching eighty thousand feet, far exceeding the limits of conventional piston-driven engines. Gas dynamics and wind tunnel facilities were subsequently added to the Tullahoma center to evaluate new airframe designs at hypersonic speeds and also to test aircraft-installed ramjet and turbojet power plants. Expansion of these facilities to achieve faster speeds at higher simulated altitudes proceeded accordingly throughout the rest of the decade in response to the Air Force requirement that industrial contractors test their prototype aircraft and propulsion systems at Tullahoma. Tests conducted for the Army and the Navy—on the propulsion systems for the *Sergeant, Pershing,* and *Polaris* missile systems, for example—also added to the workload during this period.[56]

Although AEDC engineers tested new airframes and the propulsion units that powered them at supersonic and hypersonic speeds, their counterparts at the Armament Test Center at Eglin Air Force Base—located on the gulf coast of Florida, fifty miles east of Pensacola—carried out similar investigations to determine the effects of such high velocities on the operation and effectiveness of conventional ordnance. "[N]ew high-speed airplane designs have raised a slew of armament problems that haven't even been tackled yet," *Business Week* reported in 1949. Little was known, for example, about the effects of protruding gun barrels on the aerodynamic stability of aircraft flying at supersonic speeds. Similarly, in the case of free-fall bombing, it was unclear whether standard ordnance inherited from the war would be suitable for delivery from high-speed aircraft. Conventional bomb sights were also outdated, prompting Eglin's test engineers to work with private manufacturers to develop automatic, radar-guided targeting systems for supersonic aircraft.[57] The rapid increase in the Armament Test Center's budget was one likely measure of the significance attributed to the operational limits placed on weapon systems as aircraft velocities passed the sound barrier: It quadrupled between 1952 and 1957, from $5 million to $20 million.

Construction of the Armament Test Center (later shortened to Armament Center) at Eglin Air Force base commenced in 1950, but work in this field had already been underway since the mid-1930s, when the Army Air Corps established a bombing and gunnery range on the same site. In 1951, Air Force headquarters transferred the test center from the Air Materiel Command to the

---

[55] Sturm, *The USAF Scientific Advisory Board*, 6; A. McSurely, "AF Planning Huge New Research Center," *Aviation Week* 51 (21 November 1949): 11–12; D. A. Anderton, "AF Reveals Plans for Engineering Center," *Aviation Week* 55 (2 July 1951): 13–14. On the transfer of German aircraft and rocket technology and scientific personnel to the United States, see Clarence Lasby, *Project Paperclip: German Scientists and the Cold War* (New York: Atheneum, 1971); and Karen J. Weitze, *Command Lineage, Scientific Achievement, and Major Tenant Missions,* vol. 1 of *Keeping the Edge: Air Force Materiel Command Cold War Context, 1945–1991* (Wright-Patterson Air Force Base, Oh.: Headquarters, Air Force Materiel Command, August 2003), 162–86.

[56] G. W. Newton, "AEDC Provides Huge Jet Engine Test Facility," *S. A. E. Journal* 62 (July 1954): 28–32; J. Trainor, "Arnold Center Tests All Big Systems," *Missiles and Rockets* 9 (14 August 1961): 32.

[57] "Weapon Center," *Business Week* (30 April 1949): 26, 28 (quote on 28).

new Air Research and Development Command.[58] The test center at Eglin was essentially composed of bombing, rocket, and gunnery ranges lined with sensitive instruments to measure the movement, tracking capabilities, trajectories, and explosion patterns of all types of bombs, rockets, and projectiles fired by jet aircraft and other advanced delivery systems. By the late 1950s, the center's missions had expanded into the compilation of firing and bombing tables, using ballistics, terminal effect, blast, and fragmentation data gathered during the testing of bombs, gun projectiles, rockets, and air-launched missiles.

Private contractors carried out most of the Armament Test Center's work, operating on-site. The center's in-house laboratories managed programs that provided technical support to these outside vendors. The Armament Test Facilities Laboratory, for example, developed some of the optical instruments used on the test ranges, but most equipment of this type was produced by commercial firms. "The general policy," *Aviation Week* reported in 1953, "calls for the lab to produce its own items with in-shop capability only when industry—through lack of available instruments or reluctance to produce a small quantity—is not able to do the job." A similar policy guided the activities in the center's Air Munitions Development Laboratory. In one particular case, laboratory personnel assisted in the development of the 20 and 30 mm. versions of the *Vulcan* Gatling cannons built under contract for the Air Force by the General Electric Company.[59]

The Special Weapons Center at Kirtland Air Force Base, located along the southeastern edge of Albuquerque, New Mexico, handled the nuclear equivalent of Eglin's testing functions for conventional ordnance. Established at the beginning of World War II as a flight training center for the Army Air Forces, Kirtland expanded rapidly during the 1950s as the Air Force incorporated into its growing fleet of supersonic aircraft the latest advances in nuclear weapons technology.[60] The Special Weapons Center mated the atomic weapons manufactured in nearby production facilities owned by the Atomic Energy Commission to the aircraft and other delivery systems maintained by the Air Force. Originally established in 1947 as a liaison office to transmit Air Force requirements for nuclear weapons to the AEC (primarily to the nearby Sandia and Los Alamos laboratories), the newly named Special Weapons Center added its own R&D and testing functions in 1951.[61] Although it ranked second behind the Wright Air Development Center in R&D expenditures that year, Kirtland, like the other ARDC's test centers, outsourced most of its research and development to industrial firms and universities.

---

[58] "Center Tests USAF Armament Systems," *Aviation Week* 59 (17 August 1953): 210–11; Karen J. Weitze, *Installations and Facilities*, vol. 2 of *Keeping the Edge: Air Force Materiel Command Cold War Context, 1945–1991* (Wright-Patterson Air Force Base, Oh.: Headquarters, Air Force Materiel Command, August 2003), 106–07, 114–15.

[59] "Center Tests USAF Armament Systems," 215–16 (quote on 216), 219; "AFAC Sharpens Air Force Armament," *Aviation Week* 66 (3 June 1957): 99.

[60] Weitze, *Installations and Facilities*, 264–65.

[61] Although owned by the Atomic Energy Commission, the nuclear weapons laboratories typically operated under contract with universities and industrial firms. The University of California held the contract for the Los Alamos laboratory, while the Western Electric Company, the manufacturing arm of the Bell Telephone System, managed Sandia.

The Special Weapons Center housed a wing to support the testing functions of the AEC's atomic proving ground—the continental test site in Nevada and the overseas operation at Eniwetok Atoll in the Pacific Ocean. Dedicated aircraft dropped the test weapons, gathered airborne data on the blast effects and fallout, and tracked radioactive cloud movement. Meanwhile, scientists and engineers employed in the Special Weapons Center's research directorate used this information and other data to produce analytical studies on current and anticipated requirements in nuclear weapons capabilities. Through the development directorate, they integrated these findings into the weapons development programs underway in the AEC laboratories and the industrial firms that produced the delivery systems under contract. In this capacity, the center essentially maintained its prior role as a clearinghouse, similar to the liaison office established in 1947. Other functions carried out by the research directorate included studies of the hazards of nuclear warfare and the corresponding effects on humans and the environment; analyses of the vulnerability of nuclear weapons to countermeasures, natural disasters, and human errors; and the compilation of data on the anticipated yields of atomic warheads currently under development.[62]

Edwards Air Force Base, located on a dry lake bed one hundred miles north of Los Angeles, conducted initial tests of complete air weapon systems on the first production models of combat aircraft. Originally used by commercial airframe manufacturers in the 1920s to test new designs, the military took over the site during World War II to serve as a secret test location for Bell Aircraft's P–59, the first American jet fighter. Edwards was designated a full-service flight test center in 1951, the year it was absorbed into the new Air Research and Development Command. The major test facilities in operation at Edwards in the 1950s included a high-altitude speed course, precision bombing range, photographic range to check the accuracy of new reconnaissance equipment, and radar and tracking facilities to record flight test data.

Following the establishment of flight characteristics at the Wright Air Development Center, production models of new aircraft were sent to Edwards to determine operational capabilities. This function entailed rigorous flight testing in various simulated combat conditions to match the contractor's performance guarantees to the operational requirements of the receiving Air Force command. After testing at Edwards, aircraft were transferred to Eglin Air Force Base, where they received tactical evaluation to determine combat capabilities. In cases where aircraft subsystems experienced technical malfunctions, on-site laboratories at Edwards were pressed into service to debug problems and overhaul critical components. Engines, for example, were routinely removed from aircraft and put through rigorous evaluation on test stands and other diagnostic laboratory

---

[62] R. Hotz, "Center Mates Planes to Atom Weapons," *Aviation Week* 59 (17 August 1953): 91–97; Hotz, "Kirtland Gives USAF Nuclear Delivery," *Aviation Week* 65 (6 August 1956): 151–53, 155–58, 161–63.

equipment. This work was carried out on a limited scale, however, typically in collaboration with the industrial contractors that manufactured the aircraft.[63]

Testing and evaluation of propulsion units for intercontinental and intermediate-range ballistic missiles constituted the other major function at Edwards Air Force Base. This work complemented the massive effort underway within the Air Research and Development Command to develop, produce, and put into operation a strategic ballistic missile force as quickly as possible. In 1954, the Air Force established the Western Development Division (WDD) in Inglewood, California, as a separate ARDC field office to manage and coordinate this accelerated program. Under the leadership of Brig. Gen. Bernard Schriever, the new division institutionalized the weapon system concept and concurrency on a grand scale to guide all phases of ballistic missile development and production. A new breed of private-sector organization that specialized in system analysis and integration handled technical direction. In this case, the Ramo-Wooldridge Corporation appropriated many of the technical functions previously assigned to the prime contractor and ARDC's Wright Air Development Center.[64]

Construction of the Rocket Test Facility at Edwards Air Force Base commenced in 1950, and a rocket motor was first fired there in 1953. Three years later, following the establishment of the Western Development Division, Edwards initiated a major expansion program to handle the increased workload prompted by the rapid growth of the ballistic missile program. Massive test stands were added to fire engines capable of generating up to fifty thousand pounds of thrust. Engineers from the Convair Division of General Dynamics, Douglas Aircraft, and North American Aviation conducted tests of the power plants still under development for the *Atlas* intercontinental ballistic missile, the *Thor* intermediate-range ballistic missile, and the *Navajo* cruise missile. In-house missile assembly facilities, machine and metal-working shops, and engineering and hydrodynamics laboratories provided technical support to the contractors working on-site.[65] Meanwhile, ARDC conducted full-scale testing of these and other short- and medium-range and intercontinental ballistic missiles at the contractor-operated test ranges at Patrick Air Force Base, located at Cape Canaveral on the eastern coast of Florida, and at Holloman Air Force Base,

[63] Industrial contractors working on-site at Edwards (as part of the test team and also to assist in the debugging of aircraft systems) included Northrop, Douglas Aircraft, and North American Aviation. W. Coughlin, "Flight Test Center Probes Aviation's Supersonic Frontiers," *Aviation Week* 59 (17 August 1953): 119, 125, 141–42; "Edwards Evaluates Weapons Systems," *Aviation Week* 66 (3 June 1957): 117.

[64] "WDD Directs ICBM, IRBM Development," *Aviation Week* 65 (6 August 1956): 101–05; Benson, *Acquisition Management in the United States Air Force and Its Predecessors*, 24–26, 29; Johnson, *The United States Air Force and the Culture of Innovation*, chap. 3. See also Jacob Neufeld, *The Development of Ballistic Missiles in the United States Air Force, 1945–1960* (Washington, D.C.: Office of Air Force History, 1990); John Clayton Lonnquest, "The Face of Atlas: General Bernard Schriever and the Development of the Atlas Intercontinental Ballistic Missile, 1953–1960" (Ph.D. diss., Duke University, 1996); and Thomas P. Hughes, *Rescuing Prometheus* (New York: Pantheon Books, 1998), chap. 3. In 1958, Ramo-Wooldridge merged with Thompson Products, a diversified electronics and mechanical components manufacturer, to form the Thompson-Ramo-Wooldridge Corporation (TRW). On the history of TRW, see David Dyer, *TRW: Pioneering Technology and Innovation Since 1900* (Boston: Harvard Business School Press, 1998).

[65] "Edwards Rocket Base to Test Captive Ballistic Missile Powerplants," *Aviation Week* 65 (6 August 1956): 143–45.

situated near Alamogordo, New Mexico. Both installations had been established and operated by the Army Air Forces during World War II, and they were transferred to the Air Research and Development Command in 1951.[66]

The introduction of supersonic aircraft, intercontinental ballistic missiles, and other state-of-the-art weapon systems was driven in large part by major advances in electronics technology. According to figures published in *Aviation Week* in 1949, the Air Force expected to receive two-thirds of the $172 million set aside by government agencies for the purchase of electronic equipment in fiscal year 1950.[67] Avionics—the combination of radar, radio, computer, and other solid-state technologies that constituted the electronics infrastructure of modern jet aircraft and ground-based communications and surveillance systems—consumed an increasingly larger portion of the Air Force's procurement budget during the same period. According to one estimate, the fulfillment of avionics requirements accounted for nearly half the total cost of a new jet-powered bomber in the early 1950s.[68] Although most of the sophisticated electronics technology acquired by the Air Force originated in the private sector, the Air Research and Development Command maintained its own institutionally diversified R&D program in this field after World War II to complement rather than replace the work already underway in industry.[69] This effort was concentrated in two major facilities: the Air Force Cambridge Research Center in Boston (later moved outside the city to nearby Hanscom Air Force Base) and the Rome Air Development Center at Griffiss Air Force Base in central New York State.

The Cambridge Research Center grew out of two major R&D institutions that supported the electronics requirements of the Army Air Forces during World

---

[66] For a review of the testing programs and activities at Patrick and Holloman Air Force Bases during the 1950s, see "Missile Center Expands for Long-Range Flights," *Aviation Week* 59 (17 August 1953): 170–84; "Holloman Tests Missiles and Pilotless Aircraft," *Aviation Week* 59 (17 August 1953): 186–209; D. A. Anderton, "Patrick Prepares for Ballistic Missiles," *Aviation Week* 65 (6 August 1956): 106–16; Stone, "Holloman Evaluates Missile Systems," 123–38; "Patrick Tests Air Force, Army Missiles," *Aviation Week* 66 (3 June 1957): 97; and "Canaveral Supports Space Exploration," *Aviation Week* 68 (16 June 1958): 187–95.

[67] Such equipment was needed for ultra-high-frequency aircraft radio communication, target identification, global communications, air navigation, coding and decoding, and radar warning. "$172 Million for Electronics," *Aviation Week* 50 (13 June, 1949): 34.

[68] "Avionics in the Air Force," *Aviation Week* 59 (17 August 1953): 249.

[69] A review article in the March 1960 issue of *Aviation Week and Space Technology* highlighted major electronics R&D programs underway in industry: identification, study, and production of new classes of electronic materials to replace germanium as the primary constituent in semiconductor devices; ongoing improvement of vacuum-tube technology to raise operational reliabilities and lower power consumption levels; and development of a new generation of microelectronic circuits, otherwise known as *molecular electronics*. Spearheading work in these and related fields were the large electronics firms: Westinghouse Electric, International Telephone and Telegraph, General Electric, American Telephone and Telegraph (Bell Telephone Laboratories), and the Radio Corporation of America. See B. Miller "Solid-State Electronics Trend Goes On in Plant and Laboratory," *Aviation Week and Space Technology* 72 (7 March 1960): 237–39, 243. Also by the 1960s, these and other established companies were joined by a growing number of entrepreneurial firms seeking to exploit the market potential of the electronics revolution spawned by the invention of the transistor in 1947. See, for example, Christophe Lécuyer, *Making Silicon Valley: Innovation and the Growth of High-Tech, 1930–1970* (Cambridge, Mass.: MIT Press, 2005); Ross Knox Bassett, *To the Digital Age: Research Labs, Start-Up Companies, and the Rise of MOS Technology* (Baltimore: Johns Hopkins University Press, 2002); and Michael Riordan and Lillian Hoddeson, *Crystal Fire: The Birth of the Information Age* (New York: W. W. Norton, 1997).

War II: the Radio Research Laboratory at Harvard University and the Radiation Laboratory at the Massachusetts Institute of Technology (MIT). In 1945, the AAF's Air Technical Service Command (ATSC) dispatched recruiters to the Harvard and MIT laboratories to hire technical personnel and acquire equipment for the electronics programs already underway at Wright Field and the Watson Laboratories at Red Bank, New Jersey.[70] Employee resistance to the anticipated move from Boston, however, prompted ATSC to establish a separate field station of the Watson Laboratories at Cambridge to conduct R&D on the radar and radio technologies previously supported by the wartime Office of Scientific Research and Development. In 1947, when the Air Force separated from the Army, the station's mission broadened to include more fundamental scientific studies in the electronics field, though not wholly divorced from specific applications. The following year, the station was granted permanent status as an Air Force research installation. The newly named Air Force Cambridge Research Center transferred to the Air Research and Development Command in June 1951.[71]

Organizationally, the R&D program at Cambridge comprised two directorates: electronics and geophysics.[72] Despite an early emphasis on fundamental research, the electronics directorate gradually moved toward hardware development in the 1950s, even though this latter function was already the assigned mission of Cambridge's sister facility—Rome Air Development Center. At Cambridge during this period, a substantial R&D effort focused on digital communication and data processing to support the development of systems for air defense and tactical air control. Although work on some of these technologies, such as the SAGE (Semi-Automatic Ground Environment) air defense system, was outsourced to private-sector institutions (including MIT in the case of SAGE), the directorate nevertheless operated its own in-house laboratories to pursue a multitude of related R&D programs. The propagation laboratory, for example, studied the effects of transmission media on the behavior of electromagnetic radiation, while physicists, chemists, and optical specialists working in the components and techniques laboratory examined the properties of new classes of semiconductor and magnetic materials slated for use in avionics equipment.[73] Meanwhile, other technology-oriented labo-

---

[70] The Watson Laboratories had been founded during the war as part of the expansion of the Army Signal Corps laboratories at nearby Fort Monmouth, New Jersey. The Signal Corps transferred Watson to the AAF's Air Service Technical Command in 1945. On the origins of the Watson Laboratories, see Weitze, *Installations and Facilities*, 402–03. On wartime R&D in the Signal Corps, see George Raynor Thompson et al., *The Signal Corps: The Test*, in *United States Army in World War II, The Technical Services* (Washington, D.C.: Office of the Chief of Military History, 1957); and George Raynor Thompson and Dixie R. Harris, *The Signal Corps: The Outcome*, in *United States Army in World War II, The Technical Services* (Washington, D.C.: Office of the Chief of Military History, 1966).

[71] Cambridge was officially designated the Air Force Cambridge Research Laboratories in July 1949. "Laboratories" changed to "Center" two years later but reverted back to the former when ARDC and AMC merged into the new Air Force Systems Command in 1961. I. Stone, "Cambridge's Bailiwick: Earth, Sky, and Sea," *Aviation Week* 59 (17 August 1953): 229; Sigethy, "The Air Force Organization for Basic Research," 28–29, 55.

[72] Cambridge added an atomic warfare directorate in October 1951 but deactivated it three years later. Sigethy, "The Air Force Organization for Basic Research," 55.

[73] Like their counterparts working in the laboratories operated by the large electronics firms, researchers

ratories focused on the design of ground-based and airborne radio and radar antennas and the development of more sensitive detection systems capable of evading enemy countermeasures.[74]

Cambridge's geophysics directorate studied the composition and behavior of the atmosphere, focusing specifically on the effects of severe weather, air composition, turbulence, temperature, ionization, and solar radiation on the performance of jet aircraft and electronic communication and guidance systems operating at high altitudes. Most of this work—about two-thirds of the directorate's annual expenditures in 1953—was outsourced to private-sector organizations, with the remainder conducted in-house at Cambridge. One of the major R&D programs underway in the directorate's atmospheric physics laboratory explored the gaseous composition of the upper atmosphere to predict the effects of higher aircraft speeds and altitude ranges on engine performance, airframe durability, and pilot health and safety. Meanwhile, researchers working in the ionospheric physics research laboratory studied aurora effects in the arctic region, and the extent to which they disrupted (through scattering and absorption) long-distance radio transmissions. At very high frequencies (VHF), however, auroras behaved like large reflectors, making transmission possible. Consequently, the laboratory's primary effort in the 1950s focused on the development of techniques to predict the occurrences of auroral phenomena "to permit the use of lightweight, long-distance, high-frequency sets for communication."[75]

The hardware end of the Air Research and Development Command's electronics R&D program was handled by the Rome Air Development Center in New York State. Like the Cambridge Research Center, Rome traced its roots to the wartime Watson Laboratories in New Jersey. In 1950, the entire operation at Red Bank (except for the staff and equipment that had transferred to Cambridge five years earlier) moved to Griffiss Air Force Base, which had been established in 1941 to serve as a maintenance depot for the Army Air Forces. From this core organization at Rome emerged the Air Force's ground-based avionics program, which included the development and procurement of integrated equipment for navigation, communication, direction finding, missile guidance, electronic countermeasures, and airborne identification. Rome added the procurement function was added to Rome in 1951, when the Air

---

at Cambridge studied the properties of silicon to determine its suitability as a replacement material for germanium in semiconductors. At the time, germanium-based materials dominated the commercial semiconductor market. See Miller, "Solid-State Electronics Trend Goes On in Plant and Laboratory," 237.

[74] "Cambridge Advances Art of Air War," *Aviation Week* 66 (3 June 1957): 105. On SAGE and Cambridge's collaboration with MIT, see Johnson, *The United States Air Force and the Culture of Innovation*, chap. 4; and Hughes, *Rescuing Prometheus*, chap. 2.

[75] Stone, "Cambridge's Bailiwick: Earth, Sky, and Sea," 232–36, 240 (quote on 240). Studies of the ionosphere at Cambridge diversified into the field of plasma physics in the early 1960s. A new laboratory was constructed on-site at Hanscom Air Force Base to house facilities for plasma production, diagnosis, and interaction experiments. Researchers studied the properties and behavior of the plasma sheath surrounding the nose cones of missiles and spacecraft during re-entry into the earth's atmosphere. Special attention focused on determining optimum radio frequencies capable of penetrating the sheath. Other studies explored the use of plasmas for space-vehicle propulsion and electronic applications. "OAR Upgraded, Up-Funded for Research," *Missiles and Rockets* 10 (26 March 1962): 123; "New Plasma Lab," *Missiles and Rockets* 9 (13 November 1961): 28.

Materiel Command transferred purchasing, supply, and maintenance functions for ground-based avionics from Wright-Patterson Air Force Base to Griffiss. Approximately half of Rome's technical effort during this period focused on the management and analysis of external R&D contracts. Support of AMC's procurement functions—through, for example, the preparation of specifications, monitoring of pilot production at contractor factories, and field introduction of avionics equipment—consumed another 40 percent, while the remaining 10 percent supported Rome's in-house R&D operations.

Although it rendered technical assistance to the Cambridge Research Center's continental air defense programs, Rome's primary mission in the early 1950s focused on the development of avionics equipment for tactical air power, specifically local combat area defense and ground support. Guiding this effort was the concept of an integrated network of electronic systems—mobile radar sets, centralized computers, and radio data links—to maximize the coordination and timely execution of communication, navigation, guidance, and intelligence-gathering functions between ground commanders and the tactical aircraft that provided air support. Development of these "super-systems," which commenced at Rome in 1953, relied heavily on outside contractors; in-house participation in the program was limited to 20 percent of the R&D performed that year.[76] By the end of the decade, expansion of the Air Force's operations prompted Rome to diversify its technical base into global communications systems. It also moved beyond the development of ground-based avionics equipment for tactical requirements to the development of guidance system technology for ballistic missile defense.[77]

Reintegration: R&D in the Air Force Systems Command, 1961–1991

On October 4, 1957, just as the Rome Air Development Center embarked on a new program of ballistic missile defense, the Soviet Union launched *Sputnik*, the world's first artificial satellite, into low earth orbit. This landmark event stunned the citizens of the United States and prompted an immediate response that transformed the federal research establishment. Early in 1958, just four months after the Soviet launch, the Department of Defense established the Advanced Research Projects Agency (ARPA) to fund private-sector R&D for military space programs and other high-priority projects.[78] That same year, the National Advisory Committee for Aeronautics was abolished and replaced by the National Aeronautics and Space Administration. The founding of these and other Cold War institutions, and the allocation of seemingly limitless resources to support their operations, signaled the nation's commitment to permanent

---

[76] P. Klass, "Rome Guides AF Avionics Development," *Aviation Week* 59 (17 August 1953): 251, 255–56; "Rome Expands Role of Ground Avionics," *Aviation Week* 59 (17 August 1953): 274; "Avionics Team Spends Half a Billion Dollars," *Aviation Week* 59 (17 August 1953): 262–70.

[77] "Aerial Warfare Reshapes Rome's Task," *Aviation Week* 66 (3 June 1957): 110.

[78] On the early history of ARPA, see Richard J. Barber Associates, *The Advanced Research Projects Agency, 1958–1974* (Washington, D.C.: Advanced Research Projects Agency, December 1975).

military preparedness. They also had a major impact on the Air Force, especially given the service's expanding role in the development, production, and deployment of intercontinental and intermediate-range ballistic missiles. Much of the propulsion and materials technology built into the missile force complemented the hardware requirements of the new space program. Consequently, the Air Research and Development Command's in-house facilities broadened their programming functions to include space-based R&D for military applications. Organizational changes followed. In April 1959, Bernard Schriever, now a major general, assumed command of ARDC. Guided by the success of the ballistic missile program managed by the Western Development Division, Schriever separated weapons production and procurement from the Air Materiel Command and merged both functions into ARDC, resulting in the formation of the Air Force Systems Command in 1961. The remaining functions of AMC—supply and maintenance—were consolidated into the new Air Force Logistics Command.

The driving force behind the formation of the Air Force Systems Command was the ongoing struggle between ARDC and AMC to work out a mutually agreeable division of labor at the often-disputed point in the procurement process where weapons development ceased and production commenced. The adoption of ideas about concurrency—the process of overlapping R&D and production stages to accelerate the development of weapon systems—had only exacerbated this conflict. New institutional mechanisms, such as the Weapon System Project Office, provided a temporary solution to this problem by managing all phases of R&D and procurement through on-site collaboration of ARDC and AMC personnel. Still, even in cases where this solution was effective—at the Western Development Division, for example—a tenuous relationship continued to exist between the commands. Typically, the Air Staff had to intervene to resolve disputes on a case-by-case basis.[79]

Other organizational problems persisted, which prompted Air Force Chief of Staff Gen. Thomas White to request, shortly after the launch of *Sputnik*, that the Scientific Advisory Board form a special committee to review ARDC policies, functions, and procedures. Submitted in the summer of 1958, the Stever Committee Report (named after the committee's chairman, MIT physicist H. Guyford Stever) recommended sweeping changes to ARDC's highly centralized management structure. Day-to-day oversight and micromanagement of programs, the committee concluded, should not be the function of the headquarters staff. Rather, headquarters should focus on program coordination and long-term policymaking. The committee advised General White to decentralize ARDC's command structure and grant full control of program functions and resource allocation to the weapon system project offices operating in the field. To facilitate this transition and improve operating efficiencies at the program level, the committee urged the Air Staff to reorganize ARDC

---

[79] Johnson, *The United States Air Force and the Culture of Innovation,* 52–54; Gorn, *Vulcan's Forge,* 63–66.

into four major functional divisions: research, technical development, testing, and weapons systems.[80]

The Air Force high command reacted favorably to the Stever Committee's recommendations. Yet it was not until Schriever's arrival as ARDC commander in the spring of 1959 that lasting changes were put in place. Based on the recommendations of an internal review conducted by his predecessor, Lt. Gen. Samuel Anderson, Schriever scrapped the functional scheme proposed by the Stever Committee and chose instead to replicate throughout ARDC the organizational structure of the Western Development Division. Direct management authority of R&D programs passed from ARDC headquarters in Washington to four new operating divisions. The Ballistic Missile Division retained WDD's functions, while the Office of Air Research and the Wright Air Development Center were elevated to division status. The former Office of Air Research thus became the Research Division and managed ARDC's in-house and extramural basic research programs. The Wright Air Development Center became the Wright Air Development Division (WADD) and directed the development of aeronautical systems. Work on electronic and communication systems was vested in the Command and Control Development Division, located at the Cambridge Research Center in Boston.[81]

This divisional structure remained largely intact when the Air Research and Development Command and the Air Materiel Command merged in April 1961 to form the Air Force Systems Command. The newly named Ballistic, Space, Electronics, and Aeronautical Systems Divisions assumed complete managerial responsibility for major weapons technologies, from R&D through full-scale production to delivery to the user commands.[82] Meanwhile, the research division, which had been established two years earlier, was separated from AFSC and assigned to Air Force headquarters, reporting directly to the Chief of Staff. The new Office of Aerospace Research included ARDC's extramural contracting units—the Office of Scientific Research and the European Research Office in Brussels, Belgium. OAR also acquired managerial control of ARDC's in-house basic research programs, concentrated in the electronics and geophysics directorates at the newly renamed Cambridge Research Laboratories at Hanscom Air Force Base outside Boston and the Aeronautical Research Laboratory at the Wright Air Development Division.[83]

Although the reintegration of R&D and production in the Air Force Systems Command ended more than a decade of jurisdictional squabbling between the now-defunct Air Materiel Command and Air Research and

---

[80] J. S. Butz Jr., "Stever Proposes ARDC Reorganization," *Aviation Week* 69 (21 July 1958): 23–25.

[81] "ARDC Consolidates Research Management," *Aviation Week* 69 (20 October 1958): 37; C. Lewis, "ARDC Shifts Project Authority to Four New Operating Divisions," *Aviation Week and Space Technology* 71 (12 October 1959): 33–34; "New ARDC Divisions Formed," *Aviation Week and Space Technology* 71 (21 December 1959): 21. See also Gorn, *Vulcan's Forge*, 55–63.

[82] The Air Force System Command also managed two other divisions: bioastronautics and foreign technology.

[83] "Systems Command Given New Functions," *Aviation Week and Space Technology* 75 (25 September 1961): 71–73, 77–79; "USAF Sifts Advanced Research Concepts," *Aviation Week and Space Technology* 75 (25 September 1961): 82–86.

Development Command, it did not prompt a massive reorganization of the in-house laboratories and testing facilities previously assigned to ARDC. To be sure, the political fallout resulting from the launch of *Sputnik* in 1957 left its imprint on the Air Force, primarily through an across-the-board expansion of R&D programming in space-related fields. The laboratories, however, continued to provide technical support to industrial contractors through the newly formed System Command divisions. They also diversified into leading-edge fields of science and technology relevant to the Air Force's evolving requirements. Representative examples to be discussed in this section include the expansion of testing and evaluation functions at the Arnold Engineering Development Center and Edwards Air Force Base, development of conventional armaments at Eglin Air Force Base, work on artificial intelligence technologies at the Wright Air Development Division and the Rome Air Development Center, and R&D on high-energy laser and particle-beam weapons at Kirtland Air Force Base.

By the early 1960s, the mission of the Arnold Engineering Development Center had changed to accord with the Air Force's mandate to support the Defense Department's military space program. Consequently, the testing and evaluation of air-breathing engines, which had dominated the technical activities at Tullahoma for nearly a decade, faded quickly, surpassed by new programs to develop rocket motors for missiles and spacecraft. In 1961, for example, 70 percent of the workload at Arnold was committed to the testing of rocket propulsion systems for the AFSC Ballistic and Space Systems Divisions, the Army, the Navy, NASA, and ARPA. The remaining 30 percent focused on conventional air-breathing engines for aircraft and other near-surface weapons. Between 1958, when the first test chambers in the original engine (later renamed rocket) test facility were modified, and 1960, the number of rocket motor firings increased sharply, from 15 to 761. Meanwhile, the increasing size and power of propulsion technologies pushed the operational limits of the testing facilities even higher. The engine test facility's original thrust limit of 50,000 pounds had quadrupled by 1961. New facilities under construction were expected to raise the ceiling to 500,000 pounds and eventually triple that figure again, to 1.5 million pounds, by the end of the decade. Among the major weapon systems tested at Tullahoma during this period was the Air Force's *Minuteman* intercontinental ballistic missile. In addition to test firings of the solid propellant motors at simulated altitudes, wind tunnel tests were conducted to evaluate the stability of the entire missile assembly at velocities reaching Mach 8 (eight times the speed of sound). Aerodynamic studies of the re-entry vehicle were carried out at subsonic speeds and velocities exceeding Mach 20. Similar tests were completed for the Army's *Redstone* and *Nike Zeus*, NASA's *Mercury* and X–15, and the Navy's *Polaris* programs.

Although the testing of rocket motors displaced similar work on air-breathing engines, the rocket test facility still managed a substantial workload for aircraft propulsion systems. Representative examples included tests to determine the combustion efficiency, blowout and re-ignition limits, and component reliability of the following: the J57 and TF33 jet engines manufactured by the Pratt and Whitney Division of the United Aircraft Corporation for the Convair F–106 interceptor; the Republic Aircraft F–105 fighter-bomber; and the Boeing B–52 strategic heavy bomber. Data extracted from these tests verified in-flight thrust calculations and assisted in the compilation of fuel consumption rates.[84] Testing and evaluation of this type continued throughout the remainder of the 1960s and into the following decades, especially as new military aircraft entered service, such as the McDonnell-Douglas F–15 tactical fighter and the B–1 bomber manufactured by Rockwell International. By the 1980s, AEDC engineers and outside contractors were conducting separation tests on the external fuel tank and solid-propellant rocket boosters that carried NASA's shuttle orbiter into space. Giant motor-driven compressors generated the 95,000 horsepower required to produce the 7,000-mile-per-hour winds that passed over the boosters and fuel tank during testing to ensure safe separation of the shuttle from the launch vehicle.[85]

The post-1960 diversification of the testing and evaluation functions at the Arnold Engineering Development Center matched a corresponding expansion of similar work on rocket propulsion technologies at Edwards Air Force Base. In 1963, the rocket test facilities at Edwards were consolidated into a new Rocket Propulsion Laboratory, whose civilian and military personnel worked in collaboration with industrial contractors to improve the propulsion units and requisite solid propellants for ballistic and air-launched missiles and satellite space systems. The laboratory also provided technical support in the development of upper-stage assemblies for launch vehicles. By the mid-1970s, much of this in-house expertise was directed at the development of the MX intercontinental ballistic missile.[86] The multiple-contractor-produced MX, also known as *Peacekeeper*, entered service in 1986.

Although the ballistic missile program consumed a sizable portion of the Air Force System Command's in-house laboratory resources, it did not preclude ongoing development of conventional aerial weapons. Technical progress in this field was guided by the Armament Laboratory at Eglin Air Force Base. Contractor-manufactured weapons technologies under development in the laboratory in the 1960s included aircraft guns and rockets, air-delivered mines, fuzes, explosives and gun propellants, incendiary and flame weapons, defoliants, suspension and release equipment, and munitions ground-handling equipment. Meanwhile, the escalation of the war in Vietnam prompted a sharp increase in the laboratory's workload in the 1960s; the budget increased sixfold between

[84] J. Trainor, "Arnold Center Tests All Big Systems," *Missiles and Rockets* 9 (14 August 1961): 31–34; "Arnold Validates Systems Early in Design," *Aviation Week and Space Technology* 75 (15 September 1961): 221–29.

[85] M. L. Yaffee, "AEDC Facilities Busy, Despite Cuts," *Aviation Week and Space Technology* 94 (26 April 1971): 36; C. Pugh, "Riding the Winds of Change," *Airman* 27 (October 1983): 21. See also "Test Facility to Boost Arnold Capability," *Aviation Week and Space Technology* 110 (29 January 1979): 203–4; C. Covault, "New USAF Division to Stress Research," *Aviation Week and Space Technology* 112 (23 June 1980): 47–53; and B. Wanstall, "USAF Doubles Engine-Test Capability: $625 Million Boost for Arnold Facility," *Interavia* 40 (February 1985): 138–41.

[86] "Rocket Lab Focuses on Advance Needs," *Aviation Week and Space Technology* 101 (15 July 1974): 94–95, 97; D. E. Fink, "Minuteman Experience Aiding MX," *Aviation Week and Space Technology* 105 (19 July 1976): 113–14.

1962 and 1967, from $10 million to more than $60 million.[87] Out of this wartime effort emerged the first generation of *smart* weapon systems that combined conventional explosives—free-fall bombs and other ordnance—and precision electronic guidance technologies capable of filtering, processing, computing, and transmitting target information almost instantaneously during flight. The GBU–15 glide bomb, which entered production under contract to Rockwell International in 1983, consisted of a television camera or infrared imaging sensor (for nighttime deployment) placed on the front of a general-purpose, 2,000-pound bomb and a small data transmitter fixed to its back end. Electronic display and sensor control in the cockpit of the carrying aircraft enabled the bomb to be delivered to the target with precision accuracy. Similar weapons technologies that entered service during this period included a new family of 500- and 2,000-pound laser-guided bombs used to destroy reinforced concrete targets and the GBU–89 antitank and antipersonnel mine dispenser.[88]

Unlike Eglin, which continued to support the development of conventional ordnance, the Special Weapons Center at Kirtland Air Force Base diversified into new fields outside its core capabilities of mating nuclear weapons technologies to aircraft and missile delivery systems and conducting environmental impact studies of atomic warfare. Out of the center's nuclear effects testing and simulation studies emerged a major program, located in the new Weapons Laboratory established at Kirtland in the early 1960s, to develop high-energy laser and particle-beam weapon systems for airborne and space-based applications. Though highly speculative, this research program complemented a much larger, coordinated effort among other federal agencies, universities, and industrial firms to develop an interconnected network of tracking satellites and orbiting laser weapon platforms to repel a ballistic missile attack. Later known as the Strategic Defense Initiative (SDI), this controversial program and its institutional antecedents consumed a significant share of the in-house resources and technical personnel at Kirtland's Weapons Laboratory throughout the 1970s and 1980s. In 1974, for example, weapons-oriented laser R&D consumed one-quarter of the Weapons Laboratory's technical manpower. By 1987, SDI projects alone consumed 60 percent of the laboratory's budget.[89]

In the early 1970s, researchers in the Weapons Laboratory began studying the output properties and operating features of the gas-dynamic carbon dioxide laser. Despite its high-power capabilities, however, the carbon dioxide laser proved too inefficient for practical use. The laboratory investigated other configurations throughout the remainder of the decade. Chemical lasers, for example, showed

---

[87] "New Organization Planned to Stabilize Arms R&D, Funding," *Aerospace Technology* 21 (25 March 1968): 98–99.

[88] E. Ulsamer, "The Steady Evolution of Armaments," *Air Force Magazine* 68 (December 1985): 79–81; C. F. Surba and D. Ballou, "Armament Division at Eglin AFB," *National Defense* 71 (July-August 1986): 48–49. See also "Non-Nuclear Research Under Way at USAF Laboratory," *Aviation Week and Space Technology* 123 (2 December 1985): 161–68; and C. Rabb, "Air Force Labs Work to Make Today's Innovations Tomorrow's Routine," *Defense Electronics* 18 (September 1986): 95–100.

[89] "Weapons Lab Plays Key Nuclear Role," *Aviation Week and Space Technology* 101 (15 July 1974): 287; Weitze, *Installations and Facilities*, 305.

promise as suitable substitutes because of their higher efficiencies, even though they lacked the operational simplicity of gas-dynamic devices. One line of research focused on pushing the output beams of chemical lasers further into the microwave region to help meet expected size and weight restrictions for effective use in aerial operations. The electric discharge laser was also scrutinized as an alternative energy source for weapon systems during this period. Meanwhile, the development of aircraft-borne technologies capable of emitting target-destroying, high-energy electron beams progressed alongside the laser program. Work in this field centered on a fundamental problem that had preoccupied physicists for decades, namely the interaction between electromagnetic radiation and matter. The introduction and proliferation of particle accelerators in academic and industrial laboratories before World War II had enabled physicists to study in detail the processes and outcomes of high-energy bombardment of materials by electrons, protons, ions, and other subatomic species.[90] In the Air Force, direct application of accelerator-produced particle beams was initially carried out at Kirtland to complete nuclear effects tests and simulation studies. These investigations were scaled up in the 1970s and early 1980s to meet the planned operational requirements of projected high-energy weapon systems.[91]

Laser and particle-beam weapons represented the state of the art in advanced weapons concepts at Kirtland Air Force Base during the 1970s and 1980s. These technologies constituted, in effect, a direct extension of the Special Weapons Center's core technical capabilities—the development of nuclear weapons delivery systems and analytical studies of the environmental effects of atomic warfare. A similar evolutionary cycle guided the diversification of R&D at the Wright Air Development Division. The major stages of organizational change at Wright touched on a broad range of subjects, from systems engineering and avionics in the 1960s and 1970s to artificial intelligence in the 1980s. Throughout this period, however, weapons innovation at Wright, Kirtland, and the other laboratories operated by the Air Force Systems Command was guided by a gradual realignment of mission priorities. Beginning in the 1970s, in-house basic research was scaled back and increasingly outsourced to the private sector, while the laboratories forged a stronger and more direct link between R&D programming and production requirements. Although the extent to which this new policy was institutionalized varied widely across organizations and

[90] On the development of particle accelerator technology for high-energy physics research before World War II, see, for example, Daniel J. Kevles, *The Physicists: The History of a Scientific Community in Modern America* (Cambridge, Mass.: Harvard University Press, 1987), chap. 15; J. L. Heilbron and Robert W. Seidel, *Lawrence and His Laboratory*, vol. 1 of *A History of the Lawrence Berkeley Laboratory* (Berkeley: University of California Press, 1989); and Thomas D. Cornell, "Merle Tuve and His Program of Nuclear Studies at the Department of Terrestrial Magnetism: The Early Career of a Modern American Physicist" (Ph.D. diss., Johns Hopkins University, 1986).

[91] B. M. Elson, "USAF Weapons Lab Mission Expanded," *Aviation Week and Space Technology* 110 (29 January 1979): 212–13; "Weapons Laboratory Aids Beam Effort," *Aviation Week and Space Technology* 113 (4 August 1980): 56–58; A. L. Batezel, "Best Kept Secrets," *Airman* 26 (April 1982): 43–45; "Air Force Labs Concentrate on SDI Research," *Aviation Week and Space Technology* 127 (2 November 1987): 50. See also Robert W. Seidel, "From Glow to Flow: A History of Military Laser Research and Development," *Historical Studies in the Physical and Biological Sciences* 18 (1987):112–47; and Seidel, "How the Military Responded to the Laser," *Physics Today* 10 (October 1988): 36–43.

individual laboratories, its introduction marked the beginning of a protracted transformation that culminated in the merger in 1992 of all Air Force R&D, procurement, and logistical functions into one large organization—the Air Force Materiel Command. This outcome resembled a similar transformation that had occurred in 1946, when the same functions were combined for the first time into a single organization, the Air Materiel Command in the Army Air Forces.

By 1960, one year before the establishment of the Air Force Systems Command, the Wright Air Development Division had already institutionalized the weapon system concept. Wright split into three new divisions. The systems management division incorporated the weapon system project offices (now called system program offices [responsible for aeronautics technologies]) formerly attached to ARDC headquarters. Technical support—essentially hardware development—for the system management division was provided by the system engineering division, staffed by the engineers and scientists who had worked in the commodities laboratories previously assigned to the now-defunct laboratories directorate. The largest of the three divisions was the advanced systems technology division. Each of its four divisions managed four separate laboratories responsible for advancing the state of the art in weapon system technology. The avionics division, for example, operated navigation and guidance, reconnaissance, electronics technology, and communications laboratories, all of which focused on space-based applications. Scientists and engineers in the navigation and guidance laboratory adapted conventional air defense technologies to handle similar functions on satellites and manned space vehicles.[92]

In 1963, WADD reorganized the avionics division (through the merger of several smaller laboratories) into a new avionics laboratory.[93] Within a decade, the Wright Air Development Division's entire in-house R&D operation had been restructured and split into six laboratories: avionics, aeromedical, aerospace, aero-propulsion, materials, and flight dynamics. All of these laboratories maintained in-house and contract research programs, although the extent to which one type dominated the other varied widely in each case. In 1974, for example, nearly 70 percent of the operating budget for the flight dynamics laboratory supported in-house R&D programs. The remaining funds were distributed to private-sector contractors, some on behalf of other government agencies. Similarly, 80 percent of the R&D budget in the aerospace research laboratory that year supported in-house programs in energy conversion, fluid mechanics, metallurgy and ceramics, hypersonics, chemistry, and solid-state and plasma physics. Moreover, nearly half of the members of the technical staff working on projects in these fields held doctorates in science or engineering. In the aeropropulsion laboratory, by contrast, most of the development work on turbines, ramjets, fuels, and lubricants was contracted out to commercial engine manufacturers. The

---

[92] P. J. Klass, "Major Reorganization Designed to Broaden WADD Capabilities," *Aviation Week and Space Technology* 72 (9 May 1960): 27; Klass, "WADD Avionics Division Aims at Space," *Aviation Week and Space Technology* 73 (1 August 1960): 72–73; "WADD Reorganizes for Increased Capabilities," *Aviation Week and Space Technology* 72 (23 May 1960): 95.

[93] See P. J. Klass, "Avionics Lab Expanding Applications," *Aviation Week and Space Technology* 101 (15 July 1974): 206.

R&D activities in these laboratories through the 1970s covered a broad range of topics, from testing and standardization—Wright's traditional field of expertise dating back to World War I—to the development of semiconductor devices for avionics systems and high-strength, temperature-resistant metal alloys and composite materials for critical aircraft components used on the McDonnell-Douglas F–15 tactical fighter, General Dynamics F–111 fighter-bomber, and the Rockwell B–1 strategic bomber.[94]

By the mid-1970s, while these and other programs proceeded at the Wright Air Development Division, the headquarters staff of the Air Force Systems Command executed a sweeping reorganization of its in-house laboratories. Several factors had prompted action: tightening budgets, rising inflation, and ongoing debates within the Department of Defense, Congress, and AFSC about the extent to which research and development should be more narrowly focused on practical results applicable to service requirements.[95] R&D facilities closed, merged, or were transferred to other locations in response to this realignment of mission priorities.

In 1970, the Office of Aerospace Research was abolished, and its constituent organizations—Office of Scientific Research, electronics and geophysics directorates at the Cambridge Research Center, and WADD's Aeronautical Research Laboratory—were reassigned to AFSC headquarters, though no longer reporting directly to the Air Force chief of staff. Declining funding levels "forced [OSR] to focus more sharply on contracting for basic research with clear links to present and future [Air Force] requirements," *Aviation Week and Space Technology* reported in 1974. Some seemingly esoteric fields that had received substantial support in the past, such as nuclear physics, were dropped entirely

---

[94] W. C. Wetmore, "Flight Laboratory Pushes Joint Projects," *Aviation Week and Space Technology* 101 (15 July 1974): 136, 138; "Research Lab Studies Air Force Needs," *Aviation Week and Space Technology* 101 (15 July 1974): 251, 253–54; "Propulsion Lab Refines Engine Designs," *Aviation Week and Space Technology* 101 (15 July 1974): 247–48; "Materials Lab Focuses on Top Priorities," *Aviation Week and Space Technology* 101 (15 July 1974): 235, 237–38. Electronics R&D at Wright also included pilot production of new semiconductor materials in the avionics laboratory's electronics technology division. By the late 1970s, division researchers and their counterparts working on contract at Hewlett-Packard, McDonnell-Douglas, Rockwell, and Thompson-Ramo-Wooldridge, had identified gallium-arsenide as a possible replacement for silicon devices used in aircraft avionics systems, such as signal processors in radar and electronic countermeasures equipment. Gallium-arsenide microcircuits operated at higher speeds than silicon devices (while maintaining high power and low noise levels), but work with these microcircuits in the civilian sector had been limited because of silicon's dominance in the consumer and industrial markets served by the major semiconductor firms. The manufacturing facility in the electronics technology division was built to help encourage industrial participation in the development of advanced semiconductor materials. In addition to serving as a conduit for the exchange of technical information between researchers at Wright and their collaborators in industry, the facility also enabled the Air Force to procure critical semiconductor materials for operational systems no longer produced in the private sector. "Weapon System Capabilities Explored," *Aviation Week and Space Technology* 110 (29 January 1979): 186–89; Klass, "Avionics Lab Expanding Applications," 213–15.

[95] For an insightful analysis of how changing views about the relevance of R&D to military requirements affected industrial contractors during this period, see Glen R. Asner, "The Linear Model, the U.S. Department of Defense, and the Golden Age of Industrial Research," in *The Science-Industry Nexus: History, Policy, Implications*, ed. Karl Grandin, Nina Wormbs, and Sven Widmalm (Sagamore Beach, Mass.: Science History Publications, 2004).

from OSR's funding program.[96] That same year, the Air Staff commissioned a laboratory utilization study (under the direction of Maj. Gen. Kenneth Chapman, assistant deputy chief of staff for research and development) to assess the current operational status of the AFSC laboratories and recommend procedures for the most effective long-term allocation of R&D resources. Out of this review emerged specific proposals to realign the in-house laboratories to focus primarily on product development and, at the same time, increase the percentage of total R&D outsourced to the private sector.

In its effort to reduce in-house R&D, the Chapman Committee focused on the laboratories previously attached to the now-defunct Office of Aerospace Research. In 1975, the Aerospace Research Laboratory closed, and the four remaining development laboratories at Wright-Patterson Air Force Base—flight dynamics, materials, aeropropulsion, and avionics—merged into the newly named Air Force Wright Aeronautical Laboratories (AFWAL). This organizational unit provided technical support to AFSC's aeronautical systems division.[97]

Given the critical role of electronic command, control, and communication technologies in strategic and tactical air operations, the Chapman Committee had originally proposed that the R&D supporting these functions should move from the Rome Air Development Center to the Cambridge Research Laboratories at Hanscom Air Force Base. The committee also recommended that the Special Weapons Center at Kirtland Air Force Base take over the operation of Cambridge's geophysics directorate. Opposition from disgruntled laboratory employees, local officials, and the politicians representing the affected districts in Congress, however, prompted the Air Force to scrap this plan in favor of a less disruptive alternative. Rome received a reprieve and became the development center for command, control, and communications equipment, reporting directly to AFSC's electronics system division.[98] Cambridge, which employed more physicists than any other laboratory in the Air Force Systems Command at the time, was not so fortunate. Early in 1976, the geophysics directorate transferred to Kirtland, and the remaining electronics R&D programs—constituting the old electronics directorate—moved to Rome.[99]

---

[96] At the time, OSR operated six directorates: aerospace sciences, chemical sciences, electronic and solid-state sciences, life sciences, mathematical and information sciences, and physics. "AFOSR Focuses on Pertinent Research," *Aviation Week and Space Technology* 101 (15 July 1974): 142.

[97] "New Group Coordinates Lab Activities," *Aviation Week and Space Technology* 105 (19 July 1976): 171. See also M. L. Yaffee, "Materials Lab Gears to Meet User Needs," *Aviation Week and Space Technology* 105 (19 July 1976): 177–80.

[98] "Rome Air Development Center Deactivated in USAF Cutbacks," *Aviation Week and Space Technology* 101 (2 December 1974): 26; A. I. Robinson, "Basic Research in the Air Force: A Tale of Two Laboratories," *Science* 189 (12 September 1975): 862–65.

[99] "New Lab Geared to Support of Divisions," *Aviation Week and Space Technology* 105 (19 July 1976): 215–17; "OSR Given Single Manager Role for All AFSC Basic Research," *Aviation Week and Space Technology* 105 (19 July 1976): 226, 229. Only managerial responsibility of Cambridge's former geophysics directorate was assigned to Kirtland. The laboratory facilities remained at Hanscom. In line with the revised R&D policies set down by the Air Staff, the newly named geophysics laboratory focused less on exploratory research, which was increasingly outsourced to private-sector institutions, in favor of application-oriented development work. See "Geophysics Laboratory Stressing Development," *Aviation Week and Space Technology* 110 (29 January 1979): 231–33.

Since its founding in 1950, the Rome Air Development Center had functioned primarily as a testing and evaluation organization for avionics technologies manufactured in industry. Component and device development was also part of Rome's mission but only to the extent that it supported the electronics programs outsourced to private contractors. The transfer of more than two hundred R&D personnel from Hanscom to Griffiss Air Force Base, however, "expanded [Rome's] activities in the research end of the field," *Aviation Week and Space Technology* reported in the summer of 1976. Practically overnight, Rome acquired a more extensive knowledge base in solid-state science and technology, which complemented the center's ongoing programs to develop integrated electronic systems for ground and airborne avionics—a function collectively known at the time as command, control, communications, and intelligence (C^3I).[100] R&D in these fields had originated at the Cambridge Research Laboratories during World War II and expanded rapidly during the postwar period, especially after the invention of the transistor at the Bell Telephone Laboratories in 1947 and then amid the proliferation of semiconductor technology in the decades that followed. By the early 1960s, for example, Cambridge researchers were busy synthesizing and purifying single crystals and other electronic materials, studying their properties and behavior, fabricating experimental solid-state devices, and investigating the effects of radiation exposure on semiconductors. By the late 1970s, these and related fields of electronics R&D were firmly entrenched at Rome.[101]

In the mid-1980s, the Rome Air Development Center's C^3I program expanded to include a new R&D initiative in artificial intelligence (AI) funded by the Advanced Research Projects Agency. Carrying out this expansion largely through contracts with universities and industrial firms, Rome awarded a five-year, $8.2 million contract to a consortium of eight, regional academic institutions, led by Syracuse University, to fund AI research and development and encourage more students to enter the field.[102] Rome also worked closely with the Wright Aeronautical Laboratories to promote industrial participation. Work at Wright proceeded along two different but related lines. The flight dynamics and avionics laboratories collaborated with industrial contractors—primarily McDonnell-Douglas, Lockheed, Martin-Marietta, and Honeywell—to develop pilot assistance systems, based on parallel processor technology funded by ARPA's strategic computing program. Representative examples included

---

[100] A. T. Culbertson, "Scheduling Electronic Invention," *Astronautics and Aeronautics* 4 (March 1966): 42–44; "Rome Develops New Relations with ESD," *Aviation Week and Space Technology* 105 (19 July 1976): 203–05; "Electronic Technology Aims Changed," *Aviation Week and Space Technology* 110 (29 January 1979): 221.

[101] "OAR Upgraded, Up-Funded for Research," 123; C. Pugh, "On Discovery's Threshold," *Airman* 26 (January 1982): 29–35. *Aviation Week and Space Technology* reported in 1979 that "expertise [at Rome] is being applied to more general fields, such as improving the radiation resistance of semiconductor devices, which has application to airborne and spaceborne avionics." See "Electronic Technology Aims Changed," *Aviation Week and Space Technology* 110 (29 January 1979): 221.

[102] In addition to Syracuse, the consortium included the University of Massachusetts, University of Rochester, State University of New York at Buffalo, Rochester Institute of Technology, Rensselaer Polytechnic Institute, Clarkson University, and Colgate University.

mission planning, threat awareness, monitoring of aircraft subsystems, and tactical coordination of friendly aircraft in combat conditions. The laboratories also focused their AI efforts on the development of automatic target recognition technology and expert systems to improve aircraft maintenance and diagnostic functions. The materials laboratory, by contrast, sought to apply AI concepts to aerospace manufacturing, especially to the development of automated technologies for flexible assembly. Although much of this work was contracted out to Honeywell and Martin-Marietta, the laboratory did operate an in-house facility that applied AI programming to manufacturing processes with the objective of reducing production times, lowering costs, and improving output quality.[103]

As the decade of the 1980s drew to a close, the Air Force Systems Command employed more than half of the service's scientists and engineers who worked in eight divisions: space systems; aeronautical systems; munitions systems; human systems; electronic systems; flight testing; foreign technology; and, lastly, the Arnold Engineering Development Center.[104] Further consolidation of the Air Force Systems Command's in-house R&D functions had also culminated in the formation of four "super laboratories." In addition to meeting required reductions in overhead and personnel precipitated by the end of the Cold War, Air Force leaders expected the consolidation of previously independent laboratories into four major centers would improve the responsiveness of R&D to the specific requirements of the weapons development divisions, a process that had been underway since the 1970s.[105] Those laboratories that did not provide direct technical support to weapons programs were simply absorbed into the new laboratories as auxiliary functions.[106] Meanwhile, ongoing efforts to streamline the weapons acquisition process as defense contractors resumed low-volume production prompted a merger of the Air Force Systems Command and the

---

[103] "Air Force Systems Command Accelerates R&D Efforts," *Aviation Week and Space Technology* 122 (22 April 1985): 67; "Wright Laboratories Broadens Advanced Technology Initiatives," *Aviation Week and Space Technology* 122 (22 April 1985): 77–78; "Rome Air Development Center Focuses on Expert Systems Applications for C³, Natural Speech Technology," *Aviation Week and Space Technology* 122 (22 April, 1985): 84; "Research at Aeronautical Systems Division Points to Airborne AI," *Defense Science and Electronics* 6 (February 1987): 30–34. On DARPA's strategic computing program, see Alex Roland with Philip Shiman, *Strategic Computing: DARPA and the Quest for Machine Intelligence, 1983–1993* (Cambridge, Mass.: MIT Press, 2002).

[104] "Air Force Systems Command," *Air Force Magazine* 73 (May 1990): 67.

[105] See J. W. Canan, "The Labs Move into the Mainstream," *Air Force Magazine* 67 (April 1984): 55–59.

[106] The Wright Laboratory served the aeronautical systems division through the management of six laboratories: the former materials, aeropropulsion and power, avionics, flight dynamics, and electronics laboratories at Wright-Patterson Air Force Base and the armament laboratory located at Eglin Air Force Base. The Phillips Laboratory at Kirtland Air Force Base provided technical support for the space division. This newly named facility combined Kirtland's weapons laboratory and the geophysics and astronautics laboratories located at Hanscom and Edwards Air Force Bases. Essentially unchanged, the Rome Air Development Center continued to support C³I technology development for the electronic systems division. Finally, the human systems division drew its technical support from the Armstrong Research Laboratory at Brooks Air Force Base in San Antonio, Texas. This facility managed the human research, drug testing, and occupational and health laboratories at Brooks and the aerospace medical research laboratory at Wright-Patterson. D. F. Bond, "Air Force to Reduce Research Overhead with Mergers, Creation of Four 'Superlabs,'" *Aviation Week and Space Technology* 133 (3 December 1990): 68–70.

Air Force Logistics Command into a newly reconstituted Air Force Materiel Command (with headquarters at Wright-Patterson Air Force Base) in 1992, thus completing a cycle that had begun with the institutional separation of these functions more than four decades earlier.[107]

Coming Full Circle: Patterns of Organizational Change in Air Force R&D Since 1945

In 1997, Gen. Lew Allen, retired Air Force chief of staff, commented on what he believed to be the challenges facing the in-house laboratories managed by the new Air Force Materiel Command:

[The] consolidation reduces personnel and is consistent with the reduction in force required by the Air Force. However, R&D tends to be subordinated to logistics, because logistic problems are often urgent and affect readiness. The danger is that the long-term view is sacrificed to short-term issues. The Air Force laboratories have encountered their share of criticism and recently have been judged unresponsive to the needs of the operational Air Force. The laboratories are now placed under the control of the product centers. It is hoped that leaner, more nimble laboratories will result but, again, the risk is a focus on the immediate problems at the expense of long-term research.[108]

Effectively managing this "risk" had been an ongoing effort in the Air Force since 1947. To be sure, Allen's views were neither atypical nor necessarily misinformed. They had perhaps derived from his experience as a practicing physicist in the Special Weapons Center at Kirtland Air Force Base in the 1950s and then were developed and refined over the course of his subsequent rise through the administrative ranks to become commander of the Air Force Systems Command in 1977. Allen followed a long line of Air Force officers, who, in consultation with experts in the scientific community, had argued that successful weapons innovation depended upon the separation of R&D from procurement. Except for the decade of the 1950s, however, these functions operated side by side within the same organizational unit—the Air Materiel Command until 1950; the Air Force Systems Command between 1961 and 1992; and finally, the Air Force Materiel Command in the decade of the 1990s.

R&D in the laboratories managed by these organizations proceeded along two separate but related lines. Throughout the postwar period, much of the work focused on technical support for the industrial contractors that manufactured the bulk of the weapon systems for the Air Force. Although testing, evaluation,

---

[107] H. Viccello Jr., "The Past, Present, and Future of AFMC," *Aviation Week and Space Technology* 146 (16 April 1997): 38, 41; Benson, *Acquisition Management in the United States Air Force and Its Predecessors*, 2.

[108] L. Allen, "Science Remains Key to Air Supremacy," *Aviation Week and Space Technology* 146 (16 April 1997): 60.

and standardization predominated, scientific and engineering studies of all types, regardless of the definitions or categories (e.g., *basic, applied, fundamental, product-oriented*) assigned to them by the Air Staff, were also supported by the service laboratories in line with evolving Air Force requirements. The laboratories focused on three major technologies after World War II—jet propulsion systems for tactical and strategic aircraft, microelectronics for ground-based and airborne avionics, and long-range ballistic missile systems equipped with nuclear weapons. At the same time, they diversified into state-of-the-art fields, ranging from laser and particle-beam weapons to artificial intelligence.

Because it lacked the same type of institutional infrastructure that constituted the Army's arsenal system and the Navy's network of shipyards, the Air Force relied much more heavily on the private sector for the requisite technical expertise and manufacturing know-how required to turn out aircraft and other advanced weapon systems. According to one estimate reported in *Aviation Week* in 1953, the Air Research and Development Command allocated nearly 90 percent of its R&D funds to civilian contractors that year, while the Army and the Navy distributed 45 percent and 65 percent, respectively, to external vendors.[109] The absence of an in-house production capability, however, did not preclude the existence of a significant internal R&D function in the Air Force. Since its establishment as the Army Air Corps before World War II, the Air Force had maintained a broad knowledge base in science and engineering, initially concentrated at Wright Field in Ohio, but later replicated and dispersed among laboratories and testing facilities located throughout the United States. The institutional structure of Air Force R&D after 1945 differed from its Army and Navy counterparts in degree, not in kind. Throughout all three services, with the exception of the Naval Research Laboratory, in-house studies were conducted in direct support of weapons development programs. The content and scope of such work typically covered a broad range of mutually supporting subjects, from less-frequent fundamental investigations of scientific phenomena to the far more common functions of testing, evaluation, standardization, and prototype production of weapon systems and components. Similarly, in the case of speculative research *unrelated* to specific weapons requirements, the services established special program offices, such as the Air Force Office of Scientific Research, to manage contracts distributed to universities and other private-sector R&D organizations.

The evidence presented in this chapter suggests that institutional change in the Air Force's R&D establishment after World War II was driven more by strategic considerations and evolving weapons requirements than by broad policies designed to resolve the seemingly intractable conflict between advocates of an independent R&D operation separate from production and procurement and those who favored the merger of these functions into a single organization. Because the laboratories at Wright Field were not equipped to test jet engines and their components, the Air Force established a new facility to fulfill this

---

[109] "ARDC Molds U.S. Air Development," *Aviation Week* 59 (17 August 1953): 75.

function—the Arnold Engineering Development Center—in Tennessee in 1950. In the 1960s, after R&D had been recombined with production in the new Air Force Systems Command, Arnold's technical support functions remained intact but expanded beyond testing and evaluation of air-breathing engines to include work on a new generation of rocket motors and solid propellants required by the rapidly expanding ballistic missile and space programs.

Prompted by evidence of major advances in Soviet air power in the 1950s and the introduction in the United States of smaller and lighter nuclear warheads suitable for missile payloads, the Air Force initiated an expeditious program to accelerate development of intermediate and long-range ballistic missiles. Making use of the weapon system concept, which sought to merge R&D and production into a single, overlapping process, Bernard Schriever managed to bypass the jurisdictional conflicts that had strained relations between the Air Materiel Command and the Air Research and Development Command. Although the weapon system concept was not without its limitations—most notably its chronic reliability problems and cost overruns—Schriever nevertheless adopted its institutional equivalent—the Western Development Division—as the model for effective weapons development and procurement. In the late 1950s, he spearheaded the effort to recombine the Air Research and Development Command and the production and procurement functions of the Air Materiel Command into a new organization—the Air Force Systems Command. Given the high but largely unrealized expectations that preceded ARDC's founding in 1950 and its demise ten years later, it is not unreasonable to conclude that, despite claims to the contrary, the introduction of new weapon systems into the Air Force's operating commands during the Cold War depended on the interaction of research, development, and production.

CHAPTER FIVE

Conclusion: Review and Retrospect

On 30 June 1953, Donald Putt became the commanding general of the Air Research and Development Command (ARDC), which had been established three years earlier to manage and coordinate the Air Force's entire research and development (R&D) program. In an article about Air Force R&D published in *Aviation Week* shortly after his appointment, Putt commented on ARDC's role in the development of new weapon systems:

ARDC's job is not to actually do the research and development job. . . . For that we rely primarily on industry, universities, and civilian research organizations. Our job is to tell these groups the problems the Air Force wants to solve and to program, finance, monitor and evaluate the work necessary to solve them. In turn, we keep the Air Force informed on the kind of equipment they are likely to get at any given time because of the "state of the art" in any particular field.[1]

Putt's comments were not unique to the Air Force. A similar institutional strategy guided weapons innovation in the Army and the Navy after World War II. Although less dependent on the private sector than the Air Force, both services relied on universities and industrial firms to generate the scientific and engineering expertise required to develop and manufacture new weapons technologies, ranging from high-strength materials for conventional ordnance to nuclear-powered propulsion systems for ballistic missile submarines. The expanding role of private-sector institutions in weapons development and production during the Cold War was driven by separate but mutually reinforcing causal events: the waning influence of the Army's technical services and the Navy's material bureaus and the increasing centralization of decision-making authority within the Office of the Secretary of Defense (OSD); continued expansion of research universities in the United States; and the rapid growth and diversification of the research, development, and production functions in America's science-based industries.

These events and the sweeping changes prompted by their occurrence proceeded alongside an internal debate that continued to alter the institutional landscape of research and development in the Army, the Navy, and the Air Force after 1945. Vannevar Bush, Theodore von Kármán, Louis Ridenour, and other civilian experts acting on behalf of the military services believed that the separation of the management of R&D from production was a necessary prerequisite to effective weapons innovation. Critics of this viewpoint, such as Air Force generals

---

[1] Putt quoted in "ARDC Molds U.S. Air Development," *Aviation Week* 59 (17 August, 1953): 75.

Benjamin Chidlaw and Kenneth Wolfe, argued that it was crucial for all of these functions to remain organizationally unified. Separation, they cautioned, would limit the ability of researchers in the laboratory to solve critical technological problems on the factory floor. All sides claimed victory at various points and times during the Cold War as the Defense Department's R&D infrastructure expanded and diversified to meet evolving weapons requirements.

Established in 1946 and modeled on the wartime Office of Scientific Research and Development, the Office of Naval Research contracted directly with universities and industrial firms to accumulate new scientific and engineering knowledge unrelated to specific weapons requirements but broadly correlated to Navy interests. The Army and the Navy set up contracting offices guided by the same strategic mission. Meanwhile, the in-house laboratories owned and operated by the services provided technical support—the solution of short-term production problems and the testing and evaluation of complete weapon systems—to industrial contractors. At the same time, they maintained extensive internal R&D programs to complement industrial development of electronics, jet engine, rocket propulsion, and other critical technologies relevant to military applications. Periodic organizational realignments of these internal laboratories, however, undermined efforts to maintain a clear division of labor between R&D and weapons production. In 1961, eleven years after it was founded as a separate organization, the Air Research and Development Command absorbed the Air Force's procurement arm—the Air Materiel Command (AMC)—to form the Air Force Systems Command. One outcome of this merger was a more intimate connection between the content and scope of in-house and outsourced R&D and the weapons requirements handed down by the Air Staff.

The periodic managerial separation and subsequent recombination of R&D and production functions in the Air Force illustrate the extent to which the Air Staff struggled to reconcile competing points of view among R&D policymakers and also maintain the institutional continuity needed to improve the weapons innovation process over the long term. R&D management policies put in place by the Air Staff and its counterparts in the Army and the Navy did not always translate into practice at the laboratory level. In many cases, research, development, and production proceeded simultaneously in the service laboratories. The laboratories managed by the Air Force, for example, provided technical support to the contractors that developed and manufactured aircraft, ballistic missiles, and other weapon systems. This mandate, however, did not preclude the conduct of more cutting-edge research in fields that emulated studies underway in industry and academia. Representative examples include semiconductor and high-energy radiation research at the Wright Air Development Division and at Kirtland Air Force Base in the 1970s and 1980s. The program of solid-state physics research that had originated at Frankford Arsenal during World War II to solve the problem of season cracking in artillery shells complemented ongoing efforts to develop stronger and more battle-effective ordnance materials in the other Army arsenals and university and industrial laboratories after 1945. Similarly, in the Navy, the technical bureaus were not the sole sources of product-driven R&D tied to specific weapons requirements, even though that function constituted their primary mission. Some work along this line, such as applications-driven materials testing and analysis, was also carried out intermittently by the technical staff at the Naval Research Laboratory, which had been established in 1923 as a separate organization independent of the bureaus to support long-term studies broadly related to the Navy's interests. Even the long-range studies supported through external contracts to private-sector institutions by the chemistry division of the Air Force Office of Scientific Research (AFOSR) in the 1950s were expected to yield results directly relevant to Air Force requirements.[2] In some cases, AFOSR program managers manipulated the language of the funding categories to meet these requirements without altering the scope and content of R&D contracts.

Although most likely frustrating to the managers and policymakers who sought to maintain some degree of organizational continuity in the weapons innovation process, the institutional vagaries of R&D in the Army, the Navy, and the Air Force after World War II were nevertheless indicative of broader patterns of technological change in the United States during the twentieth century. Given how much the service laboratories relied on industrial contractors to develop and build weapons to meet service requirements, it is perhaps not surprising that they adopted, either intentionally or by coincidence, some of the practices and organizational forms of industrial innovation that had driven the rise of big business since the late nineteenth century. The conduct of industrial R&D has always been an inherently messy process, one in which the branches of science and engineering and the many disciplines they inhabit in the laboratory are constantly overlapping and fragmenting in accordance with the changing scope, content, and goals of a given research program.[3] As a general rule, such behavior in the industrial laboratory militated against efforts to impose a clear division of labor among research, development, and production, even in cases where corporate management established specific policies designed to achieve that outcome.[4]

The evidence presented in the preceding chapters suggests that similar constraints guided the conduct of research and development in the laboratories and testing facilities owned and operated by the Department of Defense after World War II. In this case, however, the profit motive was replaced by military

---

[2] See R. G. Gibbs, "Chemistry Division of New Air Force Research and Development Command Will Emphasize Basic Research," *Chemical and Engineering News* 30 (3 March 1952): 855. The Air Staff mandated a similar realignment of AFOSR functions in the early 1970s. See "AFOSR Focuses on Pertinent Research," *Aviation Week and Space Technology* 101 (15 July 1974): 142–51.

[3] See, for example, Leonard S. Reich, *The Making of American Industrial Research: Science and Business at GE and Bell, 1876–1926* (Cambridge: Cambridge University Press, 1985); W. Bernard Carlson, *Innovation as a Social Process: Elihu Thomson and the Rise of General Electric, 1870–1900* (Cambridge: Cambridge University Press, 1991); George Wise, *Willis R. Whitney, General Electric, and the Origins of U.S. Industrial Research* (New York: Columbia University Press, 1985); David A. Hounshell and John Kenly Smith Jr., *Science and Corporate Strategy: DuPont R&D, 1902–1980* (Cambridge: Cambridge University Press, 1988); and Ronald R. Kline and Thomas C. Lassman, "Competing Research Traditions in American Industry: Uncertain Alliances between Engineering and Science at Westinghouse Electric, 1886–1935," *Enterprise and Society* 6 (December 2005): 601–45.

[4] See David A. Hounshell, "The Evolution of Industrial Research in the United States," in *Engines of Innovation: U.S. Industrial Research at the End of an Era*, ed. Richard S. Rosenbloom and William J. Spencer (Boston: Harvard Business School Press, 1996), 41–51.

requirements for weapon systems. Successful weapons innovation, like its commercial equivalent in industry, depended on the efficient allocation of human capital and institutional resources to meet specific product requirements, often without regard to organizational and disciplinary allegiances. Because the development of guided missiles cut across the rigid boundaries separating the Navy's technical bureaus—in this case, the bureaus of Ordnance and Aeronautics—the Secretary of the Navy established in 1955 a temporary expedient—the Special Projects Office—to develop the *Polaris* ballistic missile system. A similarly accelerated program to develop the first generation of land-based intercontinental and intermediate-range ballistic missiles for the Air Force prompted the Air Staff to set up in 1954 a separate management organization—the Western Development Division (WDD)—within the Air Research and Development Command. WDD merged the research, development, and production functions—a management strategy known as concurrency—to accelerate the entire missile procurement process. So successful were the Western Development Division and its leader, General Schriever, in mediating the often tenuous relationship between ARDC and AMC that the Air Staff authorized Schriever's proposal for the reintegration of both organizations into the Air Force Systems Command seven years later. It is precisely for this reason—that is, changing organizational and managerial responses to evolving weapons requirements—that the sweeping R&D policy directives handed down by the headquarters staffs of the Army, the Navy, and the Air Force did not always align with the division of labor in the individual service laboratories, thereby driving subsequent realignments of those laboratories and programs. An intrinsically muddled process that defied routinization, weapons innovation—from concept to production—continuously recast the institutional landscape of the military R&D infrastructure that nurtured it during the Cold War.

Unpublished Documents

Converse, Elliott V. "The Air Force and Acquisition, 1945–1953." Unpublished manuscript. October 2003. U.S. Army Center of Military History, Fort Lesley J. McNair, Washington, D.C.

Converse, Elliott V. "The Army and Acquisition, 1945–1953." Unpublished manuscript. March 2003. U.S. Army Center of Military History, Fort Lesley J. McNair, Washington, D.C.

Fusfeld, Herbert I. Interview by Thomas C. Lassman. Unedited transcript. 2–3 April, 2005. Niels Bohr Library, Center for History of Physics, American Institute of Physics, College Park, Md.

Raines, Edgar F., Jr. "U.S. Army Historical Publications Related to the U.S. Army in the Cold War Era: A Preliminary Bibliography." Unpublished manuscript. 22 July 1994. Histories Division, U.S. Army Center of Military History, Fort Lesley J. McNair, Washington, D.C.

Government Publications

Amato, Ivan. *Pushing the Horizon: Seventy-Five Years of High-Stakes Science at the Naval Research Laboratory.* Washington, D.C.: Naval Research Laboratory, 1998.

Arsenal for the Brave: A History of the United States Army Materiel Command, 1962–1968. Washington, D.C.: U.S. Army Materiel Command, 30 September, 1969.

Barber, Richard J., Associates. *The Advanced Research Projects Agency, 1958–1974.* Washington, D.C.: Advanced Research Projects Agency, December 1975.

Benson, Lawrence R. *Acquisition Management in the United States Air Force and Its Predecessors.* Washington, D.C.: Air Force History and Museums Program, 1997.

Booz Allen Hamilton Inc. *Review of Navy R&D Management, 1946–1973.* Washington, D.C.: Department of the Navy, 1 June 1976.

Brown, Shannon, ed. *Providing the Means of War: Historical Perspectives on Defense Acquisition, 1945–2000.* Washington, D.C.: U.S. Army Center of Military History and Industrial College of the Armed Forces, 2005.

Bush, Vannevar. *Science—The Endless Frontier: A Report to the President on a Program for Postwar Scientific Research.* Washington, D.C.: United States Government Printing Office, 1945.

Carlisle, Rodney P. *Navy RDT&E Planning in an Age of Transition: A Survey Guide to Contemporary Literature.* Washington, D.C.: Navy Laboratory/Center Coordinating Group and the Naval Historical Center, 1997.

———. *Where the Fleet Begins: A History of the David Taylor Research Center, 1898–1998.* Washington, D.C.: Naval Historical Center, 1998.

Christman, Albert B. *Sailors, Soldiers, and Rockets: Origins of the Navy Rocket Program and of the Naval Ordnance Test Station, Inyokern.* Vol. 1 of *History of the Naval Weapons Center, China Lake, California.* Washington, D.C.: Naval History Division, 1971.

Cochrane, Rexmond C. *Measures for Progress: A History of the National Bureau of Standards.* Washington, D.C.: U.S. Department of Commerce, 1966.

Collins, Martin J. *Cold War Laboratory: RAND, the Air Force, and the American State, 1945–1950.* Washington, D.C.: Smithsonian Institution Press, 2002.

Duncan, Francis. *Rickover and the Nuclear Navy: The Discipline of Technology.* Annapolis, Md.: Naval Institute Press, 1990.

England, J. Merton. *A Patron for Pure Science: The National Science Foundation's Formative Years, 1945–57.* Washington, D.C.: National Science Foundation, 1982.

Fowler, William A. "Charles Christian Lauritsen." In vol. 46 of *Biographical Memoirs.* Washington, D.C.: National Academy of Sciences, 1975.

Friedman, Norman. *U.S. Naval Weapons: Every Gun, Missile, Mine, and Torpedo Used by the U.S. Navy from 1883 to the Present Day.* Annapolis, Md.: Naval Institute Press, 1982.

Gerrard-Gough, J. D., and Albert B. Christman. *The Grand Experiment at Inyokern.* Vol. 2 of *History of the Naval Weapons Center, China Lake, California.* Washington, D.C.: Naval Historical Division, 1978.

Gorn, Michael H. *Harnessing the Genie: Science and Technology Forecasting for the Air Force, 1944–1986.* Washington, D.C.: Office of Air Force History, 1986.

———. *Vulcan's Forge: The Making of an Air Force Command for Weapons Acquisition, 1950–1985.* 4th pr., vol. 1. Andrews Air Force Base, Md.: Office of History, Air Force Systems Command, 1989.

Green, Constance McLaughlin, Harry C. Thomson, and Peter C. Roots. *The Ordnance Department: Planning Munitions for War.* In *United States Army in World War II, The Technical Services.* Washington, D.C.; Office of the Chief of Military History, 1955.

Hewes, James E. *From Root to McNamara: Army Organization and Administration, 1900–1963.* Washington, D.C.: U.S. Army Center of Military History, 1975.

A History of the Army Research Laboratory. Adelphi, Md.: Army Research Laboratory, August 2003.

A History of the Department of Defense Federally Funded Research and Development Centers. Washington, D.C.: Office of Technology Assessment, June 1995.

A History of Rock Island and Rock Island Arsenal from Earliest Times to 1954. Vol. 3 (1940–1954). Rock Island, Ill.: Rock Island Arsenal, 1965.

A History of Watervliet Arsenal, 1813 to Modernization 1982. Watervliet, N.Y.: Watervliet Arsenal, 1982.

Holley, Irving Brinton, Jr. *Buying Aircraft: Materiel Procurement for the Army Air Forces.* In *United States Army in World War II, Special Studies.* Washington, D.C.: Office of the Chief of Military History, 1964.

Johnson, Neil M., and Leonard C. Weston. *Development and Production of Rocket Launchers at Rock Island Arsenal, 1945–1959.* Rock Island, Ill.: U.S. Army Weapons Command, 1962.

Johnson, Stephen B. *The United States Air Force and the Culture of Innovation, 1945–1965.* Washington, D.C.: Air Force History and Museum Program, 2002.

Jones, Vincent C. "Manhattan: The Army and the Atomic Bomb." In *United States Army in World War II, Special Studies.* Washington, D.C.: U.S. Army Center of Military History, 1985.

Komons, Nick A. *Science and the Air Force: A History of the Air Force Office of Scientific Research.* Arlington, Va.: Historical Division, Office of Information, Office of Aerospace Research, 1966.

Maurer, Maurer. *Aviation in the U.S. Army, 1919–1939.* Washington, D.C.: Office of Air Force History, 1987.

McCollum, Kenneth G., ed. *Dahlgren.* Dahlgren, Va.: Naval Surface Weapons Center, 1977.

Nalty, Bernard C. ed. *Winged Shield, Winged Sword: A History of the United States Air Force.* Vol. 1. Washington, D.C.: Air Force History and Museums Program, 1997.

Passaglia, Elio, with Karma A. Beal. *A Unique Institution: The National Bureau of Standards, 1950–1969.* Washington, D.C.: U.S. Department of Commerce, 1999.

Raines, Edgar F., Jr. *Eyes of Artillery: The Origins of Modern U.S. Army Aviation in World War II.* Washington, D.C.: U.S. Army Center of Military History, 2000.

Roland, Alex. *Model Research: The National Advisory Committee for Aeronautics, 1915–1958.* 2 vols. Washington, D.C.: National Aeronautics and Space Administration, 1985.

Rowland, Buford, and William D. Boyd. *U.S. Navy Bureau of Ordnance in World War II.* Washington, D.C.: Bureau of Ordnance, 1953.

Schooley, James F. *Responding to National Needs: The National Bureau of Standards Becomes the National Institute of Standards and Technology, 1969–1993.* Washington, D.C.: U.S. Department of Commerce, 2000.

Shiman, Philip. *Forging the Sword: Defense Production During the Cold War* Champaign, Ill.: Construction Engineering Research Laboratories, U.S. Army Corps of Engineers, July 1997.

———. "Defense Acquisition in an Uncertain World: The Post–Cold War Era, 1990–2000." In *Providing the Means of War: Historical Perspectives on Defense Acquisition, 1945–2000*, edited by Shannon A. Brown. Washington, D.C.: U.S. Army Center of Military History and Industrial College of the Armed Forces, 2005.

Slaton, Amy E. "Aeronautical Engineering at Wright-Patterson Air Force Base: A Historical Overview." In *The Engineering of Flight: Aeronautical Engineering Facilities of Area B, Wright-Patterson Air Force Base, Ohio*, edited by Emma J. H. Dyson, Dean A. Herrin, and Amy E. Slaton. Washington, D.C.: HABS/HAER, National Park Service, 1993.

Smaldone, Joseph P. *History of the White Oak Laboratory, 1945–1975*. White Oak, Md.: Naval Surface Weapons Center, 1977.

Smith, R. Elberton. *The Army and Economic Mobilization*. In *United States Army in World War II, The War Department*. Washington, D.C.: Office of the Chief of Military History, 1959.

Splendid Vision, Unswerving Purpose: Developing Air Power for the United States Air Force During the First Century of Powered Flight. Wright-Patterson Air Force Base, Oh.: Air Force History and Museums Program, 2002.

Strum, Ron. *Sidewinder: Creative Missile Development at China Lake*. Annapolis, Md.: Naval Institute Press, 1999.

Sturm, Thomas A. *The USAF Scientific Advisory Board: Its First Twenty Years, 1944–1964*. Repr. ed. Washington, D.C.: Office of Air Force History, 1986.

Thompson, George Raynor, and Dixie R. Harris. *The Signal Corps: The Outcome*. In *United States Army in World War II, The Technical Services*. Washington, D.C.: Office of the Chief of Military History, 1966.

Thompson, George Raynor, et al. *The Signal Corps: The Test*. In *United States Army in World War II, The Technical Services*. Washington, D.C.: Office of the Chief of Military History, 1957.

Thomson, Harry C., and Lida Mayo. *The Ordnance Department: Procurement and Supply*. In *United States Army in World War II, The Technical Services*. Washington, D.C.: Office of the Chief of Military History, 1960.

Trask, Roger R., and Alfred Goldberg. *The Department of Defense, 1947–1997: Organization and Leaders*. Washington, D.C.: Historical Office, Office of the Secretary of Defense, 1997.

Trimble, William F. *Wings for the Navy: A History of the Naval Aircraft Factory, 1917–1956*. Annapolis, Md.: Naval Institute Press, 1990.

Weart, Spencer R. "The Physics Business in America, 1919–1940: A Statistical Reconnaissance." In *The Sciences in the American Context: New Perspectives*, edited by Nathan Reingold. Washington, D.C.: Smithsonian Institution Press, 1979.

Weinert, Richard P., Jr. *A History of Army Aviation, 1950–1962*. Fort Monroe, Va.: Office of the Command Historian, U.S. Army Training and Doctrine Command, 1991.

Weitze, Karen J. *Command Lineage, Scientific Achievement, and Major Tenant Missions*. Vol. 1 of *Keeping the Edge: Air Force Materiel Command Cold War Context, 1945–1991*. Wright-Patterson Air Force Base, Ohio: Headquarters, Air Force Materiel Command, August 2003.

————. *Installations and Facilities*. Vol. 2 of *Keeping the Edge: Air Force Materiel Command Cold War Context, 1945–1991*. Wright-Patterson Air Force Base, Ohio: Headquarters, Air Force Materiel Command, August 2003.

Theses and Dissertations

Asner, Glenn Ross. "The Cold War and American Industrial Research." Ph.D. diss., Carnegie Mellon University, 2006.
Baucom, Donald R. "Air Force Images of Research and Development and Their Reflections in Organizational Structures and Management Policies." Ph.D. diss., University of Oklahoma, 1976.
Cheng, Christopher C. S. "United States Army Aviation and the Air Mobility Innovation, 1942–1965." Ph.D. diss., University of London, 1992.
Cornell, Thomas D. "Merle Tuve and His Program of Nuclear Studies at the Department of Terrestrial Magnetism: The Early Career of a Modern American Physicist." Ph.D. diss., Johns Hopkins University, 1986.
Lassman, Thomas C. "From Quantum Revolution to Institutional Transformation: Edward U. Condon and the Dynamics of Pure Science in America, 1925–1951." Ph.D. diss., Johns Hopkins University Press, 2000.
Lonnquest, John Clayton. "The Face of Atlas: General Bernard Schriever and the Development of the Atlas Intercontinental Ballistic Missile, 1953–1960." Ph.D. diss., Duke University, 1996.
Neushul, Peter. "Science, Technology, and the Arsenal of Democracy: Production Research and Development During World War II." Ph.D. diss., University of California, Santa Barbara, 1993.
Sigethy, Robert. "The Air Force Organization for Basic Research, 1945–1970: A Study in Change." Ph.D. diss., American University, 1980.

Articles from Military and Industry Trade Journals and News and Business Periodicals

"$172 Million for Electronics." *Aviation Week* 50 (13 June 1949): 34.
"Aerial Warfare Reshapes Rome's Task." *Aviation Week* 66 (3 June 1957): 110.
"AFAC Sharpens Air Force Armament." *Aviation Week* 66 (3 June 1957): 99.
"AFOSR Focuses on Pertinent Research." *Aviation Week and Space Technology* 101 (15 July 1974): 142–51.
"Air Force Labs Concentrate on SDI Research." *Aviation Week and Space Technology* 127 (2 November, 1987): 50.
"Air Force Systems Command." *Air Force Magazine* 73 (May 1990): 66–67.
"Air Force Systems Command Accelerates R&D Efforts." *Aviation Week and Space Technology* 122 (22 April 1985): 67.
Allen, L. "Science Remains Key to Air Supremacy." *Aviation Week and Space Technology* 146 (16 April 1997): 58–60.
"AMRA Goal: New Materials to Transform Ideas into Materiel." *Army Research and Development New Magazine* 6 (September 1965): 32–35.

Anderton, D. A. "AF Reveals Plans for Engineering Center." *Aviation Week* 55 (2 July, 1951): 13–14.

———. "Patrick Prepares for Ballistic Missiles." *Aviation Week* 65 (6 August, 1956): 106–16.

"ARDC Consolidates Research Management." *Aviation Week* 69 (20 October, 1958): 37.

"ARDC Molds U.S. Air Development." *Aviation Week* 59 (17 August, 1953): 73–81.

"ARDC Trades Secrets for Progress." *Aviation Week Buyer's Guide* 63 (Mid-December 1955): 10–13.

"Army Puts Research, Development on Top General Staff Level." *Iron Age* 158 (3 October, 1946): 95–96.

"Army Research Office." *Science* 128 (19 September, 1958): 645–46.

"Army Reveals Plans to Industry." *Chemical and Engineering News* 25 (3 February 1947): 306.

"Arnold Validates Systems Early in Design." *Aviation Week and Space Technology* 75 (25 September, 1961): 221–29.

"ARO Coaching Army Research." *Chemical and Engineering News* 36 (15 September, 1958): 38–39.

"ATSC Review and Long-Range Air-Research Program." *Aeronautical Engineering Review* 5 (February 1946): 73.

Aurand, H. S. "The Army's Research Program." *Mechanical Engineering* 68 (September 1946): 785–86, 833.

"Avionics in the Air Force." *Aviation Week* 59 (17 August, 1953): 249.

"Avionics Team Spends Half a Billion Dollars." *Aviation Week* 59 (17 August, 1953): 262–70.

Barclay, H. W. "General Motors Defense Research Laboratories." *Automotive Industries* 127 (1 December, 1962): 43–46.

Barnes, G. M. "Research Needs for Weapons." *Mechanical Engineering* 68 (March 1946): 196–98, 211.

Batezel, A. L. "Best Kept Secrets." *Airman* 26 (April 1982): 43–48.

Bayer, W. L. "The Signal Corps Aircraft Radio Laboratory." *Journal of Applied Physics* 16 (April 1945): 248–50.

Beller, W. "Army Research and Development in Missiles, Aviation, and Avionics." *Aero Digest* 73 (October 1956): 22–25.

Bennett, R. D. "Wartime History of the Naval Ordnance Laboratory." *Review of Scientific Instruments* 17 (August 1946): 293–96.

Bond, D. F. "Air Force to Reduce Research Overhead with Mergers, Creation of Four 'Superlabs.'" *Aviation Week and Space Technology* 133 (3 December, 1990): 68–70.

Bonvillian, C. A. "Naval Boiler and Turbine Laboratory." *Journal of Applied Physics* 15 (March 1944): 236–39.

Brett, G. H. "Materiel Division of the U.S. Army Air Corps," *Aero Digest* 35 (August 1939): 47–51, 157.

Butz, J. S., Jr. "United Has Proved Value of Research." *Aviation Week* 66 (3 June 1957): 200–13.

———. "Stever Proposes ARDC Reorganization." *Aviation Week* 69 (21 July 1958): 23–25.

"Cambridge Advances Art of Air War." *Aviation Week* 66 (3 June 1957): 105.

Canan, J. W. "The Labs Move into the Mainstream." *Air Force Magazine* 67 (April 1984): 55–59.

"Canaveral Supports Space Exploration." *Aviation Week* 68 (16 June 1958): 187–95.

Carroll, F. O. "Research and Development at Wright Field." *Journal of Applied Physics* 16 (April 1945): 199–202.

Case, R. W. "Manufacturing Preparedness at Watertown Arsenal." *Machinery* 46 (March 1940): 99–101.

"Center Tests USAF Armament Systems." *Aviation Week* 59 (17 August, 1953): 210–26.

Chadwell, P. A. "DOD and Service R&D Programs." *National Defense* 66 (October 1981): 44–47.

"Chance Vought Stakes Its Future on Research Push." *Business Week*, 23 July 1960, 104–8.

Chidlaw, B. W. "New Weapons for Air Supremacy." *Aero Digest* 57 (September 1948): 50–53.

"China Lake: Navy in the Desert Is Guided Missile Laboratory." *All Hands*, no. 469 (March 1956): 60–63.

Christian, G. L. "NATTS Is World's Top Jet Test Facility." *Aviation Week* 66 (3 June 1957): 161–73.

Clark, E. "Martin's Research Is Broad, Varied." *Aviation Week* 66 (3 June 1957): 252–65.

Coates, L. D. "Chief of Naval Research Details Program." *Data* 8 (September 1963): 7–16.

Coughlin, W. "Flight Test Center Probes Aviation's Supersonic Frontiers." *Aviation Week* 59 (17 August 1953): 118–44.

Covault, C. "New USAF Division to Stress Research." *Aviation Week and Space Technology* 112 (23 June 1980): 47–53.

Craigie, L. C. "Research and the Army Air Forces." *Aeronautical Engineering Review* 4 (October 1945): 7–11, 37.

———. "AAF Plans for Engineering and Research." *S. A. E. Journal* 55 (March 1947): 19–22, 52.

Culbertson, A. T. "Scheduling Electronic Invention." *Astronautics and Aeronautics* 4 (March 1966): 42–44.

Denfield, L. E. "Research Activities of the Bureau of Naval Personnel," *Journal of Applied Physics* 15 (March 1944): 289–90.

Dittmar, R. B. "Development of Physical Facilities for Research." *Proceedings of the Institute of Radio Engineers* 37 (April 1949): 423–26.

Dobert, M. "Home of the Impossible." *Flying* 40 (March 1947): 32–34, 98.

"DoD Announces Frankford Arsenal Closing, AMC Depot System Realignment." *Army Research and Development News Magazine* 16 (January-February 1975): 4.

Drewry, I. O. "Atomic Applications Laboratory: Newest Addition to Picatinny Arsenal." *Sperryscope* 14, no. 5 (1957): 20–23.

————."Army Ordnance Tackles Task of Marrying Atomics with Artillery." *Army Information Digest* 13 (December 1958): 12–17.

"Edwards Evaluates Weapons Systems." *Aviation Week* 66 (3 June 1957): 117–19.

"Edwards Rocket Base to Test Captive Ballistic Missile Powerplants." *Aviation Week* 65 (6 August 1956): 143–45.

"Electronic Technology Aims Changed." *Aviation Week and Space Technology* 110 (29 January 1979): 221–24.

Elson, B. M. "USAF Weapons Lab Mission Expanded." *Aviation Week and Space Technology* 110 (29 January 1979): 212–15.

Elwers, G. "Ordnance Using X-Rays to Inspect Complex Assemblies." *Iron Age* 168 (25 October, 1951): 95–99.

Engel, L. H. "U.S. Air Center Speeds Research," *Science News Letter* 36 (8 July, 1939): 26–28.

"The Far-Flung Navy Research Network." *Missiles and Rockets* 10 (1 January, 1962): 16–17.

"Federal Labs Lose Key Men." *Chemical and Engineering News* 37 (11 May 1959): 42–43.

Fink, D. E. "Minuteman Experience Aiding MX." *Aviation Week and Space Technology* 105 (19 July 1976): 113–20.

Fletcher, L. S. "Research at a Government Arsenal in Cooperation with Universities." *Journal of Engineering Education* 33 (June 1943): 781–93.

Flood, W. A. "The Army Research Office." *IEEE Antennas and Propagation Magazine* 33 (February 1991): 17.

"For the Technical Superiority of Our Weapons." *Aero Digest* 45 (1 June 1944): 51–55.

Furer, J. A. "Research in the Navy." *Journal of Applied Physics* 15 (March 1944): 209–13.

Gardner, J. H. "Aircraft Radio Labs." *Radio News* 27 (February 1942): 8–9, 56.

Gentry, G. C. "Aircraft Armament." *Journal of Applied Physics* 16 (December 1945): 771–73.

"Geophysics Laboratory Stressing Development." *Aviation Week and Space Technology* 110 (29 January 1979): 231–33.

Gibbs, R. G. "Chemistry Division of New Air Force Research and Development Command Will Emphasize Basic Research." *Chemical and Engineering News* 30 (3 March, 1952): 854–55.

Gillmore, W. E. "Work of the Materiel Division of the Army Air Corps." *S. A. E. Journal* 25 (September 1929): 233–39.

Gillon, P. N. "Army Ordnance Research." *Army, Navy, Air Force Journal* 92 (20 November, 1954): 337, 339.

Greenall, C. H. "Non-Ferrous Metallurgical Research at Frankford Arsenal." *Journal of Applied Physics* 16 (December 1945): 787–92.

Gude, W. G. "Foundry Research at Watertown Arsenal." *Foundry* 73 (December 1945): 104–06, 186–88.

Hammill, J. P. "Research in Ballistics." *Ordnance* 44 (September-October 1959): 235–8.

Hammond, P. H. "The U.S. Navy Radio and Sound Laboratory." *Journal of Applied Physics* 15 (March 1944): 240–42.

Hartmann, G. K. "Naval Ordnance Laboratory: From Concept to Hardware." *Defense Industry Bulletin* 6 (December 1970): 9–12, 29.

Harwood, J. J. "Metallurgy Research Program of the Office of Naval Research." *Journal of Metals* 9 (May 1957): 673.

———. "Some Aspects of Government-Sponsored Research in Metallurgy." *Journal of Metals* 9 (May 1957): 665–70.

Hawkes, R. "Convair Seeks Lead Through Research." *Aviation Week* 66 (3 June, 1957): 215–30.

Haywood, O. G., Jr. "The Air Research and Development Program." *Journal of Engineering Education* 43 (March 1953): 373–77.

Hedrick, D. I. "Research and Experimental Activities of the U.S. Naval Proving Ground." *Journal of Applied Physics* 15 (March 1944): 262–69.

Hinrichs, J. H. "Army Ordnance Arsenals." *Ordnance* 43 (September-October 1958): 210–11.

Hodges, W. D. "New Role for Aberdeen." *Ordnance* 56 (September-October 1971): 132–35.

"Holloman Tests Missiles and Pilotless Aircraft." *Aviation Week* 59 (17 August 1953): 186–209.

Hoppock, D. W. "How Army Ordnance Develops Weapons for Its 'Customers.'" *Product Engineering* 16 (June 1945): 361–66.

Hotz, R. "Center Mates Planes to Atom Weapons." *Aviation Week* 59 (17 August 1953): 91–97.

———. "USAF Expands Basic Research Program." *Aviation Week* 63 (18 July 1955): 12–13.

———. "Kirtland Gives USAF Nuclear Delivery." *Aviation Week* 65 (6 August 1956): 151–65.

"How ARDC 'Buys' Scientific Ideas." *Aviation Week* 66 (3 June 1957): 358.

Howard, H. S. "The David Taylor Model Basin." *Journal of Applied Physics* 15 (March 1944): 227–35.

"Industry-Military Link Forged." *Business Week* (16 November 1946) 20–26.

Ingram, H. A. "Research in the Bureau of Ships." *Journal of Applied Physics* 15 (March 1944): 215–20.

"Keeping Federal Labs Staffed." *Chemical and Engineering News* 11 (11 November 1957): 42–46.

Kerst, D. W. "Historical Development of the Betatron," *Nature* 157 (26 January 1946): 90–95.

Klass, P. J. "Rome Guides AF Avionics Development." *Aviation Week* 59 (17 August 1953): 251–70.

———. "Bell Advances Avionics on Wide Front." *Aviation Week* 66 (3 June 1957): 235–51.

———. "Major Reorganization Designed to Broaden WADD Capabilities." *Aviation Week and Space Technology* 72 (9 May 1960): 27.

———. "WADD Avionics Division Aims at Space." *Aviation Week and Space Technology* 73 (1 August 1960): 72–74.

————."Avionics Lab Expanding Applications." *Aviation Week and Space Technology* 101 (15 July 1974): 206–15.

Klinker, L. G. "Metallurgical R&D in the Army," *Journal of Metals* 13 (February 1961): 129–31.

Kosting, P. R. "Metallurgy Research Program of the U.S. Army Office of Ordnance Research." *Journal of Metals* 9 (May 1957): 664.

Kozaryn, L. D. "Watervliet Arsenal: Birthplace of the Army's Big Guns." *Soldiers* 36 (February 1981): 40–44.

Kranzfelder, E. "Naval Boiler and Turbine Laboratory." *Marine Engineering and Shipping Review* 52 (June 1947): 66–75.

Kresge, M. W. "Research and Development, Military Explosives and Propellants." *Journal of Applied Physics* 16 (December 1945): 792–97.

Kurie, F. N. D., and G. P. Harnwell. "The Wartime Activities of the San Diego Laboratory of the University of California Division of War Research." *Review of Scientific Instruments* 18 (April 1947): 207–18.

Leggin, A. "Army Air Forces Research and Development." *Chemical and Engineering News* 24 (10 November 1946): 2914–15.

————. "Ordnance Department Research and Development." *Chemical and Engineering News* 24 (25 December 1946): 3350–51.

Lewis, C. "ARDC Shifts Project Authority to Four New Operating Divisions." *Aviation Week and Space Technology* 71 (12 October 1959): 33–34.

Loring, B. M. "Nonferrous Foundry Research at the Naval Research Laboratory." *Foundry* 74 (February 1946): 98–101, 247–49.

Luellig, P. P., Jr. "Arsenals." *Field Artillery Journal* 42 (March-April 1974): 50–53, 59.

Lynch, W. J. "Combat Superiority Aim of Army Research Program." *Defense Industry Bulletin* 5 (July 1969): 13–18.

Maggio, C. S. "Since 1813, Watervliet Arsenal Has Pioneered the Logistics of Cannon Manufacture." *Army Logistician* 5 (September-October 1973): 18–23.

Mason, H. C. "Navy Electronics Lab Serves BuShips." *Data* 8 (September 1963): 54–59.

————."Navy's Electronics Laboratory." *Sperryscope* 16, no. 6, (1963): 10–14.

"Materials Lab Focuses on Top Priorities." *Aviation Week and Space Technology* 101 (15 July 1974): 235–38.

"Materiel Development and Readiness Command Replaces AMC." *Army Research and Development New Magazine* 17 (January-February 1976): 4–5.

Matthews, N. A. "Ferrous Metallurgical Research." *Journal of Applied Physics* 16 (December 1945): 780–87.

McLarren, R. "Largest Aero Research Program." *Aviation Week* 48 (23 February 1948): 42–48.

McSurely, A. "Wright Field Tests New Air Weapons." *Aviation News* 1 (20 March 1944): 11–12.

————. "AF Planning Huge New Research Center." *Aviation Week* 51 (21 November 1949): 11–12.

————. "WADC: $200-Million Research Key." *Aviation Week* 59 (17 August 1953): 99–116.

Meader, J. W. "The Naval Air Material Center, Philadelphia, Pennsylvania." *Journal of Applied Physics* 15 (March 1944): 273–77.

"Metallurgical Activities at Aberdeen Proving Ground," *Metal Progress* 59 (April 1951): 499–502.

Miller, B. "Solid State Electronics Trend Goes On in Plant and Laboratory." *Aviation Week and Space Technology* 72 (7 March 1960): 237–43.

"Missile Center Expands for Long-Range Flights." *Aviation Week* 59 (17 August 1953): 170–84.

"Mobilization of Scientific Resources—IV, the U.S. Navy." *Journal of Applied Physics* 14 (March 1944): 203–8.

Mordoff, K. F. "China Lake Facilities Dedicated to Diverse Weapons Tasks." *Aviation Week and Space Technology* 124 (20 January 1986): 49–56.

Moses, W. M. "Research in the Bureau of Ordnance," *Journal of Applied Physics* 15 (March 1944): 249–54.

"Munitions: A Permanent U.S. Industry." *Business Week* (27 September 1952): 27–28.

Murphy, D. J. "Metallurgical Activities at Frankford Arsenal." *Metal Progress* 62 (August 1952): 67–72.

Muzzey, D. S. "How the Project Manager System Works at the Naval Ordnance Lab." *Armed Forces Management* 4 (August 1958): 29–32.

"The Naval Research Laboratory, White Oak, Maryland." *Science* 104 (13 September 1946): 237–38.

"Naval Weapons Center." *Sea Technology* 30 (November 1989): 66.

"Navy Believes Cost of R&D Can Be Cut." *Aviation Week* 66 (3 June 1957): 131–137.

"Navy Dedicates New Research Laboratory at Inyokern, Calif." *Civil Engineering* 18 (June 1948): 44–45, 88, 92.

"Navy Establishes R&D Center." *Journal of the Armed Forces* 104 (8 April 1967): 2.

"Navy Research Helps Industrial Progress." *Business Week* (30 October 1948) 48–56.

"New ARDC Divisions Formed." *Aviation Week and Space Technology* 71 (21 December 1959): 21.

"A New Command Is Born." *Flying* 48 (May 1951): 87.

"New Group Coordinates Lab Activities." *Aviation Week and Space Technology* 105 (19 July 1976): 171–73.

"New Lab Geared to Support of Divisions." *Aviation Week and Space Technology* 105 (19 July 1976): 215–17.

"New Organization Planned to Stabilize Arms R&D, Funding." *Aerospace Technology* 21 (25 March 1968): 98–99.

"New Plasma Lab." *Missiles and Rockets* 9 (13 November 1961): 28.

Newton, G. W. "AEDC Provides Huge Jet Engine Test Facility." *S. A. E. Journal* 62 (July 1954): 28–32.

"NOL—Where the Arctic and Equator Meet." *All Hands*, no. 437 (July 1953): 12–15.

"Non-Nuclear Research Under Way at USAF Laboratory." *Aviation Week and Space Technology* 123 (2 December 1985): 161–68.

North, D. M. "Navy Center Expands Mission to Include Technology Management." *Aviation Week and Space Technology* 124 (20 January 1986): 46–48.

"NOTS Converts Ideas into Missiles." *Aviation Week* 66 (3 June 1957): 148–58.

"OAR Upgraded, Up-Funded for Research." *Missiles and Rockets* 10 (26 March 1962): 122–23, 141.

"ONR Guides Navy Contract Research." *Aviation Week* 66 (3 June 1957): 351.

"Ordnance Research Laboratories at the Pennsylvania State College." *Science* 102 (3 August 1945): 112.

"Ordnance Research Program." *Army, Navy, Air Force Journal* 88 (16 June 1951): 1165.

"Ordnance Test Facilities Greatly Expanded at NOL." *Product Engineering* 21 (April 1950): 152.

"OSR Given Single Manager Role for All AFSC Basic Research." *Aviation Week and Space Technology* 105 (19 July 1976): 226–29.

"OSR: Keystone of Basic Research." *Aviation Week* 59 (17 August 1953): 87–88.

"Patrick Tests Air Force, Army Missiles." *Aviation Week* 66 (3 June 1957): 97.

"The Pentagon's Top Hands." *Business Week* (20 September 1958): 39.

Pletcher, F. B. "Aberdeen Proving Ground." *Iron Trade Review* 73 (18 October 1923): 1091–96.

Power, T. S. "The Air Research and Development Team." *Aeronautical Engineering Review* 14 (April 1955): 40–42, 47.

Poynter, J. W. "Metallurgy Research Program of the Aeronautical Research Laboratory." *Journal of Metals* 9 (May 1957): 675–76.

"Progress Proves ARDC's Mission Vital." *Aviation Week* 65 (6 August 1956): 76–79.

"Propulsion Lab Refines Engine Designs." *Aviation Week and Space Technology* 101 (15 July 1974): 247–48.

Pugh, C. "On Discovery's Threshold." *Airman* 26 (January 1982): 29–35.

———. "Riding the Winds of Change." *Airman* 27 (October 1983): 20–25.

Putt, D. L. "Air Force Research and Development." *Aeronautical Engineering Review* 9 (March 1950): 41–43.

"R&D Centers/Laboratories." *Armed Forces Journal* 106 (17 May 1969): 30–31.

"R&D Command: New AF Group at Dayton Indicates Greater Stress on Basic Research." *Aviation Week* 53 (6 November 1950): 14–15.

"R&D Pattern Taking Form." *Aviation Week* 54 (7 May 1951): 13.

Rabb, C. "Air Force Labs Work to Make Today's Innovations Tomorrow's Routine." *Defense Electronics* 18 (September 1986): 95–100.

"Research at Aeronautical Systems Division Points to Airborne AI." *Defense Science and Electronics* 6 (February 1987): 30–34.

"Research Lab Studies Air Force Needs." *Aviation Week and Space Technology* 101 (15 July 1974): 249–54.

Robinson, A. I. "Basic Research in the Air Force: A Tale of Two Laboratories." *Science* 189 (12 September 1975): 862–65.

"Rocket Lab Focuses on Advance Needs." *Aviation Week and Space Technology* 101 (15 July 1974): 94–97.

"Rockets at Picatinny Arsenal." *Jet Propulsion* 26 (February 1956): 114.

"Rome Air Development Center Deactivated in USAF Cutbacks." *Aviation Week and Space Technology* 101 (2 December 1974): 26.

"Rome Air Development Center Focuses on Expert Systems Applications for C^3, Natural Speech Technology." *Aviation Week and Space Technology* 122 (22 April 1985): 84.

"Rome Develops New Relations with ESD." *Aviation Week and Space Technology* 105 (19 July 1976): 203–13.

"Rome Expands Role of Ground Avionics." *Aviation Week* 59 (17 August 1953): 274–315.

Sawyer, F. G. "Rocket Chemistry at Inyokern," *Chemical and Engineering News* 27 (18 July 1949): 2067–69.

Sawyer, R. H. "Portrait of an Arsenal." *Army Logistician* 7 (January-February 1975): 25–27.

Scanlon, W. E., and G. Lieberman. "Naval Ordnance and Electronics Research." *Proceedings of the IRE* 47 (May 1959): 910–20.

Schindler, W. G. "Research Activities of the Naval Ordnance Laboratory." *Journal of Applied Physics* 15 (March 1944): 255–61.

"Science Dons a Uniform." *Business Week* (14 September 1946): 19–24.

Smith, H. W. "Research in the Bureau of Medicine and Surgery of the U.S. Navy." *Journal of Applied Physics* 15 (March 1944): 279–88.

Smythe, A. M. "The 25 Biggest Defense Suppliers: Part One." *Magazine of Wall Street* 99 (29 September 1956): 12–14, 51–52.

———. "The 25 Biggest Defense Suppliers: Part Two." *Magazine of Wall Street* 99 (13 October 1956): 65–67, 100.

"Some Recent Advances in Ballistics." *Journal of Applied Physics* 16 (December 1945): 773–80.

Spangenberg, K. R., and W. E. Greene. "Basic Research Projects under ONR Contracts." *Electronics* 22 (June 1949): 66–69.

"Springfield Museum, Institute Replace Armory After Phaseout." *Army Research and Development News Magazine* 9 (June 1968): 5.

Stevens, L. C. "Research in the Bureau of Aeronautics." *Journal of Applied Physics* 15 (March 1944): 271–72.

Stone, I. "Cambridge's Bailiwick: Earth, Sky, and Sea." *Aviation Week* 59 (17 August 1953): 229–42.

———. "Holloman Evaluates Missile Systems." *Aviation Week* 65 (6 August 1956): 123–38.

———. "Air Test Center Speeds Navy's Missiles to Fleet Use," *Aviation Week* 66 (3 June 1957): 140–5.

———. "Caltech Eases Transfer of Air Research Burden." *Aviation Week* 66 (3 June 1957): 277–89.

Surba, C. F., and D. Ballou. "Armament Division at Eglin AFB." *National Defense* 71 (July-August 1986): 47–52.

"Systems Command Given New Functions." *Aviation Week and Space Technology* 75 (25 September 1961): 71–80.

"Technical Developments in Ordnance Department." *American Machinist* 55 (22 December 1921): 1022a.

"Test Facility to Boost Arnold Capability." *Aviation Week and Space Technology* 110 (29 January 1979): 203–4.

Tisdale, W. M. D. "It's Always Tomorrow." *Army Information Digest* 15 (December 1960): 28–31.

Trainor, J. "Arnold Center Tests All Big Systems." *Missiles and Rockets* 9 (14 August 1961): 31–34.

Tschappat, W. H. "The Manufacturing Arsenals and Their Equipment." *American Machinist* 78 (14 February 1934): 141–44.

Ulsamer, E. "The Steady Evolution of Armaments." *Air Force Magazine* 68 (December 1985): 72–81.

"USAF Sifts Advanced Research Concepts." *Aviation Week and Space Technology* 75 (25 September 1961): 82–86.

"USAF Urges Aircraft Industry to Use Own Funds for Research." *Aviation Week* 63 (5 September 1955): 14–15.

"U.S. Army Research Office Schedules Move to New Location in June." *Army Research and Development News Magazine* 3 (May 1962): 18.

Van Keuren, A. H. "The U.S. Naval Research Laboratory." *Journal of Applied Physics* 15 (March 1944): 221–26.

Viccello, H., Jr. "The Past, Present, and Future of AFMC." *Aviation Week and Space Technology* 146 (16 April 1997): 37–41.

"WADD Reorganizes for Increased Capabilities." *Aviation Week and Space Technology* 72 (23 May 1960): 95.

Wagner, W. C. "Navy Yard Laboratories, Bureau of Ships." *Journal of Applied Physics* 15 (March 1944): 243–48.

Walker, E. A. "Ordnance Research Laboratory." *Journal of Applied Physics* 18 (March 1947): 263–67.

Wanstall, B. "USAF Doubles Engine-Test Capability: $625 Million Boost for Arnold Facility." *Interavia* 40 (February 1985): 138–41.

"War Department Research and Development Division." *Science* 104 (18 October 1946): 369.

Warner, W. W. "Arsenals in Action." *Army Information Digest* 6 (September 1951): 39–44.

"Watertown Arsenal Slated for Elimination in DoD Move." *Army Research and Development News Magazine* 5 (June 1964): 20.

"Watervliet Arsenal Improves Laboratory Facilities. *Army Research and Development News Magazine* 10 (March 1969): 19.

"WDD Directs ICBM, IRBM Development." *Aviation Week* 65 (6 August 1956): 101–5.

"Weapon Center," *Business Week* (30 April 1949): 26–28.

"Weapon System Capabilities Explored." *Aviation Week and Space Technology* 110 (29 January 1979): 186–89.

"Weapon System Plan Spurs Development." *Aviation Week* 59 (17 August 1953): 82–86.

"Weapons Lab Plays Key Nuclear Role." *Aviation Week and Space Technology* 101 (15 July 1974): 287–89.

"Weapons Laboratory Aids Beam Effort." *Aviation Week and Space Technology* 113 (4 August 1980): 56–59.

Werngren, M. S. "Skills Spell Strength." *Army Information Digest* 17 (September 1962): 60–62.

Wesson, C. M. "Adequate National Defense Requires Modernized Army Arsenals." *Machinery* 45 (July 1939): 735–37.

Wetmore, W. C. "Flight Laboratory Pushes Joint Projects." *Aviation Week and Space Technology* 101 (15 July 1974): 134–41.

Witze, C. "Speed R&D, USAF Orders Industry." *Aviation Week* 63 (22 August 1955): 12–13.

———. "Industry Role in New Weapons Increased." *Aviation Week* 65 (6 August 1956): 86–91.

"Wright Laboratories Broadens Advanced Technology Initiatives." *Aviation Week and Space Technology* 122 (22 April 1985): 77–84.

"X-Ray in an Arsenal." *American Machinist* 84 (13 November 1940): 930–31.

Yaffee, M. L. "AEDC Facilities Busy, Despite Cuts." *Aviation Week and Space Technology* 94 (26 April 1971): 36–44.

———. "Materials Lab Gears to Meet User Needs." *Aviation Week and Space Technology* 105 (19 July 1976): 177–80.

Yost, C. F. "Metallurgy Program of the Air Force Office of Scientific Research." *Journal of Metals* 9 (May 1957): 671.

Yost, C. F., and E. C. Vicars. "Interdisciplinary Laboratory Program in Materials Science." *Journal of Metals* 14 (September 1962): 666–70.

Young, D. B. "Integrated Research." *Ordnance* 40 (July-August 1955): 54–56.

Young, W. B. "Research in the Bureau of Supplies and Accounts." *Journal of Applied Physics* 15 (March 1944): 278.

Articles, Book Chapters, and Monographs

Ahern, Joseph-James. "We Had the Hose Turned on Us!: Ross Gunn and the Naval Research Laboratory's Early Research into Nuclear Propulsion, 1939–1946." *Historical Studies in the Physical and Biological Sciences* 33 (2003): 217–36.

Allen, Matthew. *Military Helicopter Doctrines of the Major Powers, 1945–1992: Making Decisions about Air-Land Warfare.* Westport, Conn.: Greenwood Press, 1993.

Allison, David K. "U.S. Navy Research and Development Since World War II." In *Military Enterprise and Technological Change: Perspectives on the American Experience,* edited by Merritt Roe Smith. Cambridge, Mass.: MIT Press, 1985.

Asner, Glen R. "The Linear Model, the U.S. Department of Defense, and the Golden Age of Industrial Research." In *The Science-Industry Nexus: History, Policy, Implications*, edited by Karl Grandin, Nina Wormbs, and Sven Widmalm. Sagamore Beach, Mass.: Science History Publications, 2004.

Bassett, Ross Knox. *To the Digital Age: Research Labs, Start-Up Companies, and the Rise of MOS Technology*. Baltimore: Johns Hopkins University Press, 2002.

Bawden, Harry E., ed. *The Achievement of Rock Island Arsenal in World War II*. Davenport, Ia.: Bawden Brothers, 1948.

Bergerson, Frederic A. *The Army Gets an Air Force: Tactics of Insurgent Bureaucratic Politics*. Baltimore: Johns Hopkins University Press, 1980.

Blake, Bernard, ed. *Jane's Weapons Systems, 1987–88*. 18th ed. London: Jane's Publishing, 1987.

Brinkley, Alan. *The End of Reform: New Deal Liberalism in Recession and War*. New York: Alfred A. Knopf, 1995.

Brown, Louis. *A Radar History of World War II: Technical and Military Imperatives*. London: Taylor and Francis, 1999.

Brown, Michael E. *Flying Blind: The Politics of the U.S. Strategic Bomber Program*. Ithaca, N.Y.: Cornell University Press, 1992.

Buderi, Robert. *The Invention That Changed the World: How a Small Group of Radar Pioneers Won the Second World War and Launched a Technological Revolution*. New York: Simon and Schuster, 1996.

———. *Engines of Tomorrow: How the World's Best Companies Are Using Their Research Labs to Win the Future*. New York: Simon and Schuster, 2001.

Campbell, Levin H., Jr. *The Industry-Ordnance Team*. New York: McGraw-Hill, 1946.

Carlisle, Rodney P. *Powder and Propellants: Energetic Materials at Indian Head, Maryland, 1890–2001*. 2nd ed. Denton: University of North Texas Press, 2002.

Carlson, W. Bernard. *Innovation as a Social Process: Elihu Thomson and the Rise of General Electric, 1870–1900*. Cambridge: Cambridge University Press, 1991.

Chandler, Alfred D., Jr. *Strategy and Structure: Chapters in the History of the American Industrial Enterprise*. Cambridge, Mass.: MIT Press, 1962.

———. *The Visible Hand: The Managerial Revolution in American Business*. Cambridge, Mass.: Belknap Press of Harvard University Press, 1977.

———. "The Competitive Performance of U.S. Industrial Enterprises since the Second World War." *Business History Review* 68 (Spring 1994): 1–72.

Coben, Stanley. "The Scientific Establishment and the Transmission of Quantum Mechanics to the United States, 1919–1932." *American Historical Review* 76 (April 1971): 442–66.

Coletta, Paolo E., ed. *United States Navy and Marine Corps Bases, Domestic*. Westport, Conn.: Greenwood Press, 1985.

Danhof, Clarence H. *Government Contracting and Technological Change*. Washington, D.C.: Brookings Institution, 1968.

DeVorkin, David H. *Science with a Vengeance: How the Military Created the Space Sciences After World War II*. New York: Springer-Verlag, 1992.

Dyer, Davis. *TRW: Pioneering Technology and Innovation Since 1900*. Boston: Harvard Business School Press, 1998.

Ezell, Edward Clinton. *The Great Rifle Controversy: Search for the Ultimate Infantry Weapon from World War II Through Vietnam and Beyond*. Harrisburg, Pa.: Stackpole Books, 1984.

Forman, Paul. "Behind Quantum Electronics: National Security as Basis for Physical Research in the United States, 1940–1960." *Historical Studies in the Physical and Biological Sciences* 18 (1987): 149–229.

Friedberg, Aaron L. *In the Shadow of the Garrison State: America's Anti-Statism and Its Cold War Grand Strategy*. Princeton: Princeton University Press, 2000.

Gaddis, John Lewis. *The United States and the Origins of the Cold War, 1941–1947*. New York: Columbia University Press, 1972.

———. *Strategies of Containment: A Critical Appraisal of American National Security Policy During the Cold War*. New York: Oxford University Press, 2005.

Galison, Peter, and Bruce Hevly, eds. *Big Science: The Growth of Large-Scale Research*. Stanford: Stanford University Press, 1992.

Geiger, Roger L. *To Advance Knowledge: The Growth of American Research Universities, 1900–1940*. New York: Oxford University Press, 1986.

———. *Research and Relevant Knowledge: American Research Universities Since World War II*. New York: Oxford University Press, 1993.

Geurlac, Henry E. *Radar in World War II*. Vol. 8 of *The History of Modern Physics, 1900–1950*. New York: Tomash Publishers and the American Institute of Physics, 1987.

Goldstine, Herman H. *The Computer from Pascal to von Neumann*. Princeton: Princeton University Press, 1993.

Graham, Margaret B. W. "Corporate Research and Development: The Latest Transformation." *Technology and Society*, no. 2/3 (1985): 179–95.

Graham, Margaret B. W., and Alec T. Shuldiner. *Corning and the Craft of Innovation*. New York: Oxford University Press, 2001.

Hart, David M. *Forged Consensus: Science, Technology, and Economic Policy in the United States, 1921–1953*. Princeton: Princeton University Press, 1998.

Heilbron, J. L., and Robert W. Seidel. *Lawrence and His Laboratory*. Vol. 1 of *A History of the Lawrence Berkeley Laboratory*. Berkeley: University of California Press, 1989.

Henriksen, Paul W. "Solid-State Physics Research at Purdue." *Osiris*, 2nd ser., 2 (1986): 237–60.

Hewlett, Richard G., and Francis Duncan. *Nuclear Navy, 1946–1962*. Chicago: University of Chicago Press, 1974.

Hewlett, Richard G., and Francis Duncan. *Atomic Shield, 1947–1952*. Vol. 2 of *A History of the United States Atomic Energy Commission*. University Park: Pennsylvania State University Press, 1969.

Hewlett, Richard G., and Jack M. Holl. *Atoms for Peace and War, 1953–1961: Eisenhower and the Atomic Energy Commission*. Vol. 3 of *A History of the United States Atomic Energy Commission*. Berkeley: University of California Press, 1989.

Hewlett, Richard G., and Oscar E. Anderson Jr. *The New World, 1939–1946*. Vol. 1 of *A History of the United States Atomic Energy Commission*. University Park: Pennsylvania State University Press, 1962.

A History of Engineering and Science in the Bell System. 7 vols. Murray Hill, N.J.: Bell Telephone Laboratories, 1975–85.

Hoch, Paul K. "The Crystallization of a Strategic Alliance: The American Physics Elite and the Military in the 1940s." In vol. 1 of *Science, Technology, and the Military*, edited by Everett Mendelsohn, Merritt Roe Smith, and Peter Weingart. Dordrecht, The Netherlands: Kluwer Academic Publishers, 1988.

Hoddeson, Lillian. "The Roots of Solid-State Research at Bell Labs." *Physics Today* 30 (March 1977): 23–30.

———. "The Entry of the Quantum Theory of Solids into the Bell Telephone Laboratories, 1925–40: A Case-Study of the Industrial Application of Fundamental Science." *Minerva* 18 (Autumn 1980): 422–47.

———. "Research on Crystal Rectifiers During World War II and the Invention of the Transistor." *History and Technology* 11 (1994): 121–30.

Hoddeson, Lillian, et al. *Out of the Crystal Maze: Chapters in the History of Solid-State Physics*. New York: Oxford University Press, 1992.

Holl, Jack M. *Argonne National Laboratory, 1946–1996*. Urbana: University of Illinois Press, 1997.

Hounshell, David A. *From the American System to Mass Production, 1800–1932: The Development of Manufacturing Technology in the United States*. Baltimore: Johns Hopkins University Press, 1984.

———. "The Evolution of Industrial Research in the United States." In *Engines of Innovation: U.S. Industrial Research at the End of an Era*, edited by Richard S. Rosenbloom and William J. Spencer. Boston: Harvard Business School Press, 1996.

———. "The Medium Is the Message, or How Context Matters: The RAND Corporation Builds an Economics of Innovation, 1946–1962." In *Systems, Experts, and Computers: The Systems Approach in Management and Engineering, World War II and After*, edited by Agatha C. Hughes and Thomas P. Hughes. Cambridge, Mass.: MIT Press, 2000.

Hounshell, David A., and John Kenly Smith Jr. *Science and Corporate Strategy: DuPont R&D, 1902–1980*. Cambridge: Cambridge University Press, 1988.

Hughes, Thomas P. *Rescuing Prometheus*. New York: Pantheon Books, 1998.

Jammer, Max. *The Conceptual Development of Quantum Mechanics*. New York: McGraw-Hill, 1966.

Johnson, Leland, and Daniel Schaffer. *Oak Ridge National Laboratory: The First Fifty Years*. Knoxville: University of Tennessee Press, 1994.

Kevles, Daniel J. "The National Science Foundation and the Debate over Postwar Research Policy, 1942–1945: A Political Interpretation of *Science—The Endless Frontier*." *Isis* 68 (March 1977): 5–26.

———. *The Physicists: The History of a Scientific Community in Modern America*. Cambridge, Mass.: Harvard University Press, 1987.

————. "Cold War and Hot Physics: Science, Security, and the American State, 1945–56." *Historical Studies in the Physical and Biological Sciences* 20 (1990): 239–64.

Kline, Ronald R. "Construing 'Technology' as 'Applied Science': Public Rhetoric of Scientists and Engineers in the United States, 1880–1945." *Isis* 86 (June 1995): 194–221.

Kline, Ronald R., and Thomas C. Lassman. "Competing Research Traditions in American Industry: Uncertain Alliances between Engineering and Science at Westinghouse Electric, 1886–1935." *Enterprise and Society* 6 (December 2005): 601–45.

Knowles, Scott G., and Stuart W. Leslie. "'Industrial Versailles': Eero Saarinen's Corporate Campuses for GM, IBM, and AT&T." *Isis* 92 (March 2001): 1–33.

Kohler, Robert E. *Partners in Science: Foundations and Natural Sciences, 1900–1945.* Chicago: University of Chicago Press, 1991.

Koistinen, Paul A.C. *Arsenal of World War II: The Political Economy of American Warfare, 1940 – 1945.* Lawrence: University Press of Kansas, 2004.

Koppes, Clayton R. *JPL and the American Space Program: A History of the Jet Propulsion Laboratory.* New Haven: Yale University Press, 1982.

Kragh, Helge. *Quantum Generations: A History of Physics in the Twentieth Century.* Princeton: Princeton University Press, 1999.

Lasby, Clarence G. *Project Paperclip: German Scientists and the Cold War.* New York: Atheneum, 1971.

Lassman, Thomas C. "Government Science in Postwar America: Henry A. Wallace, Edward U. Condon, and the Transformation of the National Bureau of Standards, 1945–1951." *Isis* 96 (March 2005): 25–51.

Lécuyer, Christophe. *Making Silicon Valley: Innovation and the Growth of High-Tech, 1930–1970.* Cambridge, Mass.: MIT Press, 2005.

Leffler, Melvyn P. *A Preponderance of Power: National Security, the Truman Administration, and the Cold War.* Stanford: Stanford University Press, 1992.

Leslie, Stuart W. *The Cold War and American Science: The Military-Industrial-Academic Complex at MIT and Stanford.* New York: Columbia University Press, 1993.

————. "Blue Collar Science: Bringing the Transistor to Life in the Lehigh Valley." *Historical Studies in the Physical and Biological Sciences* 32 (2001): 71–113.

McBride, William M. "The 'Greatest Patron of Science'?: The Navy-Academia Alliance and U.S. Naval Research, 1896–1923." *Journal of Military History* 56 (January 1992): 7–33.

Misa, Thomas J. "Military Needs, Commercial Realities, and the Development of the Transistor, 1948–1958." In *Military Enterprise and Technological Change: Perspectives on the American Experience,* edited by Merritt Roe Smith. Cambridge, Mass.: MIT Press, 1985.

Mowery, David C., and Nathan Rosenberg. *Technology and the Pursuit of Economic Growth.* Cambridge: Cambridge University Press, 1989.

Neufeld, Jacob. *The Development of Ballistic Missiles in the United States Air Force, 1945–1960.* Washington, D.C.: Office of Air Force History, 1990.

Neufeld, Michael J. "The End of the Army Space Program: Interservice Rivalry and the Transfer of the Von Braun Group to NASA, 1958–1959." *Journal of Military History* 69 (July 2005): 737–58.

Owens, Larry. "The Counterproductive Management of Science in the Second World War: Vannevar Bush and the Office of Scientific Research and Development." *Business History Review* 68 (Winter 1994): 515–76.

Peck, Merton J., and Frederic M. Scherer. *The Weapons Acquisition Process: An Economic Analysis.* Boston: Division of Research, Graduate School of Business Administration, Harvard University, 1962.

Polmar, Norman, and Thomas B. Allen. *Rickover and the Nuclear Navy.* New York: Simon and Schuster, 1982.

Reich, Leonard S. *The Making of American Industrial Research: Science and Business at GE and Bell, 1876–1926.* Cambridge: Cambridge University Press, 1985.

Reingold, Nathan. "Vannevar Bush's New Deal for Research: Or the Triumph of the Old Order." *Historical Studies in the Physical and Biological Sciences* 17 (1987): 299–344.

———. "Choosing the Future: The U.S. Research Community, 1944–1946." *Historical Studies in the Physical and Biological Sciences* 25 (1995): 301–28.

Rhodes, Richard. *The Making of the Atomic Bomb.* New York: Simon and Schuster, 1986.

Riordan, Michael, and Lillian Hoddeson. *Crystal Fire: The Birth of the Information Age.* New York: W. W. Norton, 1997.

Rodgers, Thomas E. *A Good Neighbor: The First Fifty Years at Crane, 1941–1991.* Evansville: Historic Southern Indiana Project, University of Southern Indiana, 1991.

Roland, Alex, with Philip Shiman. *Strategic Computing: DARPA and the Quest for Machine Intelligence, 1983–1993.* Cambridge, Mass.: MIT Press, 2002.

Rossiter, Margaret W. "Setting Federal Salaries in the Space Age." *Osiris* 2, 2nd ser. (1992): 218–37.

Russo, Arturo. "Fundamental Research at Bell Laboratories: The Discovery of Electron Diffraction." *Historical Studies in the Physical Sciences* 12 (1981): 117–60.

Sapolsky, Harvey M. *The Polaris System Development: Bureaucratic and Programmatic Success in Government.* Cambridge, Mass.: Harvard University Press, 1972.

———. *Science and the Navy: The History of the Office of Naval Research.* Princeton: Princeton University Press, 1990.

Schweber, S. S. "The Empiricist Temper Regnant: Theoretical Physics in the United States, 1920–1950." *Historical Studies in the Physical and Biological Sciences* 17 (1986): 55–98.

———. "The Mutual Embrace of Science and the Military: ONR and the Growth of Physics in the United States After World War II." In vol. 1 of *Science, Technology, and the Military,* edited by Everett Mendelsohn, Merritt Roe Smith, and Peter Weingart. Dordrecht, The Netherlands: Kluwer Academic Publishers, 1988.

Seely, Bruce. "Research, Engineering, and Science in American Engineering Colleges, 1900–1960." *Technology and Culture* 34 (April 1993): 344–86.

————."A Home for Big Science: The Atomic Energy Commission's Laboratory System." *Historical Studies in the Physical and Biological Sciences* 16 (1986): 135–75.

————. "From Glow to Flow: A History of Military Laser Research and Development." *Historical Studies in the Physical and Biological Sciences* 18 (1987): 112–47.

————. "How the Military Responded to the Laser." *Physics Today* 10 (October 1988): 36–43.

Servos, John W. *Physical Chemistry from Ostwald to Pauling: The Making of a Science in America.* Princeton: Princeton University Press, 1990.

————. "Accelerators and National Security: The Evolution of Science Policy for High-Energy Physics, 1947–1967." *History and Technology* 11 (1994): 361–91.

Seidel, Robert W. "Accelerating Science: The Postwar Transformation of the Lawrence Radiation Labortory," *Historical Studies in the Physical Sciences* 13 (1983): 375–400

————. "Changing Partners: The Mellon Institute, Private Industry, and the Federal Patron." *Technology and Culture* 35 (April 1994): 221–57.

Smith, John Kenly, Jr. "The Scientific Tradition in American Industrial Research." *Technology and Culture* 31 (January 1990): 121–31.

Smith, Merritt Roe. *Harpers Ferry Armory and the New Technology: The Challenge of Change.* Ithaca, N.Y.: Cornell University Press, 1977.

————. "Military Arsenals and Industry before World War I." In *War, Business, and American Society: Historical Perspectives on the Military Industrial Complex,* edited by Benjamin Cooling. Port Washington, N.Y.: Kennikat Press, 1977.

————. "Army Ordnance and the 'American System' of Manufacturing, 1815–1861." In *Military Enterprise and Technological Change: Perspectives on the American Experience,* edited by Merritt Roe Smith. Cambridge, Mass.: MIT Press, 1985.

Sopka, Katherine R. *Quantum Physics in America, 1920–1935.* New York: Arno Press, 1980.

Stokes, Donald E. *Pasteur's Quadrant: Basic Science and Technological Innovation.* Washington, D.C.: Brookings Institution, 1997.

Van Keuren, David K. "Science, Progressivism, and Military Preparedness: The Case of the Naval Research Laboratory, 1915–1923." *Technology and Culture* 33 (October 1992): 710–36.

Veysey, Laurence R. *The Emergence of the American University.* Chicago: University of Chicago Press, 1965.

Wang, Jessica. "Liberals, the Progressive Left, and the Political Economy of Postwar American Science: The National Science Foundation Debate Revisited." *Historical Studies in the Physical and Biological Sciences* 26 (1995): 139–66.

Weiner, Charles. "A New Site for the Seminar: The Refugees and American Physics in the Thirties." In *The Intellectual Migration: Europe and America, 1930–1960,* edited by Donald Fleming and Bernard Bailyn. Cambridge, Mass.: Belknap Press of Harvard University Press, 1969.

Westwick, Peter J. *The National Labs: Science in an American System, 1947–1974.* Cambridge, Mass.: Harvard University Press, 2003.

Wise, George. "Science at General Electric." *Physics Today* 37 (December 1984): 52–61.

———. *Willis R. Whitney, General Electric, and the Origins of U.S. Industrial Research.* New York: Columbia University Press, 1985.

Zachary, G. Pascal. *Endless Frontier: Vannevar Bush, Engineer of the American Century.* New York: Free Press, 1997.